WEST SUSSEX CO

WE

The Old Steam Navy

VOLUME TWO

THE IRONCLADS, 1842–1885

The Old Steam Navy

VOLUME TWO

———————•———————

The Ironclads, 1842~1885

DONALD L. CANNEY

Distributed by:
Airlife Publishing Ltd.
101 Longden Road, Shrewsbury SY3 9EB, England

© 1993
by the United States Naval Institute
Annapolis, Maryland

Library of Congress Cataloging-in-Publication Data

Canney, Donald L., 1947–
    The old steam navy.

    Includes bibliographical references and indexes.
    Contents: v. 1. Frigates, sloops and gunboats,
1815–1885 — v. 2. The ironclads, 1842–1885.
    1. United States.—Navy—History. 2. Warships—United
States—History.   I. Title.
VA55.C28   1990   359'.00973   89-13675
ISBN 0-87021-004-1 (v. 1)
ISBN 0-87021-586-8 (v. 2 : acid-free)

Printed in the United States of America on acid-free
paper ∞

9 8 7 6 5 4 3 2

First printing

To my Father,
Ladd L. Canney

Contents

Illustrations

Acknowledgments

The process of writing this book was facilitated by many individuals willing to assist and lend advice. Many have given their time in both the search for materials and in the understanding of the subject itself.

First, Charles Haberlein of the Naval Historical Center; Steve Wright, editor of *Warship International;* and Stephen S. Roberts, editor of a new edition of K. Jack Bauer's book on ships of the navy, have been consistent in their advice and encouragement. Their support has been invaluable in both this and the earlier volume on the old steam navy.

At the National Archives several individuals have been of great assistance, especially Dr. Richard Von Doenhoff and Barry Zerbe at the main archives; Ray Cotton, Jeffrey Carter, and others at the Architectural and Cartographic Branch have done much to make ship plans available to me.

Thanks also to James Frazier at the New-York Historical Society; Dana Wegner and Colin Ratcliff at the David Taylor Research Center; Dr. Harold Langley and Harold Ellis of the Smithsonian Institution; the staff of the manuscript division at the Library of Congress; Jim Dolph at Portsmouth Naval Shipyard; Dr. Robert Browning and Kevin Foster at the Coast Guard history office; and Jim Mooney, Robert Cressman, and Dr. John Reilly of the Naval Historical Center. Thanks to Dr. Charles Peery of Charleston for the use of his image of the *New Ironsides* from his collection.

Elizabeth Joyner was good enough to give me a tour of the preserved gunboat *Cairo* at Vicksburg National Military Park. She also provided needed photographs and documentation concerning that vessel.

A special thanks goes to Dr. William N. Still, Jr., of East Carolina University. His long familiarity with sources in the field of Civil War naval history was an invaluable help.

On a more personal basis, thanks to Sam Hicks, an expert in the field of computer CAD programming, who was able to understand the structure of the *Monitor* sufficiently to generate three-dimensional visualizations of the vessel.

Finally, my father, Ladd L. Canney, has always been available to assist in the field of early steam technology. His library and practical knowledge of steam engines have been irreplaceable.

Introduction

Before the advent of the new all steel navy in the 1880s, steam war vessels built by the U.S. Navy fell into two categories: the conventional, nonarmored vessels and ironclad warships. For the most part, the conventional vessels might be considered steam-powered developments of the sailing warship and were the subject of the first volume of this work. On the other hand, the ironclad ships were in many instances complete departures from historical and traditional shipbuilding practice and incorporated the technological advances of the times. These vessels, spawned by the Civil War, present astounding diversity, ranging from mere casemated river scows to sophisticated turreted semioceangoing craft. They also represented vessels used in two diverse theaters of the war: those constructed for coastal operations, the majority of which were of the *Monitor* type; and the vessels of the Western River Flotilla, which were in the main casemated boats unsuited for sea service.

A second subject pertinent to this era of technological innovation is that of experimental and proposed armorclads, most notably the never-completed Stevens battery, which might have been the most revolutionary vessel ever constructed—had she ever left the ways. Included here are the various proposed designs for this vessel as well as the *E. A. Stevens,* a small steamer donated to the U.S. Revenue Service and intended to exhibit Stevens's ideas in practical form. Additionally, there were numerous other proposals, most of which never reached a stage beyond the drawing paper. These serve as glimpses of the developing technology of the times and provide insights into official and unofficial naval thinking of the era.

Another subcategory incorporated into this volume is the group of vessels converted from civilian use for the flotilla on the western rivers. Though initially under the auspices of the U.S. Army Quartermaster Department, they were later incorporated into the navy; as will be seen, the sea service played a significant role in the design of most of these vessels. The methods used to convert riverboats into tinclads, timberclads, ironclads, and rams are presented, as well as the two purpose-built rams, *Vindicator* and *Avenger.* The inclusion of the rams is somewhat artibrary. They did, however, represent a prevalent naval fashion of the times and were certainly a result of the mating of steam technology to riverine warfare.

Few ships in these categories have been treated thoroughly by naval historians. Specifically, John Ericsson's revolutionary *Monitor* and the *Cairo,* an ironclad of the Western River Flotilla recently exhumed from the bottom of the Yazoo River in Mississippi, have been the subject of much writing. Most others, however, have received only cursory attention, and no attempt has been made to weave a cohesive story of their development, characteristics, and the technological aspects of their design. I hope that this volume will fill that gap.

The Old Steam Navy

VOLUME TWO

THE IRONCLADS,
1842–1885

CHAPTER 1

Ironclad Precedents: Pre–Civil War Proposals and the Stevens Battery

After centuries of incremental progress in warship design, the Industrial Revolution and its consequences suddenly inundated the navies of the nineteenth-century world with cataclysmic and fundamental changes in naval warfare and vessels. The introduction of the steam engine in war vessels—with Robert Fulton's *Demologos* of 1815—for the first time since the advent of oars made possible the movement of warships independent of the wind. The practical shell gun and explosive projectiles then brought the imminent danger of fire to sea battles hitherto fought predominantly with solid shot. Iron armor was developed to counter the shell threat, and this, with iron hulls and the revolving gun turret, led to the profile of the modern warship. By the 1880s the major warships of the world bore little resemblance to the broadside sailing wooden walls of forty years before.

In the United States, the reflection of these world technological developments was distorted: capital ships such as the revolutionary British *Warrior* of 1860 did not play a significant part, and the emphasis was on light-draft river and coastal vessels—a consequence of the Civil War, a conflict where inland and shoal water warfare was virtually the rule (excepting only the operations of the cruisers on the high seas). An American *Warrior* would have been simply useless in this context, except in the remote possibility of intervention by a European power. Indeed, the possibility of a European conflict did generate at least one American ironclad, the huge *Dunderberg*—a vessel never commissioned by the navy and eventually sold to a European power.

The history of the use of armor in warships has been traced variously as far back as the medieval Northmen, who were said to have belted their vessels with iron or bronze, and to the fifteenth-century Koreans, whose "tortoise ships" were clad with iron turtle-backs, which deflected the projectiles of Japanese invaders. In the United States, the first notable warship ideas that incorporated extraordinary means to render vessels impervious to enemy actions surfaced before the War of 1812. In 1807 Abraham Bloodgood proposed a circular, moored floating battery to rotate on its center and be "impenetrable to common shot."[1]

Three of these early ideas involved the inimitable inventor Robert Fulton. In response to Fulton's early torpedo (floating-mine) schemes, Captain Isaac Chauncey suggested that bows of the attacked vessels might be strengthened with bars of iron.[2] Fulton himself incorporated advanced protective thinking in two wartime projects: the steam battery *Demologos* and his proposed submersible, *Mute*. The former, the world's first steam-powered war vessel, was designed with engine and boilers located deep in its twin catamaranlike hulls—unlike most contemporary steamers, which left the machinery vulnerable and on deck. Further protection was provided by layers of planking, ceiling, and frames, totaling nearly five feet of protection from enemy shot. Fulton also proposed spraying would-be boarders with boiler water and suggested a "submarine" gun—which amounted to a Columbiad suspended from the vessel and fired below the waterline.[3] The latter might be considered a primitive, *very* short-range torpedo. These last two proposals were never implemented, and the *Demologos* itself, too late for the war, maintained a sedentary existence at New York until her accidental destruction in 1829.[4]

Fulton's *Mute* was never built. This predecessor of such oddities as the Confederate *H. L. Hunley* was to have been hand cranked, around 80 feet long, fitted with air chambers to submerge itself, and armed with the above mentioned submarine guns. Topping it off was iron plating on the exposed upper surface. Fulton referred to the proposed *Mute* as his "Bullet Proof boat." The project expired with the end of the war and Fulton's death.[5]

Other inventors contributed ideas for harbor batteries during this war, in response to the British blockade of American ports. In fact, schemes for armoring war vessels—ranging from practical to harebrained—marked a constant chorus throughout the era. Most never reached fruition. A few were noteworthy, however, for the caliber of their inventors or merely the longevity of their ideas.

In the latter category was the "system of annoyance of the enemy by land and water" proposed by Uriah Brown in 1814, a plan that surfaced periodically until 1847. Brown claimed to have rediscovered Greek fire and incorporated this into a shot-proof steam vessel design, the whole system with the classical appellation "Navis Conflagrator." According to Brown, after "repeated" experiments in the "presence of a vast concourse of the citizens of Baltimore," a public subscription was begun for the construction of one of these machines, supported by many local notables. The termination of the War of 1812 ended the project, but Brown sought congressional support in the 1820s, 1836, and finally in 1846, seeking official sanction and funds.[6]

The "Greek fire" was shown to a naval committee in 1847. After one unsuccessful attempt, a stream of the mysterious liquid was projected some sixty feet by a small steam pump, successfully igniting a mast set up for the purpose. The committee was impressed not with the inventor's claimed range of the liquid (two hundred feet) but with the probability that adverse winds might throw the volatile substance (and its vapor) back on the operators.[7] One wonders about the veracity of the reports of Brown's successful experiments before the "vast concourse" of Baltimoreans over thirty years before.

The shot-proof vessel itself was to have been 200 feet by 60 feet, propelled by two engines and "submerged wheels" to the speed of "our swiftest steamboats" and presenting "the appearance of a wedge" to shot of the enemy. The sides and rounded ends were to be angled from the waterline upward, covered with sheet iron, and backed by thick oak timbers, with a flat upper deck for hatches and other openings. (In the version of 1836, Brown suggested building the vessel of iron.[8]) Mr. Brown's "submerged wheels" would have predated the successful screw propeller by decades.

Brown was successful in gaining a congressional appropriation of $10,000 to demonstrate his ideas (in the Naval Appropriation Act of 1847) and apparently exhausted this fund in the experiment noted above. Secretary of the Navy John Y. Mason declined to support building the vessel itself, ending Brown's hopes.[9] Brown was one of the first in the United States to propose sloping-sided ironclads.

Two other inventors proposed thick-sided war batteries: John Marsh of Charleston, South Carolina, whose conventional (towed) guardship was to have 3½-foot-thick wood bulwarks with an exaggerated tumble-home; and Thomas Gregg of Pennsylvania, with a plan for a shot-proof steamer with sides angled at 18 degrees, provided with hinges at the lower edges, allowing the sides to be "sprung" outward—to the consternation of boarders.[10]

Yet another prominent early American inventor's name first surfaces in naval affairs at this time—a name that echoes through the entire old navy era: Stevens. John Stevens, Jr., of Hoboken, New Jersey, was already a noted gentleman cum scientist/inventor with influential connections and money. Brother-in-law of Robert Livingston of New York, he and his son, Robert Livingston Stevens, had been tinkering with steam propulsion as early as 1791, operating a small steam launch with an experimental screw-type propeller in 1804.[11]

Stevens made two warship proposals during the War of 1812. The first was for stationary, circular floating batteries, plated with iron and rotated by steam-powered screw propellers to bring the guns to bear. The second was for several 70-foot iron-plated vessels, each propelled by a "spiral water wheel" and armed with a single large Columbiad. He proposed carrying these vessels on board larger ships for the Atlantic crossing and using them against the Barbary powers. Neither idea met with official approval.[12]

After the War of 1812, interest in steam vessels waned in the U.S. Navy. No steamers were built for the navy until the 1830s. In the interim, small steamers were hired for various purposes, including the operations against pirates in Florida waters, and a building plan for steam batteries was kept on hand (as well as appropriate steam machinery) should the need arise.[13] The fact that European navies were pushing ahead with steam-powered vessels had little impact on American naval construction.

The introduction of the practical shell gun, however, a weapon that was to lead inevitably to armored vessels, was not lost on the American navy. Explosive shells brought the threat of fire at sea, an anathema to wooden fleets and their highly flammable stores.

Though explosive shells had been used before the nineteenth century, their drawbacks were serious: the most fatal was a tendency to detonate prematurely. In Europe, General Henri-Joseph Paixhans began experiments with these guns (which were eventually named for him) in 1809, and they were authorized in the French navy in 1824. In the United States, during the War of 1812, Major George Bomford, chief of army ordnance, introduced the Columbiad, a chambered cannon suitable for shells as well as solid shot, which became standard in coastal defense fortifications through the

Civil War.[14] Many feel that Bomford should have received the credit for developing the shell gun, rather than Paixhans.

During the War of 1812, the naval use of shell guns was suggested by Stephen Decatur, who experimented with such a weapon but rejected its use as "'unfair" to the British. A few Columbiads were in naval use through the early 1830s, but to what extent is unknown. In 1818, however, the navy contracted for elongated shells produced by Robert L. Stevens, loaded with a "secret" powder formula. Twelve hundred were ordered, though the contract specified only four hundred were to be taken if they proved unsatisfactory. Fired from smoothbore guns, these shells tumbled end-for-end, indicating poor performance. As late as 1841, however, these shells were still in the inventory—as was the order requiring secrecy.[15]

The mid-1830s brought a wave of new proposals for armored vessels in the wake of rumors of war with France. The extinction of the United States debt also encouraged many proposals for the use of surplus funds. Though Congress ignored proposals to use the surplus on various military schemes, a few items stand out.

President Jackson ordered the Board of Navy Commissioners to build a steam battery, which became the *Fulton II*—the first steamer built by the navy. One of the early proposals for this vessel was by William Kemble of West Point Foundry, who suggested low placement of the engine and a "dome, covered by boiler plate" to protect this machinery.[16]

One year later, Captain James Barron submitted to Congress a plan for a steam "prow-ship for the defence of bays, rivers and harbors." This monster was to have been 250 feet long by 75 feet beam, consisting of masses of solid timber—sufficient wood to "absorb" enemy shot and shell. Her offensive power was to be in the momentum of her mass and an iron-plated pyramidal "prow," or ram, and the vessel's upper surface was to be covered with some unidentified nonflammable material. The proof cited of the efficacy of such mass on an enemy ship was the "attack made by a whale on the ship Essex of New Bedford in the year 1819."[17]

As the navy began building steam vessels in earnest, the vulnerability of steam machinery to enemy shot was a key factor in warship design, but with the common side-wheel ship it was impossible to place all of the machinery safely below the waterline. In the *Fulton II*, the engine was unfortunately placed: exposed on the upper deck. The ship came under harsh criticism for this and other reasons, and her first commanding officer, Matthew Calbraith Perry, suggested building bulwarks around the engines and covering these as well as her thick, beveled wooden bulwarks with iron to deflect shot.[18] This idea was not authorized and

eventually the ship became a test bed for guns.

The early 1840s brought a spate of experimentation in the U.S. Navy. The navy's first operational iron-hulled vessel, the USS *Michigan,* was built during this period as well as the first screw-propelled warship, John Ericsson's *Princeton*. The era brought the experiment with Lt. W. W. Hunter's horrendously inefficient horizontally mounted paddle wheels, located in casings below the ship's waterline. Part of Hunter's "system" was a curved iron protective "shield" deck, which was to render "it impossible to sink" these vessels and which would prevent shot damage to the machinery and boilers.[19] This advanced idea would reappear in steel warships decades later but remained undone in the 1840s because of the total failure of Hunter's horizontal wheels.

The Stevens Battery: Part 1

"Long a-building" and "technologically advanced" seem to be paradoxical terms but are equally apt in describing the war vessel that was begun by Robert L. Stevens in 1841 and remained in her custom-built dry dock/shiphouse until finally scrapped in 1885. The story is long and unclear in detail because of Stevens's penchant for secrecy and the paucity of surviving documentation: as an independent contractor Stevens deemed it unnecessary to supply the navy with in-depth progress reports. The narrative can be subdivided into three segments—prewar progress, the Civil War, and postwar developments—and will be presented here in the appropriate chapters.

The original proposal was made to the Board of Naval Commissioners by Robert L. Stevens and his brother Edwin A. Stevens in August 1841 and called for a "fast steamer" with machinery below the waterline and propelled by Stevens's circular "skull"—their version of the screw propeller. (A Stevens skull was used on the steamer *Princeton* after 1845 and was six-bladed with a constant pitch of 35 degrees.[20]) The vessel was to be of iron with $4\frac{1}{2}$- to 6-inch plating—without, at least in this plan, wooden backing. Armament was to be a few guns "of the largest caliber"—breechloading, rifled, and wrought iron. In startling contrast to the then nonexistent, technologically advanced guns, the vessel was to have a full sailing rig. The vessel was intended for the defense of New York harbor. The plan was submitted shortly after a board of army and navy officers had witnessed experiments made by Stevens using a "bomb and ball proof target suited to the sides of a vessel" and consisting of layers of iron boiler plate to a thickness of $4\frac{1}{2}$ inches. Sixty-four–pounders were fired at point-blank range (thirty yards) and the projectiles made "scarcely" a dent. The officers reported favorably on the trials.[21]

By January 1842, Stevens had elaborated on and modified his plans, indicating a displacement of "1500 tons or thereabouts" and incorporating "artificial ventilation" and the use of anthracite as fuel. He predicted high speed and eliminated the sailing rig at this time. Stevens estimated that the total outlay for the ship would not exceed $300,000—about the cost of the conventional steamer *Fulton II*.[22]

The case for Stevens's proposal was strengthened by a House report on harbor defense dated 15 March 1842, which compared the Stevens proposal to a competing plan submitted by Gen. Edmund P. Gaines, which called for heavily timbered floating batteries to be towed into place for harbor and inlet defense. Naval constructor Samuel Humphreys estimated a cost of $1.4 million for each of these batteries along with its attendant towboat. Needless to say, this outrageous (for the day) monetary figure, plus the expectation that Stevens's plan would be "ten times as effective," was sufficient to gain congressional support for this unbuilt iron battery.[23] Had Congress any inkling of how wildly Stevens had underestimated the eventual cost of his battery, no doubt their support would have evaporated.

In the end, Congress appropriated $250,000 toward building the Stevens battery and the contract was made on 10 February 1843. This document adds some detail to Stevens's proposal and cites the recently completed side-wheel frigates *Mississippi* and *Missouri* as standards of comparison. Stevens's vessel would withstand shot up to sixty-four pounds and have greater speed than "any of our steam vessels"; her engines would be four in number (in the parlance of the time, each engine was a single cylinder), located "out of the way of shot from an enemy." These condensing engines would exceed the power of those of the frigates *Mississippi* or *Missouri* by 50 percent and drive wrought-iron shafts. She would be pierced for six or more guns, with their "average value" the same as those of the above frigates, each of which carried eight 8-inch and two 10-inch shell guns.[24]

The hull was to be principally of iron, "not less than" 250 feet long between stem and stern post, 40-foot beam, and 28 feet deep from upper iron deck to keel. It was to be "much sharper" than the side-wheel frigates, and the "ribs" were to be of $3/8$-inch to $1/2$-inch iron, 6 inches deep, two feet apart. Plating was to be an average of $1/2$ inch thick, and her sides, above the waterline, were to be $4^1/2$ inches of plating consisting of layers of boiler iron, tapered off below. No indication has been found that the sides were to be angled (and sloping sides are not mentioned in the testing of Stevens's shells). The vessel's firerooms were to be airtight, with forced draft for the furnaces.[25]

Construction time was to be two years and the cost was only given as the "average" of that of the frigates *Mississippi* and *Missouri*, each of which had totaled about $570,000. A troublesome caveat was included: that the completion in two years was to be contingent on the balance due being paid (over and above the $250,000 appropriation) within the requisite time.[26]

Stevens apparently applied for further installments in December of the same year but was prevented from receiving further payments by the new secretary of the navy. A supplementary contract was entered into in November 1844 with the statement that the original document was "too loose and indefinite"—for the navy, at least—in both description of the vessel itself and the terms of payment.[27]

This new document provided for delivery two years from contract date and added some minor details of the vessel to the mix. Additionally, Stevens was to admit a navy-appointed inspector for the vessel. Probably the most unusual provision, however, was the security bond: Stevens presented the government the mortgage on his Hoboken property—"land, docks, wharves, ships and all their appurtenances"—to be sold by the government if the contract was not fulfilled.[28]

Contract disputes were to continue intermittently through the prewar period. On Stevens's part, complaints were based on the refusal of the navy to authorize payments—delays which suspended operations. On the government's part were two related points: Stevens showed little or no actual progress on the vessel itself, and no plans had been submitted to the department. The latter point is problematic in that a congressional report of 1852 stated that the plans were indeed submitted with the original contract, while the navy maintained that no plan was ever received. (It seems likely that the "plan" referred to by the congressional Committee on Naval Affairs was actually Stevens's written contract description rather than a construction draft.[29]

As to the lack of progress on the vessel, it is obvious now that Stevens had wildly misjudged the entire project—on all fronts: time to completion, required finances, as well as the capabilities of current technology. Even the preliminaries got out of hand: the vessel was to be so massive that normal launching was out of the question and a suitable dry dock had to be excavated and made watertight for the construction. Workshops had to be built, with steam-powered punches, drills, and other equipment, as well as a small steamboat on which to carry out various experiments, particularly with propellers. American-made materials were found unsatisfactory and Stevens made extended trips to Europe to remedy this. Further delays were a result of Stevens's impaired health in the late 1840s.[30]

In 1856, Robert L. Stevens died, leaving the unfinished project to his brother, Edwin A. Stevens. By this date, despite delays, the project was well along—as it well should have been—and a plan of the "Great Iron Steam Battery" appeared in a contemporary nautical journal. The source of the plan was not disclosed and nothing has been found to verify its accuracy. The battery was described as 400 feet long, 45 feet wide, and 21 feet deep, "to be provided with 10 boilers, and 2 propellers driven by 8 engines."[31]

That this plan was radically different from the original is obvious: 150 feet longer, six more boilers, and so on. Probably the major factor in this change was that introduced in this country by John Ericsson in the 1840s: his 12-inch guns could penetrate iron like that originally planned by Stevens. This no doubt also accounts for Stevens's scurrying to Europe to obtain better material. A larger displacement was then necessary to support the six inches of armor plating required to make the ship shot proof. The same year, 1845, also brought the *Simoom* tests in Britain, which demonstrated that iron hulls were inherently more dangerous to ships' crews than those of wood: the brittle iron would splinter easily into lethal shards. These tests did much to set back iron-hulled warship construction in the world's navies and contributed to Stevens's technological problems with the battery.

At this point, engines and boilers had not yet been installed, and armoring had not begun. $702,755 had been spent and the honor of the "first ironclads" had fallen to the British and French floating batteries of the Crimean War.[32] Shortly, with the coming of the Civil War, the Stevens battery project would again rise to the surface and Edwin Stevens would make yet another plea for funds to complete the vessel.

The Stevens battery project was indeed extraordinary for the times. The Stevens brothers had foreseen in 1842 the eventual adoption of the submerged propeller for warships—although the navy temporized on the subject until the mid-1850s. The use of iron armor was not implemented by any navy until the Crimean War (1853–56)—and that only in floating batteries whose steam engines could barely stem the tide. Had the Stevens vessel been completed on her 400-foot plan, she would have been the largest American vessel built to that date, and her size would not have been approached in the U.S. Navy until the 1890s.

In the decades following the commencement of the Stevens battery, the concept of the ironclad warship was brought to fruition by both the British and French in the floating batteries prepared for attacking Russian fortresses on the Black Sea. An example was the British *Glatton*, which was 172 feet long by 43 feet beam, displacing 1,470 tons. Though given a steam engine and temporary masting, the vessels were exceedingly unwieldy and required towing to reach their destination. They showed their worth at Kinburn, withstanding pounding from as near as eight hundred yards. The batteries ashore were silenced. By the end of the decade the French had built the *Gloire* and the Royal Navy had begun the *Warrior*—the first true ironclad warships.

Even as the entire basis of the European navies was being called into question by the appearance of ironclads, the American reaction was virtually imperceptible. James P. Baxter refers to this phenomenon in *The Introduction of the Ironclad Warship*, quoting a *U.S. Naval Gazette* article admitting that there was a "good prima facie case" that the United States had fallen behind "the age."[33]

Little notice was taken of these events—officially or unofficially. The navy did not send observers to the war fronts. An army report dutifully described the Kinburn action and the floating batteries and concluded that American seacoast weapons should be able to fire large solid as well as hollow shot. The implications for naval warships were not addressed.[34]

I have scoured large numbers of naval documents of the era immediately after Kinburn, including the Area File for the Mediterranean, and found scarcely

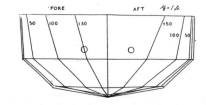

STEVENS BATTERY

The Stevens battery, the only known pre–Civil War plan. Published in U.S. Nautical Magazine and Naval Journal *in 1856, the hull cross section is quite different from the plan as it appeared during the Civil War. This plan shows the vessel to be 400 feet by 45 feet—over 150 feet longer than that of the original 1842 proposal, reflecting a radical change in the displacement needed to support significantly heavier armor plate than envisioned originally. At this stage the vessel was the largest in existence—though how much of it was actually completed is unknown. (Tracing by author)*

a mention of the conflict and no reference to the floating batteries themselves. Any significant reaction among the naval hierarchy would have made some ripple through general correspondence.

This phenomenon calls for an explanation, but that can only be speculative. Several factors were at work. First, floating batteries of any kind were far from the staple of the peacetime U.S. Navy, where cruising on foreign station was the norm. Second, at this juncture the navy was preoccupied with the Far East—building light-draft vessels for use against piratical elements in China.

A third factor may have been the long-standing obsession with speed in warships. During the mid-1850s, the big *Merrimack*-class frigates were built, the object of much media attention because of their size and expense. These vessels were roundly criticized in the press and particularly by the commercial maritime community. It might be expected that any rhetorical or reasonable tool would have been used to attack these vessels—including their lack of armor. The popular theme of the day, however, was that the *Merrimack* and her sister ships were not fast enough to catch a crack merchant ocean steamer. As Harold and Margaret Sprout point out in their volume on the rise of U.S. naval power, the navy's attitude and actions of the prewar years were a throwback to the "legend of victory" in the War of 1812. Defensive floating batteries had no place in this scheme of things.[35] This is not to say that the navy was totally ignorant of these developments. Proof of this would come in 1861, in the remarkable swiftness that marked the adoption of iron protection for naval vessels in both the Union and Confederate navies.

CHAPTER 2

Ironclads Inchoate, 1861

The force of events soon ended the navy's lassitude on the subject of ironclad war vessels—though it is evident that the navy itself was not in the forefront of the movement. The coming of the Civil War found the navy in a peculiar position: playing catch-up to the foundling Confederate navy. Without laboring familiar chords, we must remember that the Confederacy was forced to emulate the navy of the early republic: with funds for very few vessels, it was apparent that these ships would have to be of the latest and best technology, substituting quality for quantity.

As early as 2 February 1861, a Confederate congressional resolution had called for the construction of "iron plated frigates . . . and . . . gunboats" and by 26 April (less than two weeks after the firing on Fort Sumter) men in the highest places of the Confederate naval hierarchy were actively pursuing the idea of ironclad vessels.[1] (Another contributing factor may well have been the Confederates' effective use of an iron-plated wooden floating battery in the bombardment of Fort Sumter.[2]) On 10 May, Confederate naval secretary Stephen R. Mallory wrote the House Committee on Naval Affairs concerning the "first necessity" of obtaining an "iron-armored ship" and requested funds to purchase such a vessel in Europe.[3]

Because existing ironclads were unavailable, it was decided that domestic sources would necessarily suffice. On 28 June, the decision was made to resurrect the hull and machinery of the U.S. steam frigate *Merrimack* as the basis for a broadside ironclad. Renamed the *Virginia*, she would, nine months later at Hampton Roads, put the Union navy in one of the most perilous positions of the entire conflict.[4]

The direct, nonbureaucratic Confederate approach to the ironclad problem is in sharp contrast to the machinations in Washington. Certainly there was no shortage of ideas and proposals—from both within and without the department. John Dahlgren, for instance, had proposed a method of ironcladding in December 1860 (resubmitting an idea he had first proposed in 1852).[5] And, in January 1861, the U.S. Senate requested that the department outline a plan for iron-casing a vessel of the capacity and armament of the *Iroquois*-class steam sloops.

Chief constructor John Lenthall's reply was indicative of current thinking in the department and was fairly realistic. Three inches of iron was the "least" thickness of armor thought necessary—weighing about 300 tons and bringing to 1,500 tons the total for the vessel (including structural strengthening). This would result in a significantly larger vessel than the *Iroquois,* but with the same armament (two 11-inch pivot guns and four 32-pounders). The cost estimated was $558,000—some $200,000 in excess of the price of the original *Iroquois.*[6]

Nothing came of this, as evident in the naval appropriations voted the following month: $1.2 million, which was allotted to build seven (later eight) conventional screw sloops. There was some urgency in this measure because these vessels were built as repeats of the sloops of 1859 rather than developed as new designs. War with the seceding states, however, was not the stated rationale behind these ships. And though ironclads were mentioned in the debates in Congress, they were apparently only considered in comparison with the advances in European fleets, rather than in the context of the impending war.[7]

The change of administration brought no immediate decisions. The new secretary of the navy, Gideon Welles, continued to receive various proposals—some less practical than others and some from more reputable sources than others. Two days after the firing on Fort Sumter, Richard Bristol informed Welles that cotton, hydraulically pressed, was "nearly as hard as iron" and suggested it be used for armor plating.[8] Later in the conflict cotton was indeed used in just such a manner in Confederate blockade runners.

A more appropriate plan was submitted as early as 23 April by Charles W. Whitney of New York. This was the original proposal for the "mail clad" *Keokuk*, eventually laid down in April 1862.[9] (Specifics of this ill-starred vessel will be presented in chapter 6.) Other proposals came from the famed shipbuilder Donald McKay and Lt. David D. Porter. McKay proposed a 2,390-ton casemated corvette with up to 4½ inches of armor on sloping sides; Porter suggested bolting iron bars on the sides of wooden vessels.[10]

From the outbreak of hostilities until July, the department made no substantive move towards building ironclad vessels, despite a continuing influx of proposals. Chief constructor John Lenthall's opinion on ironclad vessels, written on 11 May, is instructive: "The necessarily large size, the cost and the time required for building an iron cased steam vessel is such that it is not recommended to adopt any plan at present."[11] This was written before the Battle at Bull Run and represents the generally held view that the war would be brief.

The department's first positive decision was to recommend to Congress that a committee be formed to study the subject, stating that the Congress would decide whether they would order any such vessels. Welles at this time suggested another board be instituted to make recommendations on the fate of the Stevens battery.[12] In the interim, Welles, his new assistant secretary Gustavus Fox, and others were preoccupied with the immediate dilemma: ringing the Southern coast with a legal blockade. Certainly there was sufficient work to do in both purchasing and designing the multitude of ships necessary for this task. (Inquiries were made abroad in this context—to Laird of England, who recommended iron gunboats, as opposed to wood, but did not mention ironclad ships.[13]) Furthermore, the imperative for building an ironclad would not appear until late June or early July, when the Confederates began work converting the hull of the *Merrimack* at Norfolk yard.

Though the story of the ironclads built for the western rivers will be addressed in chapter 5, their place in the chronology of armorclad construction needs to be mentioned here. These vessels, contracted and built by the U.S. Army's Quartermaster Corps, were eventually turned over to the navy and were designed by S. M. Pook, naval constructor detailed to the army, and in consultation with constructor John Lenthall and Capt. John Rodgers. Lenthall first submitted a river gunboat design, but this was not to be armored.[14] The idea (and subsequent directive) to armor these ships originated with Quartermaster General Montgomery Meigs. In his biography of Meigs, Russell F. Weigley states

that Meigs called in Rodgers (who also happened to be his brother-in-law) and demanded "that one or two at the very least be ironclads." The date of this meeting is uncertain. The completed plans for the city-class ironclad gunboats, however, are dated 2 July 1861. Therefore the honor of first authorizing Union ironclad vessels belongs to Montgomery Meigs.[15]

Meanwhile, Welles's request that Congress authorize a board came to fruition. On 3 August Congress authorized such a committee, with instructions that "should" their report "be favorable," "one or more" "iron or steel-clad" vessels should be built. Congress appropriated $1.5 million for this purpose.[16]

The committee was selected on 8 August, composed of Commodores Hiram Paulding and Joseph Smith and Commander Charles H. Davis. It would be instructive to know the reason no naval constructor was named to this board. Welles's criteria had only been that the members be "proper and competent," but Congress had been more specific, calling for "three skilful naval officers."[17] It is likely that the department had already recommended suitable members to Congress. Given Lenthall's previously stated—and decidedly negative—opinion concerning such ships and Assistant Secretary Fox's view that Lenthall needed something to "force" him into action, it is not surprising that the chief constructor was not selected for this duty.[18]

The board would evaluate proposals based on the department's public advertisement of 7 August 1861:

> For the construction of one or more iron-clad steam vessels of war, either of iron or of wood and iron combined, for sea and river service, to be of not less than ten or over sixteen feet draught of water; to carry an armament of from eighty to one hundred and twenty tons weight, with provisions and stores for from one hundred and sixty-five to three hundred persons, according to armament, for sixty days, with coal for eight days. The smaller draught of water, compatible with other requisites, will be preferred. The vessel to be rigged with two masts, with wire-rope standing rigging, to navigate the sea.[19]

To gain some idea of the department's goals as to the armament of this ironclad, the criteria in the public advertisement of 7 August can be compared to the *Wyoming* and other vessels of the *Iroquois* class mentioned earlier. These sloops had complements of 160 to 180 men and were typically armed with two 11-inch Dahlgren smoothbores (10 tons each, including pivot carriages) and four 32-pounders, and carried 30 tons of ammunition, giving a total weight of around 70 tons.[20] These figures assume the armament weight required of the proposed ironclad included ammunition as well as guns. If the 80-ton armament figure was to be guns only,

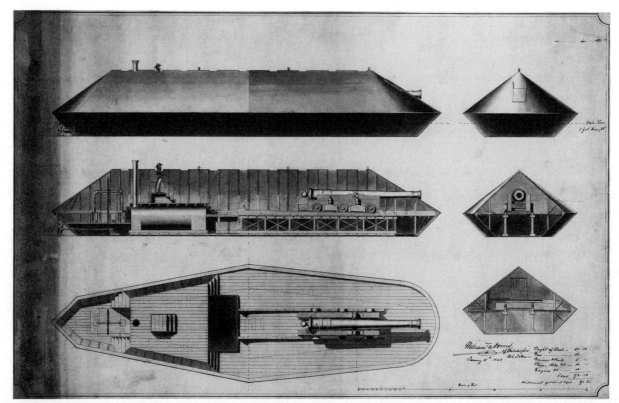

Inventors of all stripes submitted ironclad proposals as war brought the possibility of official sanction. William Norris of Philadelphia—possibly the noted locomotive builder—submitted this quaint and colorful plan and cutaway. Rejected as too small by the officiating board, it featured a chain-drive engine and single old-style smoothbore. Note the vessel commander in full dress. (NARS Plan 80-1-4, National Archives)

the ship would have been required to mount at least eight of the 11-inchers—the largest guns then in the inventory. Four other points are worthy of note in the criteria put forth by the department: no speed requirement is mentioned, a full sailing rig was to be fitted, both sea and river service were indicated, and the maximum draft was to be 16 feet.

The requirement of a sailing rig on an ironclad is not as farfetched as it appears to modern eyes. Even in the early 1860s, conventional steam warships were yet to break completely free from the need for propulsion over and above their technologically primitive simple-expansion steam engines. Steam machinery at this juncture was by definition uneconomical. Maintaining a war vessel at sea required much more than, for example, the "five days maximum steam" available to sloops such as the *Iroquois,* or the eight days required in the ironclad criteria. In any event, only two of the American Civil War ironclads were designed and built with a full-fledged sailing rig, and none were met with the operational need to remain on station on the high seas.

The phrase "not over sixteen feet draught" should be reemphasized: these few words set the American Civil War ironclad fleet apart from all other battle fleets and delimited one critical dimension in the design of Union warships. In order for an armored vessel to be of use in the shallow waters of most Southern ports, her architects must find sufficient displacement to support ammunition, guns, crew, stores, as well as significant amounts of iron armor—without exceeding 16 feet draft. Therefore other dimensions were stretched: usually breadth, resulting in unhandy, leewardly vessels. It is noteworthy that John Ericsson's approach was "off the top": his monitors solved the problem by simply excising all absolutely unnecessary superstructure. Given these salient characteristics, any attempt to compare American and European ironclad fleets of the era is infelicitous: neither fleet could meet the other on common terms.

The department's advertisement called for the submission of proposals, with drawings and description of "vessel, armor and machinery" within twenty-five days—certainly a brief interval to develop a major warship and one for which there was no precedent in naval history, European or American. The Crimean War batteries had the requisite light draft but could not "navigate the sea"; the recently completed French *La Gloire* and the nearly finished British *Warrior* both drew over 26

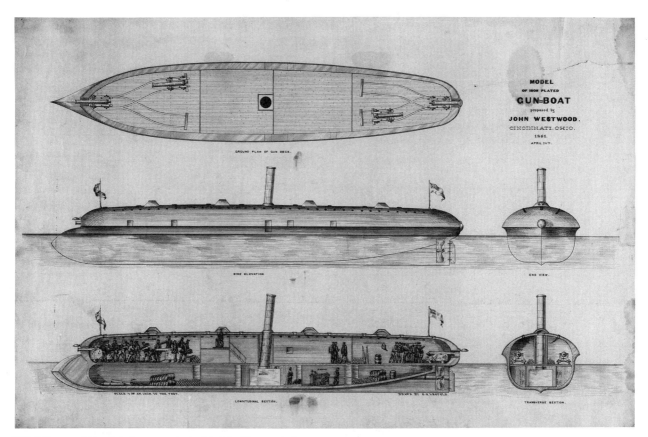

This fully crewed ironclad plan was submitted by John Westwood of Cincinnati. An unusual feature were the Y-tracks for alternating the guns at the ports. Note the side-lever engine. The board deemed the vessel insufficiently large to support the armor proposed. (NARS Plan 80-10-17, National Archives)

feet. Any sub-rosa knowledge of the Confederate *Merrimack* would have been equally unhelpful: she would draw 22 feet.

The ironclad board presented their conclusions on 16 September and selected three proposals to be awarded contracts. The committee's report was accompanied by a list and short description of each of the seventeen proposals. The three vessels (eventually to become the *Monitor, Galena,* and *New Ironsides*) that met with the committee's approval will be described in chapter 3. Whitney and Rowland's vessel (*Keokuk*), rejected at this time but later revised and built, will also be presented later.

Plans of three of the other proposed ironclads have been found. William Norris's plan was rejected as "too small" and was an iron boat without armor. It was the smallest and least expensive of all the submissions, at $32,000 and 83 feet in length and 90 tons. A plan that corresponds to this has been found in the National Archives, signed by Norris but dated 1848. The quaint hand-tinted cutaway drawing shows a single large cannon on a six-wheel carriage, firing through a port forward, with a full-dress commanding officer peering out a hatch near the stern. The two cylinders appear to operate the

screw propeller by chain drive. The old-style cannon would be appropriate to the 1848 date, so Norris may well have waited twelve years for the chance to submit his idea.[21]

John Westwood of Cincinnati also submitted a decorative plan for his gunboat. The board commented that the plan was "good enough, but the breadth not enough to bear the armor. No detailed specification; *no price or time stated.*" The vessel featured a prominent ram, rounded armored casemate, and unusual Y-shaped "tracks" for the guns—to run one gun back for reload while a second was brought up to the same gun port from the opposite side of the Y for firing.[22]

John W. Nystrom of Philadelphia submitted one of the more unusual designs—rejected by the board with somewhat cryptic remarks: "The plan of [quadruple] guns is not known, and cannot be considered. The dimensions would not float the vessel without the guards, which we are not satisfied would repel shot." The plans submitted show a 175-foot vessel, with 27-foot beam and 10-foot draft, proportions certainly too narrow for the purpose. The quadruple guns were the strangest items: four Dahlgren-like tubes crossing at the centers with one of each pair reversed—allowing (theoretically) fire in each direction of the compass. Nystrom called for these conglomerates to be cast in a single unit and bored for 6-inch, 70-pound projectiles. This unlikely looking casting was to pivot on an outsized support resembling an oarlock, with recoil to be handled by a "vulcanized india rubber packing." Each of these two quadruple guns was protected by a "battery tower"—a 10-foot *square* "turret" mounted on eight wheels and turned by manpower. There were gun ports at three corners, a door at the fourth, and a pitched roof covered by 2-inch plates.[23]

The armor arrangement was also unique: a 2-inch belt on the sides, with another four inches, referred to as "guards," at a 45-degree angle to the 2-inch belt. The angled space between the two belts was to be filled with the "hardest dry oak." The outer belt was to be removable for peacetime operations.[24]

Further eccentricity was provided by a sham "fancy house" on deck complete with "false figures" to draw enemy fire. Not as eccentric was Nystrom's intention to make significant use of mild cast steel (the Bessemer process, developed in the mid-1850s), twin screws, and a balanced rudder.[25]

A cross-sectional drawing remains of the proposal by noted shipbuilder Donald McKay of Boston. This shows an angled casemate on the 227-foot wooden vessel, with a wide 50-foot beam and draft of 14 feet.[26] McKay estimated the price at $1 million and speed at 6 to 7 knots. The department considered this overly expensive and slow. The completed *New Ironsides*, however—with similar dimensions—cost over $860,000 and averaged about the same speed.

The proposal made by William Kingsley of Washington, D.C., was the most patently outrageous (though one wonders if it was such at the time). The board's report: Kingsley "proposes a *rubber-clad* vessel, which we cannot recommend. No price or dimension stated." An explanation for this has been found among Gideon Welles's papers, with no date or further identification. This vulcanized india rubber armor proposed for forts, fortifications, and vessels was to be 8-inch thick sheets from rail to water. It was expected to be "impregnable to balls or shells" by "braking the force" of the projectiles, and, should one break through, "the rubber instantly closes the aperture made, therefore making the place perfectly watertight." An additional advantage—which no doubt would have been used—was the buoyancy of the rubber material, a characteristic useful in case of the sinking of the vessel.[27]

Of the remaining eight submissions, the largest proposed vessel was by Benjamin Rathburn, a monster ship of 15,000 tons and 24-foot draft rejected because of "incomplete specifications"; no price was stated. Next largest was a vessel by E. S. Renwick of New York that was to be 400 feet by 60 feet and attain 18 knots, but at $1.5 million, the price would have absorbed the entire congressional appropriation.[28]

Given the paucity of surviving plans and specifications, the researcher today cannot make hard and fast judgments on the merits of these proposed plans. In most instances what little is known substantiates the board's judgments. It is probably noteworthy that of the rejected designs only one was eventually built (Whitney's *Keokuk*—and that somewhat modified). Of the rejected designers only two—Donald McKay and William Perrine—subsequently built Civil War ironclads. In general, the naive assumptions on which some plans were based are striking, as well as this early manifestation of the American technology-as-panacea-for-war mind-set.

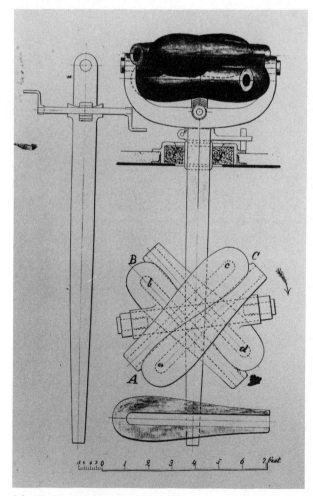

John W. Nystrom submitted a proposal for a vessel with twin manually rotated turrets, each with one of these single-casting quadruple-barrelled 6-inch guns. Recoil was to be absorbed by india-rubber packings. Other innovations included mild cast steel and a balanced rudder. The department was unimpressed by the guns and vessel, which at 175 feet and 27-foot beam was too small for the purpose. (RG 71, Bureau of Yards and Docks, National Archives)

Finally, the cover letter that accompanied the board's report gives some indication of the direction of the department's collective thinking at the time. The board first acknowledged their "scanty knowledge" of the subject at hand and noted that their request to the department for a consulting naval constructor was not acted upon. The board speculated: "It appears that they are all so employed on important service" that they were unavailable.[29]

In general the board suggested that ironclads were "formidable adjuncts" to defensive land fortifications and were necessary in the current conflict for use on "rivers and inlets." The board doubted their usefulness against "properly constructed fortification of masonry" ("notwithstanding all we have heard or seen written on the subject") but suggested they would be appropriate to "pass fortifications," reduce temporary batteries, or "run a blockade."[30]

On the question of wood versus ironclad vessels, the board suggested the former were more advantageous in a sea fight, because they were not "encumbered" with an "unyielding shield" and thus had more speed per ton of displacement. They also favored the use of "elastic" backing for armor plates—preferably soft wood—to ameliorate the shock effect of projectiles on the ship's frames.[31]

After dismissing the idea of having ironclads built abroad, the board concluded that the first priority was for light-draft armored vessels for "shoal harbors, rivers and bayous." Only after the immediate needs were met would a "more perfect system of large iron-clad sea-going vessels" be addressed. At the same time, they acknowledged the difficulty in building small, light-draft armored vessels of sufficient displacement to carry the necessary weights.[32] In all, the tone of the board's report was a grudging admission that ironclads were necessary for the conflict, combined with a large measure of doubt that such vessels could be effective.

The Stevens Battery: Part 2

Even as construction of the three contract ironclads began, a second board was studying the outsized iron battery so long in coming at Hoboken. Silas Stringham, William Inman, Thomas Dornin, Alban C. Stimers, and Joseph Henry reported on 24 December 1861. Note the composition of the committee: the first three men were line officers; the fourth, a steam engineer; and the fifth was the eminent Secretary of the Smithsonian Institution, who was subsequently a consultant to the navy on other scientific and weapons-related matters.[33]

This board reported that the vessel's plans were now "materially changed" from the plan "originally intended" by Robert Stevens and now being carried forward by Edwin A. Stevens. The plans originally submitted by Stevens are those most often seen of the vessel and differ materially from those published in the 1850s.

The major differences were in the system of armor plating and the gun mounting. In place of vertical armor and conventional gun ports, the new scheme called for inclined sides of 6¾ inches (six 1-inch and one ¾-inch layer) backed by 8-inch deep iron beams and 14 inches of locust wood. Below the waterline, the armor was thinner, but the wooden backing was up to 3 feet thick.[34] These sides did not protect the guns but sheltered the gunners: seven large guns were mounted—exposed—on the upper deck, "depending on their immense size for their own protection." The five 15-inch Rodman smoothbores and two 10-inch rifled guns were each mounted on a vertical shaft, to be turned by "steam machinery below the deck." Loading and serving were to be accomplished by dropping each muzzle 20 degrees to align with a steam cylinder below, "to the piston head of which [is] attached a rammer and sponge." Recoil was to be taken up by "india rubber springs forty inches long." The most unfortunate crewmen on this giant battery were the aimers: one man was to be assigned to each gun, to remain on the upper deck to order "by appropriate signals" the direction of fire.[35]

The loading house was to be 120 feet long with inclined ends, under a deck of 6 inches of wood with ½-inch iron below and 1½-inch iron above. A large removable smokestack rose near midships, and a "bomb-proof" grating was to be provided to ventilate boiler-room gases. Quarters for men and officers were located abaft the armored houses under a light deck.[36] An illustration from *Scientific American*, August 1861, shows eight guns and two separate loading houses.[37] Because this date precedes the date of the plans forwarded to the board, it is felt that the official description is a more accurate account of the vessel. Furthermore, the large model of the vessel displayed at the Stevens Institute of Technology at Hoboken, New Jersey—founded by the Stevens family—agrees with the official plans.

Yet another unique feature of the battery was that of "settling" the vessel an additional two feet when going into battle. This was to be done using steam pumps and tanks, bringing in 1,100 tons of water, leaving little but the guns and upper deck exposed. The water would provide additional protection without additional armor.[38]

The iron hull itself remained similar to the mid-1850s plan, though the hexagonal cross section of the earlier plan was now more rounded. A substantial ram is shown in the 1861 plan; this replaced a curved forefoot of the 1856 draft and is not evident in the *Scientific American* illustration.[39]

By 1861, the engines had been erected on the vessel—four cylinders per shaft. These were vertical, 45¾-inch diameter, working overhead beams with a 42-inch stroke. There was no connection between each set of engines, leaving the propellers completely independent. With ten fire-tube boilers, the powerplant was to produce some 8,600 horse-power.[40]

These contemporary descriptions of the vessel were quite detailed. After reading the proposals for the ship's completion and comparing that to the "work remaining to be done," however, one realizes that Stevens had completed little more than the exterior shell of the hull. Remaining undone were such things as "beams and decks," "bulkheads," a midship fore and aft keelson "the whole length of the vessel," connecting of engines and boilers, adding propellers, machinery for loading and working the guns, and—not least—armoring the vessel. At this stage, $500,000 had been supplied by the government, of a total cost estimated by Stevens of $1,283,294. Of that, $228,435 had been advanced by Stevens, and the balance desired from the government was $730,484—including the amount that would cover the Stevens's advance. This is roughly twice the original estimate—though it must be admitted that the 1861 ship was over twice the size of that specified in the 1841 proposal.[41]

The board, except for Professor Henry, disapproved completing the ship. Their conclusions were based on the excessive length-to-breadth ratio of the vessel, the vulnerability of the exposed cast-iron guns, problems expected in pumping large amounts of water in and out of the tanks (as well as the decrease in buoyancy when pumped full), the inability of the hull to support the armor, and the likelihood that the light wooden decks would be destroyed by the muzzle blast when the large guns were trained in line with the keel. Professor Henry submitted the minority report, maintaining that the hull could be strengthened to make her suitable for operation in deeper waters of the outer harbor.[42] It is important to note that the battery was never referred to in any context other than the defense of New York City—certainly her 21-foot draft eliminated her use against most Southern coastal targets.

Stevens, who was anything but easily dissuaded, did not consider this rejection as final. As we shall see, the history of the Stevens battery would continue another decade.

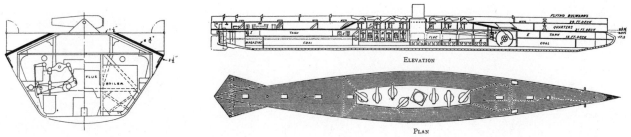

The 1861 version of the Stevens battery. The cross section shows much alteration from the plan published in the 1850s, including inclined armored sides. Elevation shows ram and large water tanks fore and aft, to be filled to lower her profile. Muzzle-loading guns, exposed on the upper deck, were to be trained and loaded from below. Note the finlike sponsons to protect the twin screws. (Elevations are from the booklet "The Stevens Battery" at the Stevens Institute of Technology. Cross section is from William Hovgaard, Modern History of Warships, *1920)*

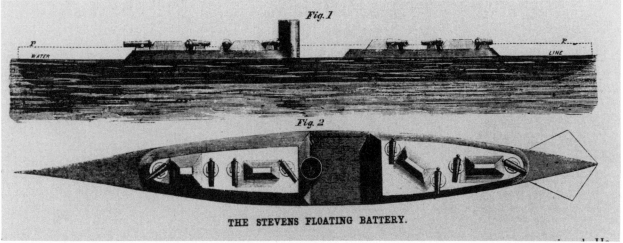

The Stevens battery, as drawn by Scientific American, *February 1861. There are several deviations from the "official" drawing above: eight instead of seven guns, pyramidal loading houses, and lack of a ram. Although the vessel was designed as a harbor defense craft for New York, the department was not convinced it would be useful—or successful.*

As the year 1861 drew to a close, three Union ironclads were well under construction on the East Coast, plus at least seven a-building for the western rivers campaigns. The sense of urgency was growing, spurred by an event of 12 October: a one-gun, armored Confederate ram, the *Manassas*, described as "something very like a whale," rammed her iron prow into the wooden hull of the federal steam sloop *Richmond* at Head of the Passes, on the Mississippi River. The impact of the collision crippled the rebel boat, the *Richmond* was grounded but was not sunk, and the *Manassas* became the first ironclad in action in the Civil War—and the first to attack a naval vessel.[43]

CHAPTER 3

First-Generation
Coastal Ironclads: *New Ironsides,*
Galena, and *Monitor*

Few warships have captured the public imagination as did the USS *Monitor,* the product of a recognized genius, John Ericsson—a vessel whose appearance "in the nick of time" single-handedly saved the Union blockade and prevented untold disasters to the Northern cause. The vessel was to exert immense influence on the course of American naval construction for not only the war years but into the next decades.

In direct contrast to the inimitable "cheesebox" were the other two vessels built as the result of the congressional directive of 1861: *New Ironsides* and *Galena.* Not only were these two ships lost in the publicity backwash of the *Monitor,* both were products of conventional ironclad thinking: they were little more than steam frigates with strengthened wooden hulls and tons of applied armor. Of these two ships, the *Galena* was not a success and in fact was more useful after she had been rebuilt as a conventional wooden ship. The *New Ironsides,* on the other hand, was singularly successful and during the war gained a considerable following of individuals who thought the monitor fever greatly exaggerated the efficacy of those vessels and who advocated building additional broadside ironclads. The debate was lively, but the well-known outcome is reflected in the present-day obscurity of the *New Ironsides.*

New Ironsides

In the postwar years, Admiral Porter described this armored vessel as "having been hammered more thoroughly than any vessel that ever floated." She was said to have been in action more days than any other Union warship of the Civil War.[1] Unfortunately, she was accidentally destroyed shortly after war's end, having spent her active days in the shadow of Ericsson's monitors.

The *New Ironsides*[2] was proposed by the Merrick firm of Philadelphia, a company with a long-standing reputation for naval steam engines, which had built power plants for the *Mississippi,* the navy's first successful side-wheel steamer; the second engine for the *San Jacinto;* and those of the large frigate *Wabash.* The company subcontracted the new ironclad's hull to William Cramp and Sons, a company that would come into its own in the steel-navy era. The ship's design was credited to B. H. Bartol, superintendent of the Merrick works.[3]

Her hull was an object lesson in the design of a conventional ironclad for shallow waters. With a length between perpendiculars of 232 feet, her extreme breadth (with armor in place) was 57 feet 4 inches: her length-to-breadth ratio was a chunky 1 to 4 (the *Ticonderoga,* a typical nonarmored ship of similar length had a beam measurement of 38 feet). *New Ironsides*'s beam without plating and planking was 55 feet 9 inches. This extreme breadth was necessary to obtain the requisite 16-foot maximum draft. The underwater form was exceedingly full both fore and aft, with a flat bottom. To carry the weight of the armor aft, a heavy counter stern extended about 2 feet below the waterline. Forward, a rectangular ram projected 6 feet from the stem. The bilge curves ended at the 8-foot waterline, and her sides extended 8 feet vertically to about the level of the gundeck. The sides were angled at 45 degrees and were capped by the spar, or weather, deck.[4]

The vessel's armor plating was built around hammered 4½-inch plates, each 15 feet by 28 inches, grooved on the edges. These indentations were to accept 1- by 1½-inch rods between each plate for mutual support. The full 4½-inch plating ran only the length of the battery, about 175 feet fore and aft. Below this, running the length of the vessel, the armor was 3 inches of iron. Wood backing was 17 inches maximum and 15 inches minimum, consisting of 8 inches of ceiling plus the depth of the hull frames. These frames were set hard against each other the length of the vessel, making the vessel's entire bottom unbroken oak—even without the planking. The 4½-inch plates may have weighed 2½ tons each.[5]

In this era, the method of attaching armor plating would become nearly as critical an issue as the armor itself, particularly in the case of wooden warships. In Britain, the *Warrior,* with an iron hull, had plating attached with through bolts. Ericsson's *Monitor* also used bolts in the turrets. The danger in the *Monitor* was that the interior nuts would break off from the shock of striking projectiles and become dangerous missiles inside the ship. The French, in the *Gloire,* used large screws to attach the iron plating to the wooden hull.[6] Cramp used the latter method, with countersunk holes for the screwheads, and a layer of *"caoutchouc"* (india rubber or gum elastic) between wood and iron, to prevent the corrosion of metal in contact with wood.[7]

Though not in the original plans, the ship was given athwartships bulkheads at the ends of the battery on the gundeck as well as on the berth deck for protection from raking fire. The gundeck bulkheads consisted of iron bars, totaling 2½ inches, laid diagonally, plus a foot of oak backing. Access from the ends into the battery deck was provided by four 4-inch-thick iron doors (two per bulkhead) mounted on rollers, operated by a rack-and-pinion system, with handwheels.[8] Forward, beyond the armor protection, were the water closets; aft were the ward room and officers' quarters.[9] An armored pilothouse (called a "Lookout" on the plans) was

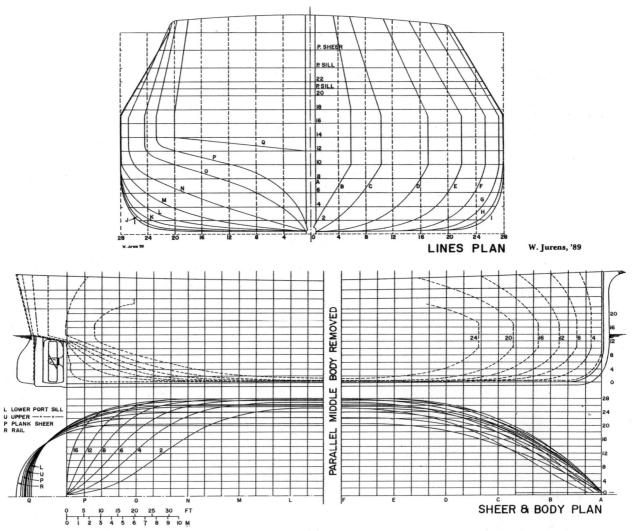

Lines of the New Ironsides. *She was flat-bottomed and exceedingly broad (55 feet 9 inches molded beam) to support her 4½-inch armor. It was no surprise that she was a leewardly vessel at sea. (Reproduced from* Warship International 26, *no. 2 [1989] and based on National Archives plans)*

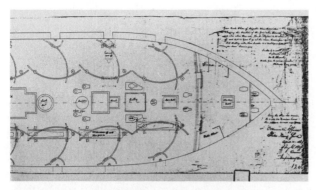

Forward gundeck of the New Ironsides. *Fore-and-aft gun stowage was patterned after the 1857 sloop* Niagara. *Armor plated doors at the ends of the gun citadel were operated on a rack-and-pinion system. Abaft the gun citadel were the wardroom and officers' quarters.* (Drawing from RG 74, Bureau of Ordnance, no. 1206, National Archives)

placed in an unusual position abaft the vessel's huge smokepipe. This structure was circular and about 5 feet in diameter. One postwar description says it was covered with 10-inch "laminated plates." The extant gundeck plan shows the base of this "look-out," as well as that of a second pilothouse added in 1863, forward of the boiler hatch, in line with the third broadside gun. A description of a second pilothouse added after the vessel went into service indicated its entrance was on the gundeck, with a spiral staircase to a platform high enough to allow a "hole for the pilot's head" through the spar deck. It is not known whether the original pilothouse had the same access arrangement, but as its base is shown on the gundeck plan, it is probable that such was the case.[10]

Port shutters were in two sections and hung pendulum style. These were 4 inches thick and designed on axles to allow them to be operated from within the casemate.[11] With a 1-inch layer of iron on the spar deck, the total weight of armor plating on the *New Ironsides* was some 900 tons.[12]

The armament for *New Ironsides* was originally to have been sixteen 9-inch Dahlgrens on the gundeck plus two 150-pounder rifles on the spar deck as chase guns. This was changed as early as 24 April 1862 (about a fortnight before launching), when Commodore Joseph Smith of the Bureau of Yards and Docks, charged with the responsibility for overseeing the construction of the 1861 ironclads, wrote Welles: "As we are aiming to take large strides in the matter of big guns," "*Ironsides*" should be armed with 11-inch Dahlgrens on iron slides and carriages, "as she will be fully able to carry them." [13] Subsequently, Smith contacted Dahlgren at the Bureau of Ordnance and invited him up to "see how many XI inch guns she can fight." This change occurred after the fight at Hampton Roads, in which the 9-inch Dahlgrens of the *Congress, Cumberland,* and *Minnesota* had slight effect on the plating of the

Virginia. The upshot was the final armament of the vessel: fourteen 11-inch smoothbores and two 150-pounder Parrott rifles, all on the gundeck. This substantially increased the broadside throw-weight of the *New Ironsides* (from around 1,400 pounds to nearly 2,000 pounds), increased the weight of the battery itself, and resulted in a complement increase from 165 to over 400.[14]

All guns were on pivot rails let into the deck. These allowed substantial facility for training the guns, as well as easing the handling of such large weights by the gun crew. Pivot rails were standard for all 11-inch guns of the era. Stowage of the guns was approximated only on the wooden frigate *Niagara* (1857), which alone in the navy inventory had a deck full of 11-inchers: the guns were brought around to a fore-and-aft position well inboard, parallel to the centerline.[15] This no doubt eased the hull strain caused by the weight of such guns when run out to the extremity of the deck.

Propulsion for the vessel was a direct-acting engine with two 50-inch cylinders and a 30-inch stroke. Direct-acting engines were relatively simple, with piston rods operating directly on the crankshaft without intermediate connections. Direct-acting engines tended to be wider athwartships than indirect- or back-acting engines, which was problematic in narrow hulls. *New Ironsides* had no such width deficit. Surface condensers were located between the cylinders. Boiler power was in four fire-tube units facing each other, exhausting into a single funnel. An auxiliary boiler was available for use when the main boilers were not operating. Auxiliary engines operated bilge pumps, feed-water pumps (for boilers), air pumps, and forced-draft blowers. A brass 13-foot, four-bladed propeller completed the power train, with an uncoupling mechanism

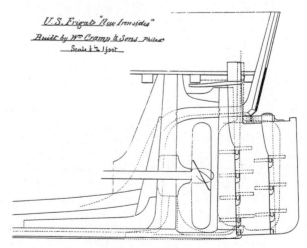

Articulated rudder of the New Ironsides. *It was designed to counteract the leewardly motion of the vessel, but it was not successful in this.* (NARS Plan 107-9-12M, National Archives. From Warship International 26, no. 2 [1989])

to reduce resistance while under sail. The 13-foot diameter prop was small for the vessel's 4,120-ton displacement but was needed because of the restrictive counter below the waterline.[16]

The vessel's rudder was unique to the navy. No doubt expecting the vessel to easily wander to leeward, Cramp designed an articulated rudder, probably to maximize its effective area. A normal rudder was mounted on the sternpost, with a second rudder hinged on the aft side of the first, giving a total width of 12 feet 1 inch. Gearing was provided (a "semicircular cog wheel") to key the movement of the outer with the inner piece.[17]

The *New Ironsides* was rigged as a bark—fairly standard for steamers of the day. She was not heavily sparred, with nothing above the topgallant sails and topmasts.[18] For action, and thus for most of her career, masts were dispensed with and poles substituted for signaling.

The vessel was launched on 10 May 1862, turned over to the navy on 10 August, and commissioned on 21 August. As completed she displaced about 4,510 tons, a figure some 495 tons greater than Merrick's original plan. The major contributions to this increase were the change in her battery (adding 301 tons) and the armored bulkheads (110 tons).[19]

As completed, the *New Ironsides* was described as "the personification of ugliness. She had neither graceful line or curve."[20] Without her masting, she was a blunt box with squat funnel and looked the part of the slow but stalwart fighter she would prove to be.

An emergency need for the vessel at Hampton Roads prevented any formal trial trip, and her salient characteristics surfaced quickly on the passage to Virginia and back to Philadelphia. In this case, two problems were intertwined: lack of speed and poor steering. Merrick had guaranteed 9½ knots in the contract; the vessel's maximum at this stage was 5.7 knots. Her engines, however, were never given maximum power, as she tended to veer badly to starboard with increased speed. The steering fault was thought to be caused by inadequate tiller ropes. After the tiller ropes were modified to gain better leverage, the problem remained. Till the end of her days, she remained unhandy and never attained anything over 6½ knots, under both sail and steam. No doubt her clumsiness was at least in part the result of her blunt lines aft, which provided poor water flow to the propeller.[21]

A report by Capt. T. Turner in January 1863 gave much insight into the sea qualities of the big vessel. He reported steaming against a gale and the ship "barely" holding her own: "Away from land, where I could use her fore-and-aft sails, assisted by the propeller, I consider her safe and seaworthy in any gale, but . . . to carry . . . directly off a lee shore against a heavy sea and high wind she is unable to do it with her present steam power and

Bow view of the New Ironsides, *probably at Philadelphia. This was one of the few times in her career she was with full sail rig. (Naval Historical Center)*

nothing could save her but her anchors." Characteristically, against a head sea she was buoyant forward but would come down with "great violence" on her counter.[22]

As to her accommodations and comfort, she was close, damp, and "scarcely more comfortable than a monitor," wrote another of her commanding officers. The gundeck was always wet in stormy conditions and the berth deck remained 93 to 103 degrees in warm weather. Capt. S. C. Rowan consequently requested the same "hardship" pay for the his crew as that paid to the monitor men.[23] These temperatures were recorded in waters off the Carolinas before October 1863 and were probably not too extreme for that climate—on shipboard or not.

Given the roles that the *New Ironsides* was assigned, questions of speed and habitability were not to be the desiderata of her success. In the coastal campaigns of the Civil War, fortifications were generally the targets of naval vessels, and thus firepower and an ability to absorb punishment were the most important criteria to be met by any ironclad. Furthermore, considering the generally sluggish pace of Confederate ironclads, both criteria would have been applicable in any theoretical meeting of such adversaries.

Though the *New Ironsides*'s broadside throw-weight was not as great as that of the larger *Merrimack*-class frigates, the deep draft of the frigates prevented their approach to within effective range of a majority of Southern coastal fortifications. In any case, their durability was limited by their wooden construction. Only the monitors, with a typical draft of around 11 feet, and the *New Ironsides* were capable of taking on such targets and sustaining a bombardment with relative safety.

The *New Ironsides*'s key advantage over the *Monitor*'s progeny was in her number of weapons and consequent greater rate of fire. The two most numerous monitor classes, *Passaic* and *Canonicus*, were two-gun vessels, the former with an 11-inch (sometimes replaced by a 150-pounder rifle) and a 15-inch gun, the latter class with two 15-inch Dahlgrens. The two 15-inch projectiles gave a "broadside" throw-weight of 880 pounds, but time between fires of these huge guns was from 5 to 7 minutes (exacerbated by the necessity of turning the turret away from the action for loading, then re-turning and realigning for the next shot). The *New Ironsides*'s broadside (seven 11-inchers and one 150-pounder) weighed around 975 pounds, but the rate of fire for the *New Ironsides* was significantly greater than the other ironclads. At Charleston, in actual combat she was able to maintain one 11-inch shot every 1.74 minutes for an hour, or one every 2.86 minutes for 3 hours in succession.[24] Between 18 July and 8 September 1863, she expended 4,439 rounds on a total of seventeen days, with the highest number on any single day being 488.[25]

"The d——d iron box" had an ability to withstand shot that was nearly legendary. At no time was her armored casemate penetrated, despite weeks of nearly constant exposure to enemy fire. One source claimed that no indentation in her plating exceeded one-half of its thickness. On one day, 8 September 1863, off Fort Moultrie in Charleston Harbor, she was hit seventy times. Her carpenter reported:

Seventy hits can be counted, but the woodwork on the spar deck is so much cut up that we were probably struck near a hundred times. Thirty four shots struck the plating and port shutters, twenty-one of which were X-inch solid shot, the others 32-pounder shot and rifle bolts. . . . One of the port shutters was shot away, and two others damaged.

The most serious damage was where two shots struck the same area of a single plate, leaving signs of cracks in the iron.[26] The only interior areas penetrated in combat were those fore and abaft the armored casemate. As far as can be determined, she retained her original plating throughout the war. More importantly, she lost no men in action (her only casualties to hostile action were from Confederate torpedoes).[27]

Criticism of the vessel's protection centered around the unarmored areas: poor protection from enfilading and plunging fire. Indeed, resort was made to sandbags on her spar deck during the attacks on Charleston. These arguments—along with her deep draft, limited room for training the guns, higher profile, and clumsy handling—were used frequently by monitor supporters during the war.

The actual performance of the *New Ironsides* negated most of these judgments. In the months under fire, no plunging fire found its way into the vessel, nor did enfilading fire affect the vessel's fighting qualities. The limits to training her guns were of little consequence in bombarding fixed fortifications. Her higher profile certainly gained her a disproportionate number of hits, and a vessel of lesser protection would have suffered, much as the *Keokuk* succumbed in a single day of action. Clumsy handling was a matter that was greatly ameliorated by experienced men at her wheel, but again, she was at anchor in shelling shore positions. The most telling argument was her deep draft, which, with the limited elevation of her guns, restricted her use, particularly in Charleston's shallow waters.

A final criticism was that she did not carry the 15-inch Dahlgren—unlike the monitors. This weapon was the largest in the inventory in action during the war and was certainly the most damaging to other armored vessels. In the smooth waters of Southern harbors this was a valid criticism, though the rate of fire of the broadside frigate greatly negated this advantage.

In the context of operations in open seas, which never occurred during the Civil War, the *New Ironsides* would have had the distinct advantage: her higher freeboard would have allowed the use of her guns in a seaway. Despite some claims to the contrary, the majority of the wartime monitors would have been simply inundated—because the seal between the turret and deck could not be maintained and at the same time allow its rotation.

If being under fire for a significant part of her career can be considered a humdrum existence, that was the career of the *New Ironsides*. She was initially assigned to the South Atlantic Blockading Squadron and participated in the unsuccessful first attack on the defenses of Charleston in April 1863. Tricky currents and her steering difficulties limited her effectiveness during this attack. Later, in July, operations were resumed against the harbor defenses, and the bombardment was sustained for two months. In September, Fort Wagner on Morris Island was evacuated because of the effects of these attacks. The *New Ironsides* was singled out on 7 September, when she was placed between the Confederate batteries and the grounded monitor *Weehawken*, while tugs freed the vessel. In this instance, the

For most of her active career, the New Ironsides *appeared as here, with only light poles for signaling. Two somewhat vertical hand-inked lines, drawn by the original owner of this photograph, show the fore-and-aft ends of the gundeck. Her funnel has been cut down and it appears that her spar-deck railing has been strengthened. (Collection of Dr. Charles Peery, Charleston, S.C.)*

big frigate was hit some fifty times without significant damage.[28]

On 5 October, a Confederate spar torpedo vessel, or "David," slipped up to her starboard quarter and exploded her charge (probably from fifty to seventy pounds of black powder) near the sternpost, over six feet below water. The David escaped, leaving a leak in the ironclad. The seriousness of this can be judged by the fact that she remained on station until May 1864—over seven months later—when she steamed to Philadelphia for repairs.[29]

After refitting, she was assigned to the North Atlantic Blockading Squadron and participated in both assaults on Fort Fisher—December 1864 and January 1865. In the latter operation, the *New Ironsides* performed a remarkable feat of naval gunnery in support of ground troops, described by Admiral Porter: "The soldiers had gained two traverses, while the Admiral directed the 'Ironsides' to fire in succession on the traverses occupied by the enemy. Four, five and six traverses were carried . . . in . . . an hour." More remarkable was the time: the fighting raged until 10 P.M.[30]

The *New Ironsides* was decommissioned on 6 April 1865. Laid up at Philadelphia, she was there when an accidental fire destroyed her on 16 December 1866. This ended the career of the U.S. Navy's only seagoing broadside ironclad.

Galena

Cornelius Scranton Bushnell, Connecticut entrepreneur and railroad investor, was instrumental in the construction of two of the Union's first three ironclads. As will be seen, he would be involved in bringing John Ericsson's revolutionary ironclad plan to the attention of the Navy Department, and at the same time he himself submitted one of the other two successful proposals. Unfortunately, Bushnell's *Galena* became nearly as disastrous as Ericsson's *Monitor* was successful.

Bushnell's original proposal, dated 28 June 1861, called for a wooden ship of 162 feet on the load line, 32 feet in beam, and 10 feet 8 inches depth of hold, with an estimated displacement of 800 tons. Power was to be from one of John Ericsson's patent engines of 48-inch diameter and 36-inch stroke, built by Delamater Ironworks, which will be described thoroughly below under the heading *Monitor*.[31] Cladding for the vessel was limited by the current technology available in the American iron industry: the inability to roll thick iron (as opposed to "hammering" the plates as in the *New Ironsides*). It was therefore necessary to build the armor up in layers. Ericsson would use simple 1-inch layers in his monitors, while Bushnell opted for a baroque "rail and plate" system that at least looked impressively complicated: the lower rails, also called "chairs," were 5 inches in width and overlapped about 2 inches on their longitudinal flanges. The plates "grasped" the vertical rail and at the same time covered the bolt heads. With this arrangement a single bolt tied together two adjacent overlapping chairs as well as the plate above, totaling $3^{1}/8$ inches of iron. (See diagram). Externally, the finished product resembled ordinary planking. Bushnell's original idea was for plating of $2^{1}/2$ inches, plus a layer of $1^{1}/2$ inches of india rubber as backing. Beneath this was 18 inches of wood. The upper deck was to be $1^{1}/4$-inch iron.[32]

The ship was to be rigged as a schooner and generally built with scantling somewhat heavier than war vessels of similar dimensions. Room and space was 26 inches, with frames sided 12 inches amidships and keelsons 14 by 14 inches. Construction was to be for the most part white oak. Coincidentally, the dimensions, scantling, and general deck layout of this "Bomb Proof" gunboat are remarkably similar to those of the 90-day gunboats conceived during the same time frame (May through June 1861). The latter vessels were four feet shorter (158 feet) and four feet narrower (28 feet) but had about two feet more depth in the hold. Room and space in both designs was 26 inches (room and space indicates the distance between frames).[33] Aft to the location of the funnel, about 88 feet from the stem in both designs, port number and arrangement are the same: two ports, a wide pivot port, another gun port, and an ash port, in that order. Further aft, where the 90-day gunboat had another gun, port, and open deck, the original Galena design had only a gangway—and cabins, wardroom, and storage, all to be under protection of the armored casemate. The other major difference was the incorporation of a second pivot port aft in the ironclad in place of a standard port on the conventional ship.

These similarities are quite striking and of course do not hold up throughout: Galena, in the original design, was to be three-masted, whereas the 90-day gunboats were two-masted, and the hull forms (cross section, and so on) were totally different. The correspondence between the two designs is brought into focus by another significant factor: the 90-day gunboats were the design of Samuel Hartt Pook, the very same gentleman and naval constructor who formulated the original plan of the Galena for Cornelius Bushnell.[34]

This original design, however, was significantly different from the actual vessel. The new design as submitted to the ironclad board was substantially larger—probably because of doubts that the small increase over the 90-day gunboat displacement was not sufficient to support the armor proposed. The new length was 181 feet; extreme breadth, 36 feet; depth, 12 feet 8 inches; and the rig was reduced from three masts to two.[35] Ericsson was consulted and on his advice the armor was extended to $4^{1}/2$ feet below the waterline (in the original, it extended about $2^{1}/2$ feet), and he added one foot to the depth of hold (to 11 feet 8 inches) to accommodate the boilers.[36] Another foot was added to the hold by Pook, who also increased the room and space to 35 inches.[37]

If the later, 181-foot length plan is accurate, the hull form and amount of tumble home for the armored sides were modified greatly. The original was marked by much deadrise, compared to the flatter bottom of the later plan. Above water, the original presented a much flatter and more angled armored surface, with the angle beginning about at the waterline itself. As modified, the sides were more convex and significant tumble home began at least a foot above water.[38]

The contract for the Galena was dated 27 September 1862 and construction was at the shipyard of William Ellery Maxson and Nathan G. Fish at Mystic, Connecticut. This yard had built seven vessels since its founding in 1853, including the fast Garibaldi of 1860. This was their second naval vessel: the yard had begun one of the twenty-three 90-day gunboats earlier in the year. The size of the establishment can be judged by the fact that Mr. Maxson himself "went into the woods looking for timber."[39]

Conditions for construction were far from ideal. Winter snows, ice, and gales created unbearably painful manual work—especially for the workmen

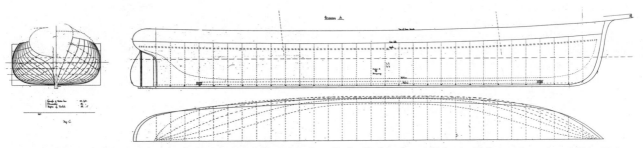

Lines and body plan of the Galena, *showing her increased dimensions from Bushnell's first plan: 181 feet by 36 feet, up from about 160 by 32 feet.* (NARS Plan 78-6-2H, National Archives)

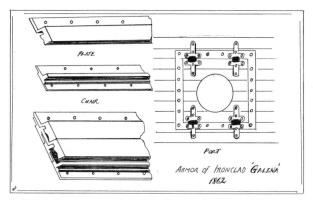

Rail-and-plate armor plating of the Galena. *Interlocking "chairs" and "plates" presented completed sides resembling conventional planking. A plan to include a layer of rubber was dropped, and total thickness was 3¹/₈ inches. (Author's tracing of drawing in* Scientific American, *19 April 1862)*

handling the iron plates, each of which was 6³/₄ inches wide by 24 feet long. The process of fitting the armor to the curves of the hull was, in the most telling sense, manual labor. T. F. Rowland, whose New York firm was to complete the vessel, visited the yard in December and reported that each plate would have to be "hoisted aboard, fitted, marked and taken to the shop to be worked." Furthermore, part of the work would be done "hanging over the ship's side." The work itself went reasonably well until January, when inclement weather forced the suspension of plating. Construction of a shiphouse was necessary to complete the hull. Launch was on 14 February 1862, with armor incomplete.[40]

The armor, battery, and deck plan were modified midconstruction. First, despite the doubts of Commodore Smith, the india rubber layer was dropped and replaced with an extra ⁵/₈ inch of iron, making a total of 3¹/₈ inches of plating. Smith contended that the vessel would not support this additional weight and was backed up in this by Pook. Compromises were suggested, one of which involved reducing the metal to a mere ¹/₂ inch from stem to 20 feet aft, and about the same distance from the stern. Another was reducing the metal to 2 inches above the port sills and making the weather deck of 2¹/₂ inches of wood plus ¹/₂ inch of iron. An undated contract addendum absolved John A. Griswold and John Winslow (the iron mongers) of responsibility for the results of the changes in armor.[41]

The final disposition of the armor-plating dilemma is not precisely clear. On 6 March, Winslow requested permission to extend the thicker armor fore and aft as the ¹/₂ inch boiler plate was "sure to be penetrated." Two days later, a letter indicated that the department preferred "extending bars" from stem to stern "if it does not increase the displacement" beyond the contract. On 31 March, it was reported that the armor was 2 inches thick above the ports, except around the stern, where it

was ¹/₂ inch. The *Galena* was commissioned on 21 April and sailed for Fortress Monroe the next day.[42] Whether the armor was over 3 inches on her sides may or may not have materially altered the extent of the disaster to come, however.

The battery for the ship was originally to have included two large pivot guns with long ports and two other large broadside guns. The addition of 18 feet to the length of the vessel resulted in moving the gundeck cabins below, clearing the deck for more broadside weapons. In October, Smith proposed four 9-inch guns in broadside and two 80-pounder pivot guns. In the end she received two 100-pounder rifles, one forward and one aft, to be shifted on rails for use on either side, and four 9-inchers. The original wide ports were eliminated to reduce the exposure of the gun crews.[43] Gun port lids were in upper and lower halves, armored exactly as the ship's sides.

The passage to Hampton Roads was the *Galena*'s only voyage under sail. At 7 and 8 knots, she rolled heavily, bringing "great quantities of water on the gun deck." On 24 April, she was inspected by L. M. Goldsborough, commander of the North Atlantic Blockading Squadron, who ordered her spars cut away.[44]

She had not been greeted with enthusiasm: Goldsborough called her a "most miserable contrivance" and ordered sheet iron to cover all the nuts on the interior of the gundeck. Another senior officer predicted that if she was used against the Confederate works, "she will be destroyed, as . . . her armor is only 2 or 2¹/₂ inches thick."[45] Capt. John Rodgers, her commanding officer, later wrote: "I was convinced as soon as I came on board that she would be riddled under fire, but the public thought differently, and I resolved to give the matter a fair trial."[46]

The new ironclad became part of the navy's support of McClellan's Peninsular campaign. With the destruction of the *Virginia* by the Confederates on 11 May, nothing stood between the navy and Richmond itself except Confederate works at Rock Wharf, Hardin's Bluff, and Drewry's Bluff on the

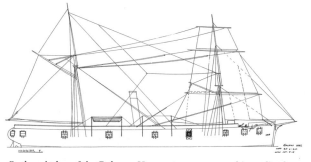

Outboard plan of the Galena. *Her masts were removed immediately on her arrival on station. (Drawing by author based on NARS Plans 28-6-2G and 107-9-11, National Archives)*

Drawing by R. G. Skerrett showing the Galena *on active service before the removal of most of her ineffective armor in 1863. (Naval Historical Center)*

James River. Rodgers in *Galena* easily defeated the first two small emplacements, then, joined by the *Monitor* and the Stevens battery (known as *Naugatuck,* or *E. A. Stevens*), attacked the latter. Manned in part by excrewmen from the *Virginia,* Fort Darling was over one hundred feet up on the bluff, with three 32-pounder and two 64-pounder rifles.[47]

With spectacular "neatness and precision" Rodgers steamed the vessel to within eight hundred yards under Confederate fire, "let go her starboard anchor, ran out the chains, put her head inshore, backed astern, let go her stream-anchor . . . [and] hove ahead . . . before firing a gun." It was quickly found that the guns of her consorts would not elevate sufficiently to allow effective fire on the Confederate position, and the *Galena* became the prime target.[48]

For three hours and twenty minutes Rodgers held his position under the guns, only withdrawing when his ammunition was exhausted. "We demonstrated that she is not shot proof," was Rodgers's sarcastic judgment. Indeed, there were precious few areas on her port side that were left untouched. Only near the waterline did shots embed themselves rather than breaking entirely through. Thirteen shots penetrated her port side, and there were three large holes (two of them a yard long) through the spar deck. The *Galena's* log gives a graphic account of the engagement: "The first shot [struck] our port bow . . . going quite through and slightly wounding two men. Shortly . . . another shot in

the bows going entirely through the ship, killing one man." Later, after the *Galena's* shells were expended and her fire on the fort was less damaging, the Confederate battery "opened on us with terrible effect, every shot taking effect—going through the iron armor." After the action, the "whole side of the ship appeared to be caved in."[49] There were thirteen killed and eleven wounded in the action.[50]

McClellan's Peninsular campaign failed, and Drewry's Bluff proved that army support was necessary to break this last outpost of the city. McClellan demurred and Richmond stood another three years. As to the Mystic-built ironclad itself, it is pertinent to quote here the opinion of the ironclad board, written 6 September 1861: "Although we are not satisfied that the armor is capable of resisting

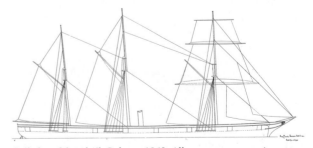

Sail plan of the rebuilt Galena, *1863. All armor was removed except that around the engines and boilers. She was then armed with eight 9-inchers and one 100-pounder rifle. (NARS Plan 78-3-3X, National Archives)*

One of two known photographs of the Galena. The date of view is uncertain, as her port side was described as "caved in" after the disastrous engagement at Drewry's Bluff. (Naval Historical Center)

the heaviest guns in Forts; the price is reasonable and the time for available purposes is short."[51]

The *Galena*, though discredited for action against such fortifications, remained on the river for another year, patrolling and engaging in minor fire support activities. In 1863, her armor was removed and she became a nondescript barkentine-rigged sloop of war. She retained the armor alongside her engines and was armed with eight 9-inchers and a 100-pounder. She was at Mobile Bay in 1864, lashed to the *Oneida*, pushing both vessels through the forts' fire when *Oneida* lost a boiler.[52]

In the postwar years, she was in commission for a short time in 1869 and was finally condemned by survey in 1870 and broken up two years later.[53] Though a "rebuilt" *Galena* appeared in 1880, this was an administrative fiction for an entirely new vessel.

The final word on this unfortunate vessel may be those of her commander, John Rodgers, some four years after the tragedy at Drewry's Bluff. Reminded of the incident, Rodgers said: "The *Galena* was a mistake. The monitor was the right principle. We could not afford mistakes, fighting in such a war, and with the danger of foreign interference. I had to prove the *Galena* a mistake. The poor fellows who died on board her that day did not die in vain."[54]

Ericsson's *Monitor*

John Rodgers's "right principle" was conceived by a Swedish-born engineer and inventor, John Ericsson, who was no stranger to the U.S. Navy. Some two decades previously he had produced the design for the *Princeton,* the first naval vessel designed from keel up as a screw-propelled steamer. Among other things, that ship had introduced the telescopic funnel, forced-draft fires, and an "automatic" form of simultaneously firing all broadside guns. Unfortunately, one of her new 12-inch shell guns exploded amidst a delegation of high officials, killing, among others, the secretary of the navy. Ericsson's star waned considerably with the navy in subsequent years, and when the nation looked for ironclad designs, Ericsson was loath to participate.

At this juncture stepped in Cornelius Bushnell, who personally presented Ericsson's idea and a small model to President Lincoln, Fox, and the navy board in Washington. Bushnell later recalled the meeting and Lincoln's typical (possibly apocryphal) humor: "All I have to say is what the girl said when she stuck her foot into the stocking: It strikes me there's something in it!" The accuracy of Bushnell's story is questionable: Gideon Welles noted that he himself had seen and been impressed by Ericsson's model, met Bushnell in Hartford, and sent him to Washington to meet the board.[55] In any event, after subsequent meetings in which Ericsson himself met the board and overcame their doubts concerning the stability of the radical little vessel, a contract was consummated.

Though the details of the story may not agree, it is fair to assume that there was substantial opposition to the plan by members of the board. In retrospect, it is amazing that the *Monitor* plan was accepted at all. As one of the board members remarked, drawing on scriptural phraseology, the vessel "was in the image of nothing in the heaven above or on the earth beneath or in waters under the earth." The plan presented in the fall of 1861 was a development of a theme Ericsson claimed to have presented to the Emperor Napoleon in 1854: a revolving gun turret amidships on a very low freeboard vessel.[56] Whereas the 1854 design used a hemispherical turret and sported a spar torpedo, the 1861 version had a cylindrical turret and deleted the torpedo.

Even apart from the innovative revolving turret, the vessel was a total departure from naval or merchant shipbuilding practice. Inspired, Ericsson said, by the "behaviour of timber rafts on our great Swedish lakes," where the operator in an "elevated cabin" experienced little motion though the seas were breaking over his "nearly submerged craft," the *Monitor* was less a warship than a rotating gun platform mounted on a steam-driven floating box.[57] Only exceedingly close displacement calculations separated this platform from total immersion, and only its pointed ends and propeller hinted at its intention to make its home in sea or river.

The original contract, dated 4 October 1861, called for an iron and wood vessel 179 feet long, 41 feet wide, having the deck 18 inches above the load line, with sufficient stability "for safe sea service in traversing the coast." It was to carry provisions for one hundred men for ninety days, 2,500 gallons of water, and eight days coal for her engines at 8 knots. A sailing rig was to be provided to allow 6 knots in a "fair breeze of wind." The vessel was to be completed in one hundred days from the contract date. Concerns about the novel vessel resulted in a warranty clause: the vessel would be proved satisfactory both in "successful working of the turret and guns with safety to the vessel and the men in the turret" under the guns of the enemy, and in its buoyancy, before the government would complete payment. In other words, she would have to go into combat to prove herself.[58] If the vessel failed to live up to expectations, she would be held as collateral until the contractor returned the funds already paid.[59] The failure of stability would probably have rendered the "collateral" inaccessible to both contract parties.

An article in *Scientific American* dated 23 November 1861 provides an excellent overview of the *Monitor*'s hull structure—a description attributed to Ericsson himself:[60]

> The structure consists of three principal parts, viz., a shallow-decked vessel with perpendicular sides, dead flat bottom and pointed ends. Under this shallow vessel a second and deeper vessel is attached with a raking stem and stern, perfectly flat bottom and sides inclined at an angle of 51 [degrees] to the vertical line. This lower vessel does not extend the entire length or breadth of the upper one. It is in free communication with the latter, the bottom of which is cut out corresponding exactly with the top line of the lower vessel. The third principal part consists of a cylindrical turret.[61]

The familiar midship cross section of the ship seems, on first glance, to belie this description, making it appear that the ship was simply a rather angular iron hull with wooden deck beams across the top and a surrounding armor shelf. From Ericsson's description and further study of the plans and Ericsson's specifications, however, the true structure of this unique ship can be delineated.

The upper part, or "vessel," was also called the "raft." This "shallow decked vessel" was composed of deck beams (10-inch square oak timbers, 26 inches between centers), covered with 7-inch pine planking and two layers of $\frac{1}{2}$-inch iron, surrounded by vertical $\frac{3}{8}$-inch iron sides, about 5 feet high, which formed the back of the armor belt and extended down some 42 inches below the bottoms of the square deck beams. The deck beams and sides were connected by roughly triangular brackets.

These were bolted to the deck beams, and, using angle iron, riveted to the sides. A 30-inch horizontal shelf was fastened at the bottom of the sides. The armor (both oak and iron) rested on this shelf, and the shelf was strengthened by other brackets filling the right angle between the shelf and the $\frac{3}{8}$-inch sides.[62]

The above paragraph has described only the top and sides of the "upper vessel." One of the most elusive pieces of this structure was what Ericsson

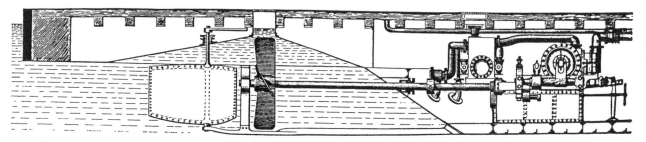

1. AFT SECTION. LONGITUDINAL PLAN THROUGH THE CENTER LINE OF THE ORIGINAL MONITOR.

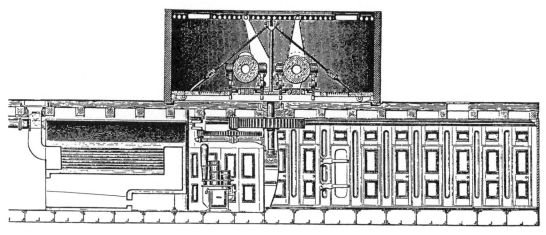

2. CENTRAL SECTION, SAME PLAN.

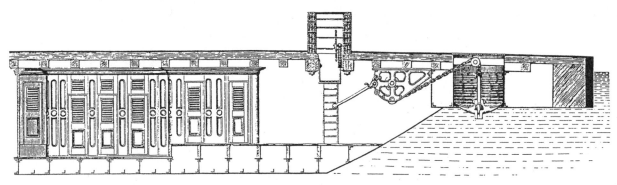

3. FORWARD SECTION, SAME PLAN.

Longitudinal section of the USS Monitor. *One inconsistency is apparent: the pilothouse is shown in its original configuration—without angled glacis—but the forward end of the deck was raised later in her career. (From* Century Magazine's Battles and Leaders of the Civil War, *1887)*

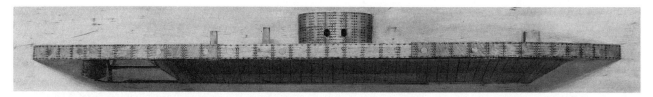

Full length view of Thomas F. Rowland's builder's half model of the Monitor, *showing scribed plating lines. The model is the property of the New-York Historical Society. (Naval Historical Center)*

called the "bottom" of the upper vessel. In the building instructions, the *bottom of the upper vessel* was to be plate iron, ¹/₂ inch thick, attached to the sides by angle iron and riveted.[63] Theoretically, if this bottom had not been "cut out" to "correspond exactly" to the outline of the lower vessel, the ¹/₂-inch iron would have formed an unbroken "dead flat" bottom for the raft or upper vessel. In actuality, where the sides of both upper and lower vessel are parallel (some 80 feet of the ship's length) this "bottom" plate is less than 5 inches wide (between lower vessel and armor shelf). The true character of this bottom plate is obvious, however, where the lower vessel tapers down to a stem and stern, leaving a dead flat surface fore and aft, measuring nearly 30 feet aft of the stern "post" and about 10 feet

forward. Forward, in the dead flat bottom, there was an aperture for the anchor; aft, the indentation and opening for the propeller.

The "lower vessel" was analogous to the bottom and bilges of a conventional ship. In the *Monitor*, the bottom was flat, broken only by a U-shaped projection where the keel would have been. This, inside, was called the "limber" and was intended to collect and carry water aft to the pumps. (Ericsson designed his ship to trim higher forward than aft.) The floor frames of the lower vessel were 3- by 3-inch angle iron and 12-inch-deep crossmembers (15 inches deep forward of the midship bulkhead), spaced 36 inches apart, with 3-by-3 frames midway between these main frames. Hull plating was ⁷/₁₆-inch iron, riveted at the laps longitudinally and to

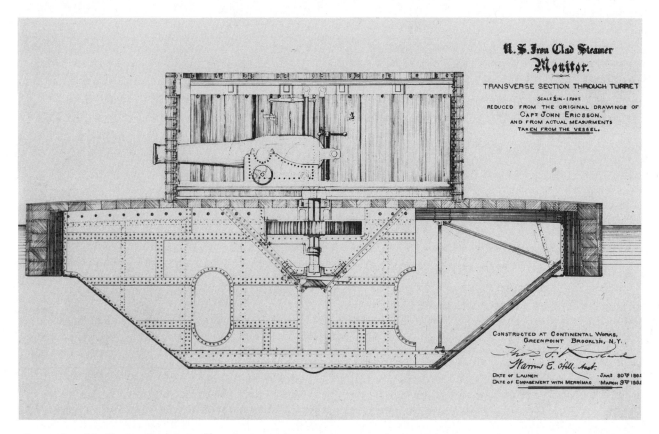

Cross section of the Monitor *through the turret, showing wood and iron side armor, main bulkhead on which the weight of the turret rested, and stanchions connecting deck beams with the frames of the lower hull. The iron gun carriage was designed by Ericsson. (Naval Historical Center)*

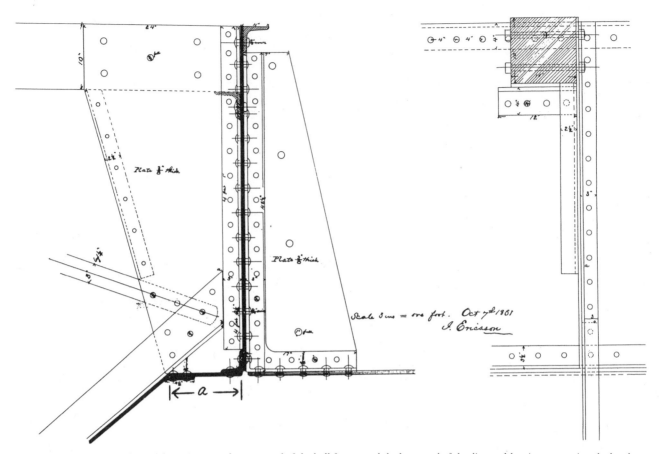

Bulwark bracket plan of the Monitor. *Seen are the upper end of the hull frames and the lower end of the diagonal bracing connecting the brackets and deck beams. The side bulwark brackets were somewhat analogous to the hanging knees of wooden vessels and connected the 10-inch-square deck beams to the hull frames of the "lower vessel." The side of the "upper vessel" (Ericsson's terminology for the deck and armored sides) was $^3/_8$-inch plate. What Ericsson termed the "bottom" of the upper vessel has been labeled a by the author. Though quite narrow for most of the length of the vessel, this bottom plating was significantly wider fore and aft, where the breadth of the lower hull narrowed. (Peterkin,* Drawings of the USS Monitor, *1985)*

butt straps transversely. For simplicity of construction, Ericsson dispensed with curved bilges and made them angular, about 36 degrees from the horizontal.[64]

The major transverse structure of the lower hull, though it tied to the upper hull also, was a midship bulkhead of $^3/_8$-inch iron. Stiffened by 3-inch angle iron on both sides, this bulkhead, and the pivot of the turret shaft, carried the entire weight of the turret.[65]

The two "vessels" forming the *Monitor*'s hull were each self-contained, making the method of interconnecting them of some importance to the integrity of the ship. Other than the fastenings around the midships bulkhead (to the deck beam, side brackets, and bottom frame), several structural elements accomplished this. First, two rows of vertical stanchions, of $2^3/_4$-inch-diameter iron, connected the floor frames to the deck beams and were intended as supports for the beams.[66] These stanchions began two deck beams aft of the anchor well, but it is not known how far they extended aft. Also,

although the connections between the tops and bottoms of the stanchions were fairly straightforward where the bottom frames and deck beams were parallel, some rather unusual connecting brackets were necessary where the stanchions met the angled bottom frames fore and aft.

A second connecting element between the vessels were five rivets at the upper end of each frame of the lower vessel, securing them to the lower ends of the vertical brackets/knees of the upper vessel.[67] A third element is described in Ericsson's specifications: "The side and ends of this vessel . . . are secured to the bottom of the upper vessel by a double rivet joint with $^3/_4$ inch rivets."[68] In other words, the rivets ran along the line where the $^1/_2$-inch iron bottom of the upper vessel was "cut out" to accept the lower vessel.[69]

There were also two bulkheads about which little is known. With the assistance of computer-generated drawings, I have been able to pinpoint a bulkhead on the aft side of the first deck beam aft of the anchor well. This formed the forward partition for the boatswain's lockers and connected the top of the lower hull, nearly at its stem, to the deck frame timber immediately above.[70] The bulkhead was pierced to receive the anchor chain. Aft, there was a bulkhead on the fore side of the deck beam directly above the farthest point aft of the lower hull. This bulkhead formed the aft side of the coal bunkers and was riveted using angle iron to the bottom of the upper vessel. In both instances, these bulkheads took the place of the corner brackets.[71] Any questions concerning the security of the upper/lower hull connection should center around all of these rather disparate structural elements.

The *Monitor's* side armor rested on the shelf outside of the upper vessel. The armor was composed of iron, pine, and oak. Ericsson's original plan was for six layers of iron, each 1 inch thick, or, alternatively, three $3/4$-inch layers covered with an outer plate of 4 inches in thickness.[72] In the end, such 4-inch iron plates could not be produced in the allotted time.[73] The completed ship had five layers of 1-inch plate from the top (deck) level to below the waterline. This was reduced to four, then three at the bottom of the armor shelf.[74]

Immediately backing the iron were five horizontally laid "strakes," the four lower of pine, the upper, oak. The iron plating was spiked to this wooden backing. Inside, between horizontal wood and the $3/8$-inch iron side bulwark, were 12-inch square vertical oak timbers, some 42 inches in length. The plans do not indicate spacing between these vertical

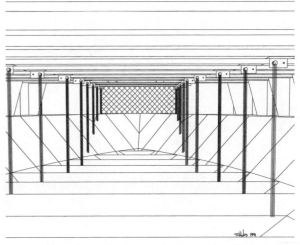

Computer-generated interior view looking forward, USS Monitor. *Shown are the floor frames and deck beams, with the side bulwark brackets and two rows of stanchions connecting the upper and lower hulls. The cross-hatched area is the forward bulkhead. Not shown are the diagonal braces from the deck beams to the side brackets. (Sam Hicks)*

blocks; therefore, the armor shelf, including wood and iron elements, was 30-some inches of solid material, measured athwartships, and 5 feet, measured vertically. The outer strakes were spiked to the inner vertical blocks, whereas the inner blocks were bolted at their tops to the iron side bulwark. The vertical timbers were also spiked to each other. No length has been found for the horizontal wooden timbers. Later, some would claim that these strengthened the ship longitudinally.[75] This was only partially true: they no doubt contributed to the structure of the upper vessel, but their location on the shelf did nothing whatever to buttress the lower hull.

The most characteristic component of this ship and later monitors was the revolving turret. While it is not the purpose here to discuss the antecedents of this innovation, it is worth noting that mounting ordnance on revolving platforms was an old idea. Indeed, a few of the maligned "Jefferson" gunboats at the beginning of the nineteenth century mounted twin cannon on a turntable amidships, with the recoil intended to revolve the platform. Later, Theodore R. Timby, of New York, patented a "Metallic Revolving Fort," which would use steam power for turning the gun platforms. In Britain, Capt. Cowper Coles patented a turret idea in 1859, and an experimental turret was erected on the ironclad *Trusty* in 1861. After a successful test, the Admiralty ordered the construction of a vessel incorporating Coles's turret. This order was part of the naval estimates dated 24 February 1862 and the ship became the *Prince Albert,* commissioned in 1864. In actual fact the first turret vessels to be completed—after the *Monitor*—were the Laird

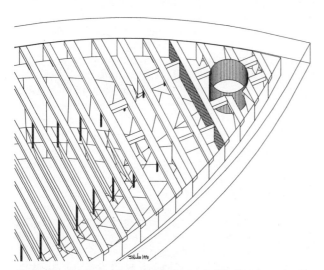

Computer-generated projection of the fore end of the Monitor, *showing the anchor well, deck beams, side bulwarks, and some bulwark brackets. The cross-hatched area represents the forward bulkhead, which also formed the fore end of the boatswain's locker. Note that this bulkhead was located nearly above the "stem" of the lower hull and therefore was a major component of the structural elements connecting the upper and lower hulls. Not shown is the aperture for the hawse pipe through the forward bulkhead: the potential for leakage through this is obvious. (Sam Hicks)*

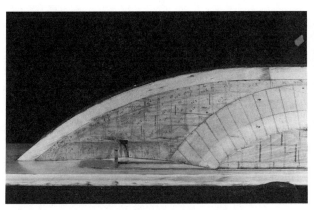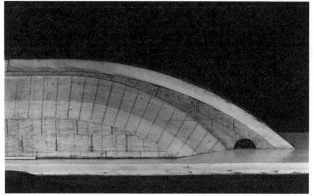

Forward (right) and aft (left) sections of the builder's half model of the Monitor, *showing the plating pattern and the width of the flat bottom of the "upper vessel" in these areas. (Naval Historical Center)*

rams *Scorpion* and *Wivern*, built for the Confederate navy but seized by the British after their launch in 1863.[76]

Therefore, John Ericsson can not be credited with inventing the naval gun turret. To this ingenious Swede, however, goes the honor of completing the first turreted naval vessel.

John Ericsson's original specifications called for a turret 21½ feet in diameter (outside dimension) and 9 feet high with 8 inches of iron plate armor, carrying two guns. He intended the plating to be of 1-inch layers or "¾ inch plates to a thickness of 3¾ inches thick riveted together and covered with plates 4¼ inches thick bolted to the former." Again, the 4-inch-plus plates could not be had in time, and 1-inch layers were used, with the inner two layers riveted and the outer layers bolted. (The bolts passed through all eight layers, to allow the removal of damaged outer plates.) The plating was attached to a 1-inch wrought iron framework. A large press at Novelty Iron Works in New York bent flat plates to fit; then the turret was assembled on the premises. The turret was then disassembled and shipped to Continental Iron Works for erection on the hull.[77] The weight of the turret rested upon a single iron crossmember some 19 feet long at the base of the structure. This member contained a socket for the upper end of the turret shaft, which was about 5 feet 10 inches in length, with its lower end supported by the central bulkhead. Note that the turret shaft did not extend through the base to the top of the turret. Four iron beams perpendicular to the main crossmember formed the support for the guns and the floor.[78]

Ericsson first intended the floor to be an open iron grating with grated hatches for passage into the vessel. The open grating (as well as the similarly pierced turret roof) was to prevent vibration and concussive pressure in the turret when the guns were fired. Plans indicate that the finished turret floor was of 7½-inch-wide, 4-inch-thick planking.

Four grated hatchways communicated with hatches in the deck below—when aligned correctly. The turret top consisted of four iron support cross-members, covered by railroad iron (track) spaced for ventilation. It originally was to have been 2-inch iron pierced with small ventilation holes. The turret top rested on an iron ring bolted to the inside of the turret wall. Its weight alone was to secure it.[79]

Holes for the gun ports were drilled through the completed turret sides (all eight layers). Judging from contemporary photos, three cuts were needed for each opening to give sufficient elevation for the guns. Pendulum-shaped port stoppers were used.[80]

Probably the most critical part of the turret, as far as the safety of the vessel at sea was concerned, was the junction between the turret base and the deck. Ericsson called for a brass ring in the deck, on which the armored cylinder rested when not in use. This, according to Ericsson, was to be a watertight junction. When the turret was to be turned, a wedge-shaped "key" was screwed under the turret shaft, lifting the entire structure, which weighed approximately 160 tons.[81] Even given the mechanical advantage of the screw threads—and a long wrench—this operation no doubt required a massive application of elbow grease.

The mechanism for turning the turret leads us to the motive power and other steam appliances incorporated in the *Monitor*. The engine itself was Ericsson's patent "double trunk," similar to the machinery built for the screw steamer *Daylight* (1860), purchased by the U.S. Navy during the Civil War.[82] This type of engine used a single cylinder, arranged athwartships, with two pistons operating in tandem back and forth in the cylinder. Piston rods working outward from the ends of the cylinder operated L-shaped rock shafts—a "monkey motion" that, with connecting rods, operated the center-mounted propeller shaft. According to Ericsson's specifications, the cylinder diameter was 40 inches, the stroke, 22 inches. With two horizontal fire-tube boilers, and blowers to provide forced draft, the machinery was to develop 400 horsepower. Though designed as low-pressure motive power with a jet condenser, as a temporary expedient the engine could operate as a high-pressure power plant.[83]

A single four-bladed propeller drove the ship. This was 9 feet in diameter and turned on a 9-inch shaft, with access provided by a hatch in the deck aft. An equipoise rudder was incorporated in the vessel. That is, the rudder was mounted on pivot points above and below rather than to a vertical rudder post. The *Monitor* was the first U.S. Navy ship so equipped.[84]

Auxiliary machinery included steam engines for the blowers as well as the turret turning mechanism. These were not totally independent power sources, however: they were dependent on the main boilers for steam. Two centrifugal blowers were used, with one providing draft for the boilers, the other drawing air in through gratings and sending it forward to the crews' quarters through vent holes in the floor frames and registers in the floor planking.[85] The turret engines operated two gears, which it was found (in February 1862) could rotate the turret at 2½ revolutions per minute.[86]

A few items were *not* part of the USS *Monitor*. Despite the other steam apparatus, neither steam steering nor steam anchor hoisting was used (though the anchor hoist could be accomplished below deck). Despite a suggestion by Commandant

Ericsson's vibrating lever, or double trunk, steam engine, of the type used in the Monitor. *Two pistons operated in tandem in the horizontal cylinder, operating horizontal shafts (left and right on the base board). These operated levers and connecting rods, which rotated the propeller shaft in the center. (Trustees of the Science Museum, London)*

Joseph Smith, a "temporary" deckhouse was not built on the ship, and, contrary to the contract, Ericsson provided no masts or rigging. Finally, one of the earliest complete plans of the ship shows a conical pilothouse, telescoping stack and ventilators, and guns firing in opposite directions. Both 11-inch Dahlgren smoothbores on the completed ship fired in the same direction, and apparently at the battle of Hampton Roads, the sole deck protrusion, other than the turret, was the square pilothouse with its eye-slits.[87]

Though the Dahlgrens were standard, their carriages were not. Ericsson designed the carriages with his own type of friction gear to absorb the recoil. A large hand wheel below the trunnion acted to spread two arms that applied pressure to friction plates on the inside of the gun slides. The presence of eye-bolts and the lack of any geared mechanism indicate the guns were run out by block and tackle, though Ericsson claimed that brass rollers made it possible for one man to run the gun out. Though it was suggested at one time that the Dahlgrens be shortened for use in the turret, in the end this was not necessary.[88]

Little needs to be said about the interior arrangement of the ship. With everything on one deck, the engine spaces, coal, and boilers were aft of the main bulkhead, and the living spaces, plus pilothouse and anchor well, forward. To aid in air circulation, partitions between officers' cabins did not extend to the ceiling. According to one crew member, the cabins, decorated in black walnut with lace and damask curtains, were fitted out at Ericsson's own expense. Though specially designed deck lights allowed enough illumination to read by on a sunny day, generally this "sub-marine cellar" was considered "too dark." Sailors, whose hammock area was in the area of the turret, had the most disagreeable quarters, because of leakage around its base in heavy weather.[89]

The *Monitor* was launched 30 January 1862, with a doubtful crowd in attendance making book on the chances this weird contraption would go straight to the bottom. On the contrary, she floated within inches of Captain Ericsson's calculations. Commissioned on 25 February 1862, she was found, after loading ammunition, to draw 9 feet 2 inches forward and 10 feet 5 inches aft, showing about a foot of freeboard.[90] Oddly enough, the only navy-built vessels with comparably light draft were the 90-day gunboats, and later the double-enders.

After an initial steering problem, the *Monitor* departed New York for Hampton Roads on 4 March 1862, towed by the tug *Seth Low*. In four days, two Union wooden warships would fall victim to another new ironclad, the CSS *Virginia* (ex-USS *Merrimack*) and the stage would be set for the most famous duel between two such vessels in history.

Some eight photos of the Monitor *are known. Dated 9 July 1862, this view shows one of the two funnels—added after Hampton Roads—(square box on the left), a gun port clearly showing the three borings required to make them (center right), and the angled glacis added around the pilothouse (behind the turret). The results of two Confederate projectiles are also plainly seen on the turret. (Naval Historical Center)*

It is hardly necessary to reiterate the famous battle at Hampton Roads and its arguable strategic outcome. Suffice it to say that Ericsson's strange vessel blunted the Confederate threat and came out of the four-hour confrontation nearly undamaged. It is conceivable that the outcome would have been more decisive had not a bureau directive limited the 11-inch gun powder charge to 15 pounds—less than half the normal loading—to prevent excessive recoil within the turret.[91]

Subsequently, the vessel's defects were delineated, leading to some modifications. One of her commanders pointed out some salient problems:

1. The officer in the pilothouse had little control over his guns (at Hampton Roads apparently a messenger was employed to carry orders to the gunners).
2. The guns could not be fired forward nearer than 30 degrees to the line of the keel without deafening the inhabitants of the pilothouse.

3. There was limited elevation of the guns—especially important in operations against elevated enemy shore positions.
4. There was lack of adequate ventilation—up to 140 degrees in the turret when in action and excessive heat in the galley area.
5. The maximum speed was only 6 knots.[92]

In the nine months of the vessel's lifespan, several modifications were carried out, a few as a direct result of the fight at Hampton Roads. The little pilothouse, which was simply an iron box of bars "log cabin" style, was strengthened with an angled glacis all around. The sole injury on board at Hampton Roads had been Captain Worden, who had been blinded temporarily by a direct hit on this structure. Smokestacks 5 feet high were added; then, in refit at the Washington Navy Yard, she was given a telescoping funnel, which branched into a Y to the two uptakes through the deck. On top of the turret, a thin boiler-iron rifle shield was erected as well as

This view of the Monitor *shows both funnels, the awning and stanchions, and the crew cooking on deck. Poor ventilation below made open-air cooking necessary in summer. (Naval Historical Center)*

stanchions and an awning. Inside, the berth deck was raised approximately four steps up from the ward room, allowing greater width to the berth deck. The most familiar longitudinal plans of the ship show the interior as thus modified, though the exterior shows the vessel as originally built—with no funnels and the early square pilothouse.[93]

After Hampton Roads, the *Monitor* was a legend in her own time. Operationally, the remainder of her career was anticlimactic. After supporting McClellan's Peninsular campaign on the James River, and the demise of her rival *Virginia* in May, little of note occurred. The final act was to be her passage south from Hampton Roads to South Carolina, in December 1862. December was no time for such a vessel to attempt passage off Cape Hatteras, especially under the necessary tow. On the night of 30 December, gale winds set in and water began streaming into the vessel—a great deal by way of the turret base. Against Ericsson's advice, oakum had been added to further seal this joint—and it

worked its way out—and allowed water in. There were indications of water entering by way of the coal bunkers, however, far aft of the turret and adjoining the aft juncture of the upper and lower hulls, and through the hawseholes. The latter brought water in via apertures in the forward bulkhead.[94] Her commanding officer, J. P. Bankhead, also later reported that she "must have sprung a leak somewhere in the forward part where the hull joins on to the armor . . . caused by the heavy shocks received as she came down on the sea."[95] The *Monitor* sank early on 31 December, carrying sixteen men with her.

The circumstances of her sinking resulted in an ongoing controversy over Ericsson's monitors. On one hand, anti-monitor people claim she sank because of Ericsson's strange upper and lower hull design, citing Bankhead's impression that the fatal leakage appeared to come from the forward joint between the hulls. Pro-Ericsson defenders of the vessel fault the navy commanders for distrusting

Ericsson's joint between turret and deck and introducing the unnecessary oakum. Certainly the most easily seen—and well reported—source of the water was the turret base. Water entering far forward or aft, however, may have contributed much to the disaster and not have been seen, simply because the crew was generally concentrated amidships during the ordeal. Since the wreck of the *Monitor* has in recent years been located and studied on the ocean bottom off North Carolina, the answer to this question may be one day be available.

This strange little vessel was the first in a long succession of monitors of various designs in the United States Navy, and in fact she gave the name itself to an entirely new class of warships: shoal water, low freeboard vessels armed with guns in revolving turrets. It can also be said that she was the first naval vessel that was designed as a naval fighting "machine," rather than as a ship adapted to warfare. As such she formed an abrupt break from tradition and represented a new concept in the construction of naval vessels.

The success of the *Monitor* brought immediate imitators and claimants. Among the latter was Theodore R. Timby of Syracuse, New York. In 1843 he had patented a "Metallic Revolving Fort" for use on land or water. This involved four tiers of guns, totaling around twenty-five, with a wood-backed, 6-inch iron casing rotated by a steam engine. Ericsson's partners, Griswold and Winslow, after negotiations, paid royalties to Timby. Ericsson later (1884) explained that they were "desirous of securing an interest in the grand revolving turret, which they supposed would be employed to protect *every* harbor in the country," and thus were loath to contest the claim.[96]

In December 1862, during the negotiations with Timby, J. L. Barnes, one of Griswold's lawyers, wrote similar words indicating that overthrowing the patent would "put an end forever . . . to any expectation of advantage to be derived from it on our part." After stating that the patent covered all aspects of the turret and method of turning, Barnes advised paying the royalty, acknowledging that Ericsson was not the "real inventor of the idea" and that Timby was "entitled to it now." Barnes contended, however, that Ericsson was entitled to the "real credit" for the practical development of the turret.[97]

CHAPTER 4

Riverboats of War: Wood- and Ironclad Conversions, 1861–1862

Throughout the Civil War the construction of ironclad vessels by the Union navy ran in two distinct threads, which in general did not intersect. Armored vessels were needed for two theaters of the war: coastal and river operations. The first armored river vessels were developed simultaneously with the *Monitor* and her consorts and spawned a genus of vessels probably unique to naval warfare.

Before describing these "riverboats-of-war," it would be appropriate to describe the typical merchant craft on which most of these were based. Resembling little more than fancy-porched, two-story Victorian houses on barges and romanticized by such stories as Mark Twain's *Life on the Mississippi*, these vessels featured exceedingly light-draft, broad-beam, scowlike hull lines, and simple (and uneconomical) operation using side- or stern-mounted paddle wheels.

The most critical design element was the light draft necessary for operation on shallow rivers. Even the largest of the riverboats (the famous *Robert E. Lee*, for instance, which was nearly 300 feet long) rarely exceeded a depth of hold of 10 feet. The typical steamboat averaged 5 feet or less draft. With such shallow, wide, and lengthy hulls, the major design problem was preventing hogging (the tendency of a hull to droop at the ends). These hulls were so limber and flexible that when a vessel was left high and dry after flood waters receded, the hull would drape itself to conform to the lay of the land; more amazingly, some of these vessels successfully regained their shape when refloated. When it came to building armored river vessels or converting existing riverboats, the enormous weight of armor and guns was many times placed well forward—greatly exacerbating the problem of hogging.

The only solution for both merchant and naval boats was the use of "hog braces" and chains. These chains, which were in actuality iron rods, formed a truss running fore and aft over the braces and were kept taut by turnbuckles: the whole system prevented the ends from drooping and the midships sections from bending upward. These chains are easily seen on contemporary photos and resembled angled clothes lines connecting the ends of beams protruding above the cabins. Though unsubstantial in appearance, they were essential to the vessel's structure.

Besides the problem of weak, shallow hulls, the necessity of shallow draft for operations in river backwaters brought another significant obstacle: obtaining sufficient displacement to support an adequate battery and protective armor and backing. Because increasing the length aggravated the hogging danger, the solution was increasing the vessels' beam. Fortunately, the width of the midwestern rivers allowed much leeway here, and the wide beam allowed significant numbers of forward firing guns. The record width was the ironclad *Tuscumbia*: 75 feet wide and merely 178 feet long, mounting three 11-inch guns across in her generous forward casemate.

From a mechanical standpoint, the American western river steamboat was primitive—even by contemporary standards. The paddle wheel—side or stern mounted—was the standard propeller: the ubiquitous river snags and shoals were likely to entangle any submarine screw propeller. High-pressure fire-tube boilers were the norm, and so were simple two-cylinder, poppet-valve engines, usually mounted on deck. Unlike the situation in ocean-going vessels where economy in fuel consumption was critical to survival, the abundance of fuel along the riverbanks made it unnecessary for the river steamer to make any pretense at fuel economy, and there was little incentive to improve the basic engine. The lack of change or improvement in the basic riverboat engine is illustrated by the fact that the cylinder casting patterns used as late as 1864 were identical to those of a quarter century before. In fact, it was stated by a contemporary that the introduction of more sophisticated engines and valve mechanisms was successfully resisted by riverboat engineers until well after the Civil War.[1]

The Tinclads and Timberclads

These basic characteristics of riverboats would come into play in various ways in the development of a riverine force. The minimum treatment to convert a river vessel to naval use resulted in a "tinclad," of which there were dozens in the inventory.

The following excerpt from a letter of December 1862 is illustrative of the conversion process:

> The commodore desires that the boats be of the lightest draft possible, to be armed with two 24-pounder and two 12- pounder or four 12-pounder howitzers; that the engines and boilers [on deck] be protected against light fieldpieces and the space between them against Minié rifle balls.
>
> That the protection be carried up from the main deck sufficiently high to prevent the enemy firing from high banks between it and the hurricane decks.
>
> If to preserve light draft it becomes necessary to take off a portion of the cabin, he desires that at least four rooms on a side, in addition to the small apartment usually found on the after part of the

river boats, be retained for the use of the captain and officers. If by placing these quarters amidships a lighter draft can be obtained, he prefers it being so placed, and that two rooms on each side be also fitted up.[2]

Note that no actual modifications to the basic vessel were directed, except if necessary to maintain a light draft. Later, in 1863, Admiral Porter described the adding of 8 inches of wood covered by 2 inches of iron plating to the sides of the "light drafts" to make them in "every respect musket proof" and to draw three feet of water.[3] An earlier directive called for the smokepipes of all purchased riverboats be made to hinge for lowering, presumably to clear low-hanging branches.[4]

The two major varieties of tinclads, as well as river steamers in general, were the side-wheel and stern-wheel vessels. Other than the obvious differences in cabin and deck arrangements between the two, the major operational distinction was the greater maneuverability of the side-wheelers, where the two wheels were independent of each other, allowing the vessel to pivot relatively quickly. The stern-wheelers' engines, on the other hand, were both connected to the single paddle wheel.

Although it is not my purpose here to catalog and describe all the tinclads, general examples can be instructive. The majority of the stern-wheelers were in the area of 150 feet in length and over 30 feet wide. No stern-wheel tinclads in federal service exceeded 175 feet in length. The average side-wheeler was similar in dimensions. There were two "super" tinclads, *Black Hawk* and *Ouachita*, with the

The stern-wheel tinclad Rattler. *Conversion to naval use amounted to closing in the main deck around the engines and boilers and the addition of sufficient light plating for protection against light field pieces and musketry. (U.S. Army Military History Institute)*

The side-wheel tinclad Ouachita. *At 227 feet she was one of the larger tinclads and one of the most powerful, mounting twenty-three or more guns, ranging from 24-pounders upwards. Note the pillboxes for riflemen. (Naval Historical Center)*

The timberclad Conestoga. *Conversion was accomplished by lowering the boilers into the hold and building 5-inch wood bulwarks around the decks. (Naval Historical Center)*

latter measuring 227 feet by 38 feet, and the former, 260 feet by 45 feet 6 inches. *Black Hawk* was the Mississippi Squadron's flagship, armed at one point with eight 24-pounders and two 30-pounder rifles and painted with false gun-port stripes. *Ouachita* was by far the heaviest armed of the tinclads, with as many as eighteen 24-pounders, five 30-pounders, and other smaller guns.[5]

The conversion of these vessels was straightforward and easily accomplished—probably without the use of formal plans. Their contribution to the war effort, however, was far from insignificant, particularly in the backwaters and bayous of the Mississippi River system. When Lincoln paid tribute to the navy after the fall of Vicksburg, no doubt he had these vessels in mind: "Nor must Uncle Sam's web feet be forgotten. At all the watery margins they have been present. . . . Wherever the ground was a little damp they have made their tracks."[6]

The term *timberclad* was applied to three vessels: the *Lexington, Tyler,* and *Conestoga.* These riverboats were purchased and converted by Capt. John Rodgers in mid-1861 for use by the army in the Mississippi River campaign and later became part of the navy's river flotilla. The dimensions of the *Tyler,* originally named *A. O. Tyler,* were 178 by 45 feet, with a 7-foot hold, displacing 525 tons. Built in 1854, she had two cylinders (typical of western riverboats): 22 inches by 8-foot stroke.[7] She was the largest of the three, carrying six 8-inchers, three 30-pounders, and four 24-pounders after March 1864. No dimensions of the *Conestoga* are known, but her greatest armament was three 32-pounders and three 30-pounder rifles. *Lexington* was 36 feet 10 inches wide and 177 feet 7 inches long and carried six 8-inchers, one 32-pounder, and two 30-pounder rifles toward the end of the war.[8]

Captain Rodgers described his conversion of these ships: "These vessels were sound and above average strength. Timbers and beams were put in to strengthen them to bear their batteries; the thin

board houses taken off and solid bulwarks of 5-inch oak plank put round them; the boilers were dropped into the hold and the steam pipes were lowered as far as possible."[9] Cabin arrangements included two mess rooms and eight staterooms on each vessel, plus an aft gun room doubling as a cabin. The joinerwork was called "exceedingly rough" and "more like the work of Irish laborers than of mechanics." Refinement could hardly have been expected: they were purchased on 5 June and all three were in action by 10 September 1861. Rodgers exceeded his orders in independently purchasing and fitting out these vessels, but all three proved very useful. Two served throughout the war and the *Conestoga* was sunk in a collision in 1864.[10]

The Ellet Rams

Another permutation of the basic riverboat, which is described here in the interest of completeness, were the Ellet rams. Col. Charles Ellet, Jr., an engineer and bridge builder, had long advocated the building of fast steam rams. With the appearance of the Confederate *Merrimack* the army authorized Ellet to immediately "take measures to provide steam rams for defense against ironclad vessels in the Western waters."[11] In a postwar article, Alfred Ellet, brother of the engineer, listed nine vessels so converted: the *Dick Fulton, Lancaster, Lioness, Mingo, Monarch, Queen of the West, Samson, Switzerland,* and *T. D. Horner.*[12] Of these, the *T. D. Horner* (123 tons) and *Samson* were converted tugs, and little is known about the *Dick Fulton.* Two, *Mingo* and *Lioness,* were small stern-wheelers (228 and 198 tons, respectively). The four remaining were the *Lancaster* (375 tons), *Monarch* (406 tons), *Queen of the West* (406 tons), and *Switzerland* (415 tons), all of which were side-wheel vessels. Known dimensions ranged from 176 feet in length to 181 feet, and 30 to 36 feet in breadth. Note two names: *Mingo* is not to be confused with *Mingoe,* a side-wheel double-ender built in 1863, and *Lancaster* was renamed *Kosciusko* when taken into the navy from the War Department (though it continued to be known as *Lancaster No. 3*).[13]

The conversion of these vessels, described by Charles Ellet, was by

> running three heavy, solid, timber bulkheads, from 12 to 15 inches thick fore and aft, from stem to stern, placing the central one directly over the keelson; in bracing these bulkheads one against the other, and the outer ones against the hull of the boat, and all against the deck and floor timbers, and staying the hull from side to side by iron rods and screw bolts; in fact, making the whole weight of the boat add its momentum to that of the central bulkhead at the moment of collision. In addition, the boilers and machinery are held by iron stays in all directions, the pilot house protected against musketry, and the engines and boilers shielded by 2 feet thickness of oak timbers, well bolted together.[14]

Ellet originally built these as pure rams, without ordnance. At the battle of Memphis in June 1862, neither *Monarch* nor *Queen of the West* were armed. Indications are that most received some weaponry as the war progressed. The *Queen of the West* was reported to have had one 30-pounder, one 20-pounder and three 12-pounders on board when lost in mid-1863.[15] Further evidence is a photograph of the *Switzerland* showing her bristling with guns on two decks. Finding accurate information on these vessels, however, is made quite difficult because of their neither-fish-nor-fowl administrative position between navy and army.

Ellet's rams met their test at Memphis, an incredible midriver melee in which the rebel fleet was decimated. *Queen of the West* immediately rammed and sank one Confederate vessel, while *Monarch* rammed another and forced her ashore. Probably the most notable later incident involving a ram was

the *Queen of the West*'s unsuccessful attempt to sink the rampaging Confederate ironclad *Arkansas* later in 1862. Their powers as rams were not again put to the test during the conflict. The army later constructed two additional rams, *Avenger* and *Vindicator*, which will be taken up in a later chapter.

USS *Essex*

One of the most unusual riverboat conversions resulted in the ironclad USS *Essex*. Before the war, she had been the *New Era*, a river ferry operating out of Saint Louis. Her small (18-inch by 6-foot) cylinders drove a recessed stern paddle wheel, mounted below her centrally located cabin area, leaving a wide open deck aft in addition to the spacious decks on the three other sides of the cabin, usually used for vehicles and cargo.[16] She measured 159 feet by 47 feet in her original form. The potential for the vessel to carry heavy ordnance was obvious.

New Era was taken in hand and became a timberclad by the simple expedient of constructing wooden bulwarks high on the perimeter of the cargo deck. Fore and aft, the bulwarks were some 6½ feet high between gun positions and at least a foot thick, with openings for nine guns. The fore and aft decks were not roofed over, but the side bulwarks were extended upward and angled to join with the central cabin, and timber protection was built over the paddle-wheel opening. At this stage she retained her original engines, boilers, and single stack. Her first battery was three 9-inch Dahlgren smoothbores.[17]

In this configuration she made a long sortie along the Cumberland River, then returned to Saint Louis to receive further modifications. Now under the command of William D. ("Dirty Bill") Porter, the

An Ellet ram. These were originally without ordnance, relying entirely on their speed and ram. The key to their strength was solid timber bulkheads running their entire length and braced for mutual support. The engines and boilers were shielded with 2 feet of wood. The vessel here is unidentified but may have been the Lancaster, Queen of the West, Switzerland, *or* Lioness. *Note the extremely sharp prow. (Naval Historical Center)*

The recessed paddle-wheel steamer New Era *being converted to the timberclad USS* Essex, *1861. As can be seen, her ferryboat origins provided copious deck space for weaponry. (Naval Historical Center)*

The **Essex** *at Baton Rouge, 1862. Note the domed pilothouse, covered with 1³/₄-inch iron, and the extremely low main deck. (Naval Historical Center)*

brother of David Dixon Porter, she received plating across her forward casemate, though apparently not to full height, and possibly ³/₄-inch plating on her sides. The major change was the addition of a light deck forward and aft over the gun deck and the completion of the side bulwarks upward to the new deck, enclosing the battery. The officers' cabins were exposed and not plated and the pilothouse opened via trap-door to the gundeck.[18]

At the battle of Fort Henry in February 1862, the *New Era*, now named *Essex* and under navy control, fought brilliantly but then took a shot through the forward casemate immediately above the armor line, thence into her center boiler, scalding several, including the men in the pilothouse above who had neglected to close the intervening door between gundeck and pilothouse.[19] She was knocked out of the action. Porter, known for precipitate action, immediately instigated yet another rebuilding of the vessel, which made her into one of the most formidable in the river flotilla.

Between early February and the end of June 1862 (she came out of the dock late in April), Porter supervised rebuilding the *Essex* into what was essentially a new ship—in appearance as well as internally: she received an *S* and an *X* painted on her funnels as distinguishing marks. The vessel now had a unique two-story casemate about 17 feet high, with the upper level devoted to quarters and stores. Above this a dome-shaped pilothouse protruded, covered with 1³/₄-inch iron, as well as the shield over the paddle wheel. The casemate itself was angled and the sides were of 16-inch timber covered with ³/₄-inch plates of iron described as "very superior"; forward, the backing was 30 inches behind

1³/₄ inches of iron. One-inch rubber was used between the side plating and the backing. A mass of solid timber was used in the bows for ramming purposes.[20] The dimensions of the vessel were now 205 feet by 60 feet: 45 feet longer and 13 feet wider than the old *New Era* and 1,000 tons compared to an original 355 tons. According to one source, the engines were now 23 inches in diameter and she had twin stacks. Certainly the increase in displacement warranted more powerful motive power. The number of boilers is unclear: some reports say the fatal shot hit her "middle" boiler, indicating three before rebuilding, whereas another lists four boilers for the ship.[21] Finally, the relative locations of stacks and paddle wheels show that her internal machinery had been relocated, vis à vis the original vessel.[22]

The additional 13 feet in width was obtained by adding "sponsons" to the sides of the bottom, forming a double wall for further protection from ramming. It is not clear, however, when this was done, since Porter referred to such sponsons at the time of Fort Henry.[23]

Porter spent in excess of $50,000 on this rebuilding, leaving no major system untouched: new engines, boilers, and machinery arrangement; over 40 feet added to length and 13 to breadth; and completely redesigned casemate and interior. It also appears that the paddle wheels were now larger—higher than the 17-foot-high casemate, as opposed to well hidden below the cabin on the old *New Era*.[24] The factor that allowed such major alterations in a short period of time was the simplicity of riverboat design and construction. The scowlike hull lines required little planning and simple carpentry if one wished to add length, and the straight

DETAILS OF THE LATER ESSEX

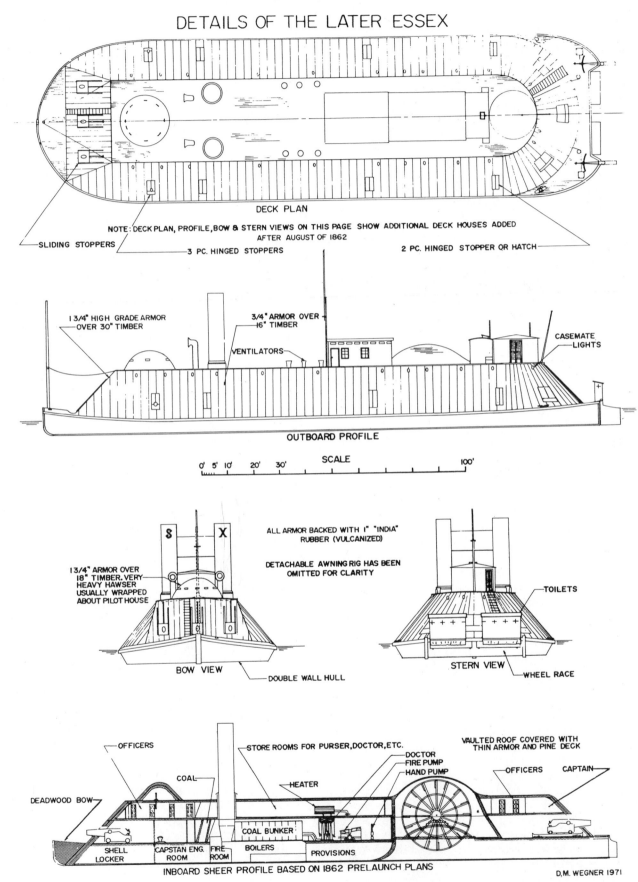

DECK PLAN

NOTE: DECK PLAN, PROFILE, BOW & STERN VIEWS ON THIS PAGE SHOW ADDITIONAL DECK HOUSES ADDED
AFTER AUGUST OF 1862

SLIDING STOPPERS

3 PC. HINGED STOPPERS

2 PC. HINGED STOPPER OR HATCH

1 3/4" HIGH GRADE ARMOR OVER 30" TIMBER

3/4" ARMOR OVER 16" TIMBER

VENTILATORS

CASEMATE LIGHTS

OUTBOARD PROFILE

SCALE
0' 5' 10'   20'   30'   100'

13/4" ARMOR OVER 18" TIMBER. VERY HEAVY HAWSER USUALLY WRAPPED ABOUT PILOT HOUSE

ALL ARMOR BACKED WITH 1" "INDIA" RUBBER (VULCANIZED)

DETACHABLE AWNING RIG HAS BEEN OMITTED FOR CLARITY

TOILETS

S   X

BOW VIEW

DOUBLE WALL HULL

STERN VIEW

WHEEL RACE

OFFICERS

STORE ROOMS FOR PURSER, DOCTOR, ETC.

VAULTED ROOF COVERED WITH THIN ARMOR AND PINE DECK

COAL

DOCTOR
FIRE PUMP
HAND PUMP

HEATER

OFFICERS   CAPTAIN

DEADWOOD BOW

COAL BUNKER

SHELL LOCKER

CAPSTAN ENG. ROOM

FIRE ROOM

BOILERS

PROVISIONS

INBOARD SHEER PROFILE BASED ON 1862 PRELAUNCH PLANS

D.M. WEGNER 1971

Stern view of the USS Essex. Taken at a later date than the 1862 picture, the photograph shows that cabins have been added fore and aft of the paddle-wheel housing. (Naval Historical Center)

hull sides would similarly facilitate additional breadth. In any case, Porter accomplished an extraordinary amount of work in short order on this vessel.

The performance of this thoroughly rebuilt vessel was not surprising for something that was hardly more than a massive floating box: "She works slowly and not very well; although running two engines and two wheels she cannot be kept under complete command; she moves so very slowly, even under full steam, that when the river rises she will be unable to double the points, making the bends without the aid of a powerful tug. In present . . . low stage . . . with scarcely any current, she does very well."[25]

At full steam, she could carry six days' worth of coal; with banked fires, one month. Provisions carried were sufficient for one month. As is obvious from illustrations, her deck was barely above water: 3 inches with normal load. This, plus the fact that all her pumps were steam driven, led to some apprehension that any accident occurring when steam was not up could result in sinking the vessel.[26]

Conditions on board were described as "wretchedly uncomfortable and unhealthy." In the rain she leaked badly, because of shrinkage of the planking beneath the plating. Since storage and living spaces were on the top deck, the result was ruined provisions and clothing.[27]

In September 1862, the *Essex* was armed with two 50-pounder rifles, one 24-pounder, one 32-pounder, three 9-inchers and one 10-inch Dahlgren. In 1864, the number of 9-inchers was six, plus two 100-pounder Parrott rifles. There were

W. D. Porter's final version of the Essex, *showing her 17-foot-high, two-story casemate. As completed, she was over twice the displacement and 45 feet longer than the original vessel.*

three ports forward, and the stern gun could be fired through any of three ports aft (center and each side).[28]

The *Essex* proved to be one of the most formidable of the river fleet, despite the fact that her casemates were "frequently penetrated" by enemy shot.[29] Her most famous encounter was with the rebel ironclad *Arkansas* in mid-1862: at fifty yards all three of her bow guns ripped into the Confederate vessel, with one shot entering the forward gun port. This fight was inconclusive: the *Arkansas* escaped, only to be found again the next day—disabled and aground. At the approach of the *Essex,* the *Arkansas*'s crew destroyed their vessel to prevent her capture. The *Essex* fought out the war only to be sold in late 1865 for $4,000.

USS *Benton*

With the USS *Benton* the history of the western river ironclads becomes intertwined with that of James B. Eads—the western theater's cognate of John Ericsson. Eads was a self-taught engineer who had invented a diving bell for salvage work on the rivers, and who would, after the war, go on to become a noted bridge builder.

That Eads was well connected was quickly evident: only three days after Fort Sumter, Edward Bates, Lincoln's attorney general wrote Eads, pressing him to "come instantly" if called to Washington, to make available his expertise on steam boats and the river.[30] Shortly thereafter, the first mention is found of what would become the ironclad *Benton,* when Eads, now in Washington, wrote Welles of a snag boat, "converted for raising sunken steamboats," owned by the Missouri Wrecking Company. She was a twin-hulled vessel, with seven watertight compartments per hull and two independent engines. Eads suggested protecting her with cotton bales as armor and arming her with 32-pounders and maintained that in this configuration she would draw only four feet (one foot less—said Eads—than the minimum depth of the Mississippi from Cairo, Illinois, to Memphis).[31]

Eads also put in a strong argument for establishing a base of operations at Cairo, at the confluence of the Mississippi and Ohio rivers. These suggestions were duly noted and forwarded to Simon Cameron, secretary of war, and thence to General McClellan, then commander of the Union army in the West. Shortly thereafter, Commander John Rodgers was detailed to the West to aid the army in establishing this river naval force.[32]

The next allusion to the vessel occurred in May, when Eads informed Welles that he had "secretly" moved her from Saint Louis to Cairo, as Bates had thought such boats would be useful to the government.[33] In August, after plans had been made for Eads's city-class gunboats, an inspection was made

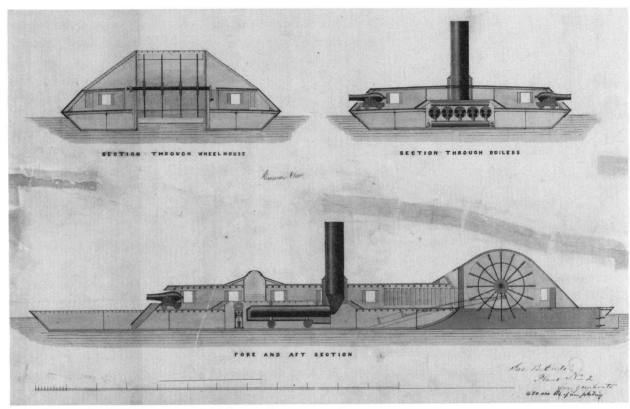

SECTION THROUGH WHEELHOUSE   SECTION THROUGH BOILERS

FORE AND AFT SECTION

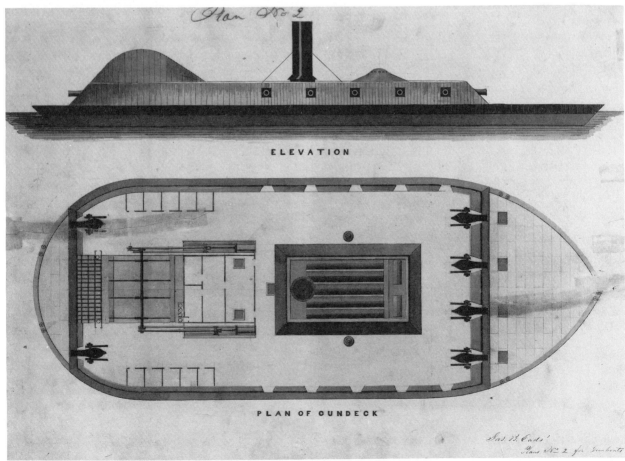

ELEVATION

PLAN OF GUNDECK

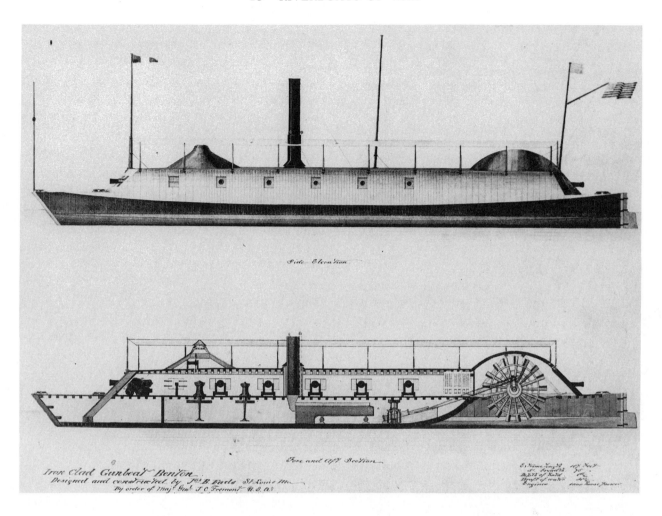

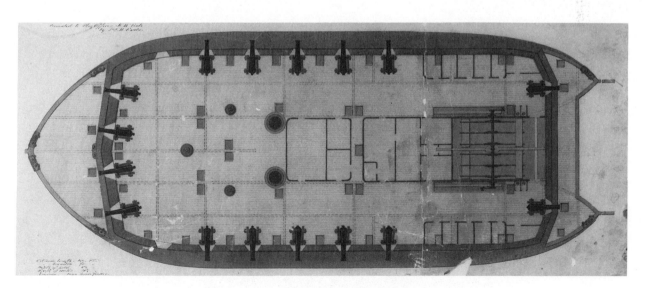

Outboard, inboard, and deck plans of the Benton. On the original plan, the lightly drawn grid on the deck plan shows below the deck bulkheads. (Naval Historical Center, outboard and inboard; Smithsonian Institution, deck plan)

Opposite: *James Buchanan Eads's gunboat Plan No. 2. This was apparently Eads's original plan for the* Benton. *Major differences from the final plan are the lack of sheer and higher placement of the boilers. Note the center section longitudinally, which recalls the vessel's origin as a catamaran snag boat. (NARS Plans 28-6-4D and 28-6-4F, National Archives)*

of "Submarine Boat No. 7" (*Benton*'s company designation) to determine her suitability for conversion to a gunboat. The vessel was duly purchased and work began. (Eads was later accused of conflict of interest in this transaction: he was part owner of the wrecking company involved.[34])

Snag boats such as No. 7 were necessities on the broad shallow rivers, where annual floods constantly altered their courses, leaving trees and miscellaneous obstructions to endanger commerce. With a twin-hulled snag boat, the offending tree was brought in between the hulls, tied off, and sawed out of the way.

Eads later described the conversion process:

> She was built with two hulls, about twenty feet apart, very strongly braced together. . . . I had the space between the two hulls planked, so that a continuous bottom extended from the outer side of one hull to the outer side of the other. The upper side was decked over in the same manner; and by extending the outer sides of the two hulls forward until they joined each other at a new stem . . . the twin boats become one wide, substantial hull. The new bottom did not extend to the stern of the hull, but was brought up to the deck fifty feet forward of the stern, so as to leave space for a central wheel.[35]

Eads described her tonnage as "quite double" that of the city-class vessels, and, unlike those ships, she would be "entirely covered with iron plates" with machinery and boilers "perfectly inaccessible to shot or shell." The armor would total about 260 tons, of which 150 tons was 2½ inches thick. The forward casemate and the forward 60 feet of the sides was 2½-inch iron, with the former backed by 34 inches of wood and the latter by 20 inches (measured "on a horizontal line," according to Eads, making the actual thickness somewhat less). The forward casemate—wood and iron—also extended 2 feet below the deck line. Indications are that the side plating aft was ⅝ inch, and the pilothouse armor was 1½ inches in thickness.[36]

Propulsion for the vessel was by provided by two inclined 20-inch cylinders, with a stroke of 7 feet, with steam from five boilers. Each cylinder drove an independent paddle wheel, allowing these paddles to assist in turning the vessel. She was provided with steam-operated pumps, which, combined with watertight compartmentation, would aid in keeping her afloat if holed by accident or gunfire.[37]

The "watertight" bulkheads used in wooden ships (ocean-going as well as river vessels) were obviously not equivalent to those incorporated into iron or steel ships, and their effectiveness was limited by the flexibility of wooden hulls, as well as the impermanence of the caulking used. On the *Benton*, Eads reported there were forty compartments, and on available plans, the bulkheads can be seen as light lines in a grid pattern fore and aft and athwartships in the hull.[38]

The resulting vessel had one of the most capacious gundecks on the river, and the only deck on which four large guns fired forward. (Only the *Tuscumbia* exceeded this weight of forward fire, with three 11-inchers.) The *Benton* began her career with two 9-inch guns, seven 32-pounders, and seven U.S.

1863 U.S.S. Benton – Lt Comdr J. A. Greer U.S.N. Comdg after running the Vicksburg batteries

The Benton, *shown after running the batteries at Vicksburg. She mounted sixteen heavy guns, making her the most heavily armed of the river ironclads. (U.S. Naval Institute)*

Army 42-pounders. In mid-1863, she mounted two 100-pounder rifles, eight 9-inchers, four 32-pounders, and two 50-pounder rifles. With a total of sixteen heavy guns, she had the heaviest battery in the river fleet.[39]

The *Benton,* measuring 187 feet overall, by 75 feet in beam, and over 1,000 tons, had her first river trial in mid-January 1862. She did not exceed 2¹/₂ knots against the current and made 5¹/₂ knots in slack water. At full steam (145 pounds pressure) she was unable to back against the current, and counter-rotating her paddles would not bring her around without assistance from her two rudders. It required a sluggish eight to twelve minutes to bring her around. The general consensus was that she was underpowered and needed larger engines and boilers. Commodore A. H. Foote commented that he had recommended more powerful machinery earlier; but construction was well under way, and in any case, he had no jurisdiction at the time because the vessel was being constructed under the auspices of the army's Quartermaster Department.[40]

In the end, the only modifications were the raising of her wheel by 18 inches and the increase of her rudder surfaces, both to improve her handling. She continued through the war "at all times an unmanageable ship" and at "her usual snail's pace" as Admiral Porter and C. H. Davis put it. She was, however, a strong bulwark for the flotilla. Her sides were notably strong, with shots "scarcely leaving a mark" according to Admiral Porter. Plunging fire was another matter: hits on her decks "went through everything."[41]

The big *Benton* served through the major campaigns of the river war, from Island No. 10 onward, including Memphis, Vicksburg, Grand Gulf, and Red River. She was decommissioned 20 July 1865 and sold for $3,000 after the removal of her plating.[42]

*Eads's ironclads under construction. In the foreground are the
boilers; on the ship in the background a few of the spar-deck beams are
in place. (U.S. Naval Institute)*

CHAPTER 5

———————— ◆ ————————

City-Class Ironclads

Within the field of Civil War history, the western theater of operations has always played the role as backdrop to the campaigns in the East. By the same token, naval history of the western river operations has long been overshadowed by the coastal campaigns. This has placed the city-class vessels in a shadow they hardly deserved. Although these seven boats were hardly perfect or technologically innovative, judged by their operational usefulness they were, ton for ton, some of the most important war vessels of the conflict.

The naval forces on the western rivers, particularly the Mississippi, were originally developed under the auspices of the U.S. Army, in particular, the Quartermaster Department, the arm of the service responsible for both supply and transportation. The role of the U.S. Navy in the formation of the river flotilla began as early as 16 May 1861, with directives from secretary of the navy Welles to Commander John Rodgers and naval constructor Samuel M. Pook to proceed to Cincinnati or Cairo, Illinois, to report to General McClellan. Rodgers was to report "in regard to the expedience of establishing a naval armament" on the rivers, and Pook was given special duty under Rodgers.[1] Rodgers proceeded immediately on arrival in the West to purchase vessels suitable for conversion to military use, notably the *Lexington, Tyler,* and *Conestoga.*

Back in the nation's capital, the higher echelons of both services were producing plans for constructing purpose-built river gunboats. A draft and description of a river war steamer, dated 1 June, was sent to Gen. Winfield Scott, then commanding the army, by way of Gen. Joseph G. Totten, the army's chief engineer, from naval chief constructor John Lenthall. Lenthall began his description with daunting words: "It does not seem to be practicable to make an armed steam vessel for the 'Mississippi'

. . . that will be very efficient. The depth of water will not permit a vessel being fitted with a propeller and the engine below deck, but it must be a side-wheel requiring the support of guard beams, braces, etc.—the cranks and shafts also exposed."[2]

Lenthall proceeded to describe a flat-bottomed "batteau" with a depth of hold just under 9 feet, containing engines, boilers, and fuel. The vessel would be 28 feet extreme breadth (not including paddle-wheel guards) and 170 feet long, with identical ends, each with a rudder. The paddle wheels would be about 24 feet in diameter, with cylinders 18 inches in diameter and stroke of 8 feet. Armament was to be four 8-inch guns, and expected draft was around 5 feet, displacing 436 tons. It is noteworthy that these dimensions, except for the draft, were quite similar to those of the 90-day gunboats designed contemporaneously. Lenthall closed with another disclaimer, effectively admitting that his expertise in seagoing vessel construction was not likely to be as useful as that of someone "engaged in this kind of work" and recommended the War Department consult with S. M. Pook, "now at Cairo, or on the Ohio." Despite Lenthall's reticence, Totten thought the plan "well adapted" for the purpose.[3]

Lenthall's plan was shelved, however, despite the support of Totten and Winfield Scott. Scott had wanted sixteen vessels to be built under the supervision of and commanded by naval "sea" lieutenants.[4] As far as is known, the only army-built unarmored Civil War gunboats were to the design of Norman Wiard in 1864. These were about 160 feet by 21 feet double-enders, characterized as "complete failures."[5]

When the subject of gunboats reached Montgomery C. Meigs, the new quartermaster general wrote to McClellan, "It will be of importance to prepare one or two iron-plated vessels." These "mere scows" would not "need much speed" and would carry three rifled 42-pounders in the bow, one astern and two on each broadside. They would be screw propelled and have 4½-inch plating for 7 or 8 feet above water.[6] Meigs emphasized forward fire and deemphasized speed. The resulting vessels would meet both expectations.

At this juncture, S. M. Pook applied his considerable talents to the problem of designing an armored light-draft river war steamer. His drawing, now in the National Archives, is the master plan for the city-class vessels, called by some "Pook's Turtles," referring to their wide, inwardly slanting shells. The dimensions were 175 feet long on deck by 50 feet extreme breadth, with center paddle wheel and angled casemate partially covered with iron plating. The noticeable differences between this original plan and the completed vessels are in the number of boilers—four in the original, five in the completed ironclads—and the number and placement of gun ports. Pook placed three across the stern and seven evenly spaced on each broadside, as opposed to two stern guns and four in broadside placed generally forward in the casemate on the actual vessels.[7]

Based on this plan, early in August eight firms placed bids for contracts from the Quartermaster Department. Of these, the highest price quoted was $110,000, by A. F. Temple of Madison, Indiana; the lowest was $75,000, by William Jones of New Albany, Indiana. The shortest construction time was fifty days, claimed by Humphreys Marine Railway and Dock Company, for $90,000. The majority offered one to five vessels. The exception was the

The USS Cairo, 1991. After the wreck of the vessel was taken in hand by the National Park Service, serious preservation work began. Using a technique known as "ghosting," the vessel was reconstructed, as much as possible from her original parts. What was missing was recreated with a modern timber skeleton, as shown here, at Vicksburg National Military Park. (Photograph by Elizabeth Joyner, National Park Service)

bid by James Buchanan Eads, who offered four to sixteen boats complete with machinery and plating at $89,000 each. The deciding factor for the government, other than the production numbers he claimed, may have been his inclusion of a penalty clause for each week beyond the contracted completion date: 5 October 1861.[8]

This was the origin of the seven city-class gunboats: *Cairo, Carondelet, Cincinnati, Louisville, Mound City, Pittsburgh,* and *St. Louis,* all named for river cities. The *St. Louis* was renamed *Baron de Kalb* on 8 September 1862, after her transfer to the navy,

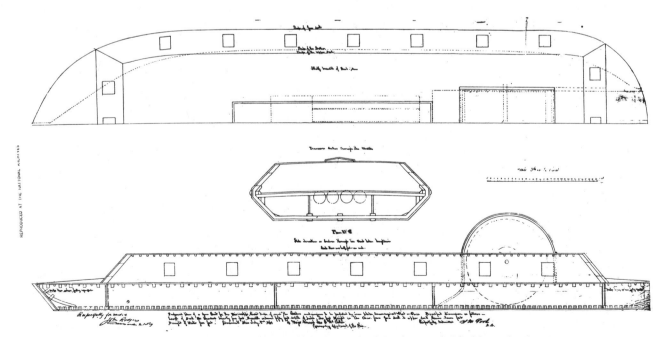

Samuel Pook's original plan for a light-draft armored river gunboat. The completed city-class "turtles" had five rather than four boilers, four ports per side, and angular knuckles at the base of the armored sides. (National Archives)

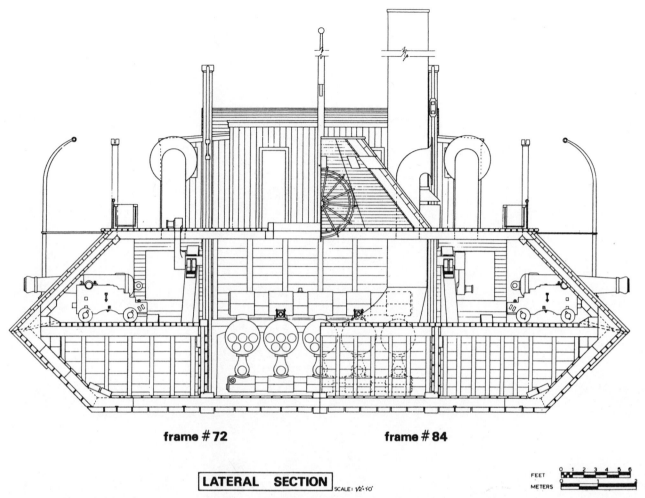

frame #72   frame #84

LATERAL SECTION   SCALE: 1/2"·10'

FEET
METERS

Cross section of the USS Cairo. *Unlike the boilers, the steam drum is above deck. This exposure caused a disaster on the* Mound City *when an enemy shot penetrated the fore quarter, then the steam drum, scalding dozens of crewmen. (National Park Service)*

which already listed a second *St. Louis,* a sailing sloop of war.

Of the entire steam-powered U.S. Naval Civil War Fleet the city-class vessels are unique in that one of their members survives today, though in an incomplete condition. The USS *Cairo,* named after the town in Illinois and pronounced by natives "Kay-ro," or "Kare-o," is now preserved at Vicksburg National Military Park, salvaged from the Yazoo River in the early 1960s, where she had lain since striking a Confederate floating torpedo in December 1862. Therefore, unlike any other vessel described in these two volumes, the *Cairo* can be to some extent described with reference to the original: though considerably modified by the ravages of time, the river, and unfortunate salvage methods. To be specific, significant portions of the vessel no longer exist: "the wheelhouse, hurricane deck, large sections of the casemate and armor plate, machinery, bulkheads, gun deck, and stern fantail" have been lost.[9]

Ameliorating this loss is the method used by the National Park Service, a restoration technique referred to as "ghosting." This is designed to incorporate and display all the surviving parts of the vessel in their proper places, with the missing portions represented by a modern framework.[10] The vessel has been the subject of extensive study and the publication of a detailed Historic Structure Report by the National Park Service. Her engines have been listed as a National Historic Mechanical Engineering Landmark by the American Society of Mechanical Engineers. The following description is based on these studies, original documents, and an observation trip to the site. The description may be considered appropriate for the entire city class, and any known significant variations among the other class members will be noted.

The flat-bottomed hull of the USS *Cairo* as built was predominantly white oak, fastened with spikes. The frames were set on 18-inch centers and measured 4 1/2 inches by 10 inches. Frames were doubled

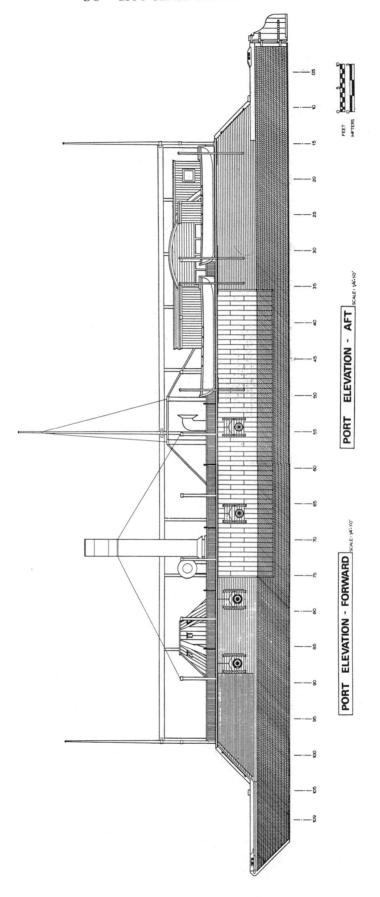

PORT ELEVATION - AFT   SCALE : ¼"=1'0"

PORT ELEVATION - FORWARD   SCALE : ¼"=1'0"

FEET

METERS

for floors and up as far as the lower port sill. The major longitudinal members were three keels and three keelsons, 14 inches wide and 6 inches thick, placed in the center and approximately 10 feet on each side of the centerline. Bottom planking was 5 inches thick; side planking, 4 inches. Gundeck beams alternated between 10 inches square and 10 inches by 4 inches, on 24-inch centers, with 4½-inch pine planking. Ceiling plank was 2½ inches thick.[11]

The original specifications called for two longitudinal bulkheads, nominally watertight, and four athwartships bulkheads, forming fifteen compartments. The lengthwise bulkheads were to continue forward from the two sides of the paddle-wheel race and terminate at the intersections with the incurving bilge timbers. On today's Cairo these bulkheads are not complete in the midships area, athwart the engines and boilers. Also, the athwartships bulkheads do not coincide with the original plans.[12] These divided the hold into various compartments, including coal bunkers, magazines, and stores. The lack of present-day compartmentation is no doubt a result of the primitive salvage methods used before the involvement of the National Park Service, including the segmenting of the vessel for ease of overland transportation. Compartmentation of the vessels was credited with preventing the sinking of the sister vessel Carondelet at Fort Donelson in February 1862, after she had been struck repeatedly in the bows between wind and water.[13] It was not sufficient to prevent the loss of the Cairo, however, which went down in twelve minutes after taking a mine in the port bow.

The major alteration made by Eads in building these vessels was in eliminating the vertical section at the beam ends, shown in Pook's original plan. Instead, Eads continued the frames of the sides of casemate and bottom to form sharp knuckles, thereby adding about two feet to the extreme width of the vessels.[14]

The hurricane deck held the octagonal armored pilothouse, paddle-wheel housing, and accompanying cabin. Skylights were located aft of the pilothouse and on each side of the wheelhouse. Eight-foot-high awning stanchions ran the length of both sides of the hurricane deck, and a line of 10-foot-high stanchions ran down the centerline. There were four ventilators, two over the fireroom and two immediately abaft the boilers. As the war continued, these broad hurricane decks acquired various other cabins and structures. The Louisville, for instance, eventually resembled a peacetime riverboat with a full-length roof. A cabin was immediately abaft the pilothouse, and the aft wheelhouse cabin was lengthened. Additionally, a "peacetime" unarmored pilothouse was erected directly above the armored battle conning tower. Another addition made to the Cincinnati for which there is no available description in detail was a cylindrical flat-topped structure aft over the wheelhousings, about as wide as the cabin itself. The one illustration of this is of the Cincinnati shown in Harper's Weekly in 1863. It appears it may have been an iron-plated riflemen's redoubt.[15]

Also visible above the hurricane deck on these ships were four vertical stanchions or braces approximately above the fourth gun port. Diagonal lines descending from these forward and aft to the deck were the hog chains (two sets: one port, one starboard). These rods were 1 to 2½ inches in diameter and passed through both decks and attached to the keelsons on either end of the engine and boiler spaces—the heaviest part of the hull. The starboard chains have been preserved and can be seen on the Cairo.[16]

The second major hull component was the iron armor. The government specifications were vague, calling only for an "estimated" 75 tons of plating to "protect the boiler and engines."[17] In fact, all seven received 2½-inch thick plating on the forward casemate as well as the sides athwart the machinery. Note, however, that the boilers as well as the cylinders themselves were below the deck line. Only the steam drum was exposed above the main deck. The plating covered approximately 60 feet of the sides, with 12 feet above the knuckle and 5 feet below the knuckle. The strakes were vertical, 13 inches wide and up to 8 feet 1½ inches long. The plates were tied together by overlapping lips—2 inches wide and ½ inch thick, with 1⅛-inch bolts passing through the laps. The forward casemate measured about 36 feet wide at its broadest point and was covered with the same type of plating. The wooden (oak) backing was 24 inches thick on the casemate, 12½ inches on the sides and aft.[18] The octagonal pilothouse was also plated. The wooden backing of the front three panels was 19 inches; the remaining panels were backed by 12-inch wood timbers.[19]

Given this armor arrangement, there were obvious weak points. First, however, a strong point: the forward casemate was, according to plans, backed by solid wood over 2 feet thick, with alternating vertical and horizontal timbers. The side backing, listed at 12 inches, was solid only at each vertical frame (the aggregate thickness of plank, frame, and ceiling). There is no indication that the intraframe space was wood filled.

Given the in-curving of the casemate sides toward the bow and the lack of plating there, it was obvious that these were the most dangerous areas of the

Port elevation of the USS Cairo. *Shown are the armor plating covering the area abreast the engines and boilers and the armored pilothouse. Hog braces are between funnels and paddle-wheel housing. (National Park Service)*

vessel when going head-on into battle. After her commissioning, the commanding officer of the *Cairo* requested that further plating be applied to these two areas. The result can be seen today on her starboard side: horizontal railroad iron (3½-inch track) bent to the appropriate shape and attached to the wooden sides beginning at the forward casemate corners and running back to the first gun port. On the *Cairo* the plating totaled 122 tons, 47 tons beyond the original specifications.[20]

Some variations have been found in the plating of these vessels after going into service. Porter reported in December 1862 that three—*Carondelet*, *Cincinnati*,, and *Baron de Kalb*—in addition to having new batteries, had their boilers "perfectly protected with heavy oak casemates, covered with iron."[21] Later, Porter had the side plating completely removed from some of these vessels in 1864, to lighten them to pass the dam in the Red River campaign. These vessels were the *Louisville, Mound City, Carondelet,* and *Pittsburgh.* Porter, incidentally, approved of the result, claiming they ran 2 to 2½ knots faster, and, "it never having been of any use to them," proposed to leave the plating off "altogether."[22] One existing photograph of the *Louisville* appears to show her late in the war, without her side plating.

The propelling machinery of the city class was a variation of the western rivers high-pressure engine and boiler plant, though initially there was some idea of alternative configurations. Three engine plans were referred to Chief Engineer Isherwood in July 1861: two designs by Thomas Merritt and one by S. H. Whitmore. The latter was for a paddle-wheel engine, whereas Merritt supplied a screw as well as a paddle-wheel design. The screw propulsion proposal included inclined cylinders mounted transversely and pinion gears to drive the propeller shafts.[23]

Isherwood responded that the best plan was the "usual" type paddle-wheel engine "used on those waters," as arranged by Merritt. The screw engine was considered inappropriate and "unreliable" because of the muddy waters and snags, and the frequency of groundings.[24] Consequently, the engines incorporated into the city-class vessels were a variety of the noncondensing western river powerplant with high-pressure boilers. Later, screw propellers would be applied to several classes of armored river vessels, and the machinery used was very much like that proposed by Merritt.

The "usual" paddle-wheel machinery had been in use on the rivers for decades before the Civil War and continued in much the same form for years afterwards. The pattern was so familiar that formal engine plans were rarely used; rather, a standard casting pattern was employed when a new

engine was built.[25] The cylinder, in the city-class boats was 22 inches in diameter, with a stroke of 6 feet, connected to the paddle wheel by an iron and wood pitman rod 110 inches in length. As with the others of this type, steam inlet and exhaust were governed by poppet valves, similar in concept to today's automobile engine valves, which were actuated by levers that lifted and dropped semicircular cams. Steam was brought in on one side of the cylinder and exhausted on the opposite side. The most significant modifications on the city-class cylinders were the use of S-shaped rather than straight valve lifting levers, as well as valves angled into the cylinder. These changes were necessitated by the 15-degree front to back inclination of the cylinders introduced to bring the engines below the deck line.[26]

Both cylinders of the *Cairo* were recovered with the vessel and are well preserved. Because of the ghosting technique used in the *Cairo* restoration, the engines as well as the boilers and pitman rods can be seen in place, connected much as they were in 1862.

Five boilers were used in these boats, each 3 feet in diameter by 25 feet long. These were fire-tube units, with five large flues in each boiler. The firebox, with furnace doors and grates at the forward end of the boilers, was built of brick and extended beyond the after boiler ends, with the brick built up to a level at least even with the boiler water. The hot gases were carried to the aft ends of the flues, then sucked forward and out by the immense draft created by the tall funnels. A steam drum above the boilers was used to collect the vapor-heavy "working water" and prevent its being carried into the cylinders. Useful steam was carried thence via steam pipes to the cylinders. Mud drums were located below to collect sediment from the water fed into the boilers.[27] Only a part of the original firebox front with furnace doors remains today, though the boilers and steam and mud drums remain intact. Each of the two smokestacks was 28 feet in length and 44 inches in diameter.

Apparently some of these vessels had significantly taller funnels than the others. By working approximate scales from photographs, it appears that the *Louisville, Pittsburgh,* and *Mound City* had stacks at least five feet taller (33 feet or more) than the sister vessels. No explanation for this has been found. One temporary modification to the *Carondelet* is referred to in March 1862, when her machinery was "adjusted to permit escape of steam through the wheelhouse" and thus muffle the loud "puffing" sound resulting from the steam passage through the normal pipes. (The puffing sound of these vessel's machinery was analogous to that made by a steam locomotive: both used a high-pressure, non-

USS Louisville. *Many of the variations on the city-class vessels can be seen here. She has significantly taller funnels than the* Cairo *and others; a full length hurricane deck has been built, along with an expanded paddle-box cabin and an elevated wooden pilothouse. Ventilation ports have been added abaft the gunports. She had her side armor removed for the passage over the Red River dam in 1864 and apparently at the date of this picture remained without it. (Kean Archives)*

condensing type of engine.) The object was an undetected night run past the batteries at Island No. 10.[28]

The steam machinery of the *Cairo* included an auxiliary engine, called in the parlance of the time the "doctor" engine. This vertical single cylinder was 8 inches in diameter with a 21-inch stroke, placed aft of the boilers between the main cylinders. Existing plans show this as a somewhat decorative beam engine with fluted supports. It worked off main boiler steam and operated cold water and boiler water feed pumps. Steam was also used to operate the vessel's capstan. A steam-operated capstan was a definite advantage on the rivers, where it provided a means to winch the vessel off after grounding, using hawsers connected to convenient trees along the bank. The doctor engine was lost during salvage.[29]

The remaining elements of the class's propulsion system were the paddle wheel and rudders. The wheel was located in an 18-foot-wide race between protective casemates, in an opening measuring about 28 feet from the stern. This was a single iron-framework wheel 22 feet in diameter, with a crank on each side operated by the pitman rods. The *Cairo*'s paddle "buckets," or blades, were wood and

are now lost. The framework had collapsed upon itself but has been reconstructed in its original form.

Because the paddle-wheel race effectively bisected the vessel's stern, a single rudder would have been impossible. Instead, rudders were fitted on sternposts on either side of the race. These were over 5 feet in width and mounted with wrought iron hinges. Given the scowlike hull characteristics and strong river currents, two rudders were still not sufficient to render the vessels particularly maneuverable.

Though the hulls had poor lines, by the same token, they allowed mounting a formidable battery. All seven vessels carried thirteen guns each, ranging from 30-pounders to 100-pounder rifles. The *Cairo* originally mounted six 32-pounders (43 cwt.), three 8-inch (64-pounder) smoothbores, and three 42-pounder army rifles, plus one 12-pounder. By the date of her loss the 12-pounder had been replaced by a 30-pounder Parrott rifle. They were arranged as follows: two 42-pounders and one 8-inch forward; three 32s and one 8-inch port side; two 32s, one 42, and one 8-inch starboard; and one 32 and one 30-pounder aft. Another battery variety can be seen in the *Baron de Kalb* after May 1863: Bow: one 10-inch and two 9-inch Dahlgrens; stern: two

30-pounder rifles; broadside; two 8-inch and six 32-pounders. Probably the heaviest battery was on the *Pittsburgh* in December 1863: one 100-pounder, four 9-inchers, two 8-inchers, four 32s, two 30s, and one 12-pounder.[30]

Finally, a few notes on the exterior appearance of these vessels. As with most naval vessels, the paint was basic black, with natural wood decks. Each of the class had a distinguishing identification stripe near the top of the stacks. The *Cairo* sported a gray stripe, with the others as follows: *Carondelet*, red; *Cincinnati*, blue; *Louisville*, green; *Pittsburgh*, light brown; *St. Louis*, yellow. The *Mound City* was reported to have had an orange stripe; however, one photograph shows her with a five-pointed star on each funnel. If these ships followed the pattern set down for the light-draft boats, the upper cabins (if such had been added, as on the *Louisville*) were buff.[31]

On many merchant riverboats a decorative symbol of some sort was frequently mounted on the spreader bar between the funnels. Illustrations of the *Baron de Kalb* show something similar to a Masonic emblem in this location. Incidentally, the ladder that is often seen leaning against one of the stacks was a lookout perch.[32]

The first of the city-class vessels launched was the *St. Louis*, on 12 October 1861. The first commissioned was the *Carondelet*, on 15 January 1862. She was the first Union ironclad and the first purpose-built iron-plated vessel in either federal or Confederate navies. (CSS *Manassas* had been converted from merchant service and was in service in October 1861.) Last commissioned was the *St. Louis*, on 31 January 1862.

The river trial of the *St. Louis* occurred in November, under John A. Winslow (later of *Kearsarge* vs *Alabama* fame). Performance of the class as a whole varied little from that of this vessel. At a draft of 5 feet 7 inches forward and 5 feet 8 inches aft, and 90 pounds pressure, Winslow credited her with 5½ knots. Though he characterized her response to the helm as "satisfactory," her handling was at the mercy of the current. When backing upstream, she was manageable as long as she was in line with the current; once caught, she would "wind" around in the stream without regard to her helm.[33] Later, the *Carondelet* exhibited similar shortcomings: when backing upstream "she would sheer from one side of the river to the other, and with two anchors astern she could not be held steady enough to fight her bow guns down-stream."[34] To negate this tendency and gain a steady gun platform, the vessels were often tied up to shore during actions against fixed fortifications.[35]

In general the effectiveness of the armor and casemate was in proportion to the thickness of the plating, or lack thereof. The *Mound City* took a heavy shot through the "larboard forequarter" in June 1862. This penetrated the steam drum. The result was a disaster of scalded men. The numbers directly attributable to the scalding are somewhat in question because the enemy gunners fired on the survivors in the water, but they were horrifying: only three officers and 22 men of a complement of 175 escaped uninjured, while 82 died.[36] This was the most disastrous boiler-related combat accident of the war (*Oneida*, at Mobile Bay, took a boiler hit but lost only eight men, and the *Sultana* explosion was after the end of hostilities). By way of comparison, a peacetime boiler explosion on the *Bennington* in 1908 killed 60 of a crew of 197.

The *Mound City* disaster exemplified the vulnerability of the unplated forward ends ("forequarters") of the casemates, and probably explains the informal railroad iron bent to the sides of the *Cairo*.

Another illustrative combat loss was the second sinking of the *Cincinnati* at Vicksburg in 1863. General W. T. Sherman happened to observe Confederate shots placed "right under her stern."[37] Plunging fire from a highly placed battery repeatedly penetrated her deck and she sank. Her commanding officer, G. M. Bache, reported that the only shots that did not penetrate "struck the bow casemate, which was well greased."[38] The fatal damage was incurred while the unarmored fantails were toward the enemy guns.[39]

The plated portions of the vessels were quite effective in stopping shot, however. On the *Baron de Kalb*, in January 1863, her commanding officer reported she was "repeatedly" struck by 8- and 9-inch shot "at very short range" (about 400 yards) and the "iron was in no case penetrated. The loss was from shot and shell entering the ports." Only one plate of the forward casemate was "badly broken by shot."[40] At similarly short ranges, however, the pilothouse was vulnerable: at Fort Donelson, the *St. Louis* lost her wheel from such fire.[41] It was

The USS Cairo, *1862. Note the identification stripe on the funnels. The demarkation line where the armor plating begins is very obvious. (Naval Historical Center)*

thought that coating the casemates with some slippery substance would deflect shot, particularly projectiles that struck at an angle. It is not certain whether one or more than one substance was used: letters refer to "tallow" and "slush" and to the casemates and pilothouse being "greased." The effectiveness of this practice is obviously questionable.[42]

The careers of these seven "Pook's turtles," in all cases except the *Cairo* and *Baron de Kalb*, were as long and eventful as the campaigns on western waters, beginning with the actions at Lucas Bend on the Mississippi, Fort Henry, and Fort Donelson in early 1862—the latter the first major Union victory in the West—through and beyond the Red River campaign of 1864. *Cairo* was sunk in December 1862 and *Baron de Kalb* in July 1863.

Cairo participated in operations against Fort Pillow and Memphis before being lost to a torpedo while on the Yazoo River. *Baron de Kalb* was first in action of the seven, engaging rebel vessels at Lucas Bend in January 1862. She was at Forts Henry and Donelson, Island No. 10, Fort Pillow, Memphis, the Yazoo River campaign, Fort Hindman, Fort Pemberton, and Haynes Bluff before being the second city-class vessel lost to a mine, on the Yazoo River on 13 July 1863.

The *Cincinnati* joined the 90-day gunboat *Sciota* in the distinction of being sunk twice during the war. *Sciota*, however, was not raised to see combat the second time. *Cincinnati* was at Fort Henry, Island No. 10, and was rammed and sunk at Fort Pillow (May 1862). After salvage and rebuild, she was in the Yazoo and White River campaigns and bombarded Fort Hindman and Vicksburg before being sunk the second time, at Vicksburg. Again salvaged, she was rebuilt and took the surrender of the CSS *Morgan* and *Tombigbee* in 1865. She finally sank again at her moorings in 1866, after being sold from the navy.[43]

The *Carondelet*, in addition to the usual fort engagements from Henry to Pillow, plus Grand Gulf and the Red River campaign, was the only city-class

ship to take on a Confederate ironclad. She engaged the CSS *Arkansas* one-on-one in July 1862 and, losing her steering, ran aground. She took a beating, with 35 casualties. After the war, she was sold, became a wharfboat at Gallipolis, Ohio, and her engines went into the towboat *Quaker*.[44]

The *Louisville* began her career at Fort Donelson and participated in actions at Island No. 10, Memphis, Fort Hindman, Vicksburg, Grand Gulf, and on the Red River. She was sold in November 1865.

The *Mound City* was at Island No. 10 and Fort Pillow before being rammed twice and put aground in the great ram melee called the Battle of Memphis. She was disabled again (see above) by a single shot to her steam drum at Saint Charles, Arkansas, in June 1862. She ran the batteries at Vicksburg, bombarded Grand Gulf and Vicksburg, and was in the imbroglio on the Red River. She was sold in 1865 and broken up a year later.

The *Pittsburgh* served at Fort Donelson, Island No. 10, Fort Pillow, Yazoo River, Vicksburg, Grand Gulf, and Red River. In the five-and-a-half-hour engagement at Grand Gulf, she was heavily damaged, taking thirty-five hits and losing six killed and thirteen wounded. She was sold in 1865 and abandoned in 1870.[45]

It can be said that the seven city-class vessels took the brunt of the fighting in the Mississippi River campaigns of the Civil War. No major engagement of the Mississippi River Flotilla was without at least one of these vessels. Thus, in terms of contribution to the service and the war effort, they were invaluable. It is equally obvious, however, that they had undeniable shortcomings, the most dangerous to the crews being the unarmored forward sections of the side casemates. Second in importance was the vulnerability of the sterns. These two factors accounted for the great loss in a single instant aboard the *Mound City*, the sinking of the *Cincinnati*, and numerous other personnel losses through the course of the war. With these caveats we can see both the importance and vulnerability of these vessels: the first American squadron of ironclads.

An artist's view of the major ironclads of the U.S. Navy. On the left is the monitor Puritan *in double-turret configuration; in the left foreground is the* Keokuk, *with inaccurately drawn gun towers; in the center is the converted* Roanoke, *the war's only triple-turret vessel, shown with an incorrectly located funnel, with the* Galena *immediately behind; and in the right foreground is an accurate depiction of the little* E. A. Stevens, *technically a Revenue Service vessel. On the right are the* New Ironsides, *with an incorrect gun on the upper deck, and the* Monitor. *Sailing steamers in the background are a 90-day gunboat and the sloop* Brooklyn. *(From an engraving published in* Harper's Weekly, *September 1862; Naval Historical Center)*

CHAPTER 6

Second-Generation Coastal Ironclads, 1862

Even as the *Monitor* was taking shape and reports filtered through that the Confederate navy was seriously pursuing its own ironclad program, the Bureau of Construction and Repair finally entered the picture with their own proposal for plated vessels. Baxter, in *Introduction of the Ironclad Warship*, takes pains to disprove the department's reluctance to move to ironclad vessels, and particularly to prove that they were not averse to adopting the revolving turret. As will be seen, he is certainly correct about the latter. As has been shown, however, they showed little enthusiasm for ironclads before the letting of the contracts for the *Monitor, New Ironsides*, and *Galena*. Only subsequently, no doubt fearing that private contractors might co-opt the navy's ironclad program, did the department develop specifications and plans for plated vessels. Additionally, Assistant Secretary of the Navy Fox, always an idea man, was applying pressure on Lenthall and other bureau heads to the same end.[1]

In March 1862, Lenthall wrote Secretary Welles referring to a Bureau of Construction and Repair ironclad proposal submitted in November of 1861.[2] The specifications are in the National Archives, dated December 1861, and plans are in the Gustavus Fox papers at the New-York Historical Society. The proposed vessel was to be 216 feet 2 inches on deck, 48 feet in breadth, and 13 feet 11 inches depth of hold, and would carry two Coles-type revolving turrets.[3]

The hull was not far removed from conventional wooden shipbuilding practices. Composed for the most part of white oak, the scantlings were substantial but not unusually robust: the keel, stem, and sternpost, for instance, were to be sided 16 inches; the throats of the floor timbers, 15 inches. Room and space was to be 26 inches. For a rough comparison, the *Merrimack*, a live-oak frigate, had room and space of 34 inches, with keel, stem, and sternpost sided 18 inches.[4]

The major departures from standard practices were seen in the deck beams and timber framework beneath the towers. Although other deck beams were 12 by 11 inches, under the towers they were sided 13 inches. Furthermore, iron was to be substituted for wood in the lodge and lap knees, and fore and aft pieces were incorporated between the deck beams under the towers. "Cross keelsons" were also incorporated, bolted to the main and bilge keelsons and measuring 15 by 18 inches. Stanchions and struts were placed between beams and the cross keelsons to add strength below the towers.[5]

One 11-inch gun was to be mounted in each of the twenty-one ½-foot-diameter "towers" to be built on the principles set down by Capt. Cowper Coles of the British navy. There were two major distinctions between Coles's and Ericsson's turrets: the former rotated on ball or conical bearings at the base, on the circumference of the tower; in contrast, Ericsson's turrets revolved on a central axle. This changed the weight distribution of the turret significantly. Second, Coles employed an armored glacis around the base of the tower, protecting this vulnerable area. A third distinction in the department's plan was the use of a 10-inch wooden backing inside the turret. Turret armor was to be two thicknesses of plates, totaling 5 inches.[6]

The hull's side armor ranged from 3¼ inches at the ends to 4¼ inches thick for the greater part of each side. The deck armor was to be two layers, each ¾ inch thick. In the specifications there is no mention of masts or rigging, and the power plant was to be a conventional low-pressure condensing unit. Draft, as built, was to be about 12 feet.[7]

In December 1861, Secretary Welles requested an appropriation to construct twenty of these vessels, costing about $500,000 each. The request was quickly passed in the House. At this juncture the bill was delayed in the Senate until February. In the interim, Ericsson and his friends invoked pressure in favor of delaying the adoption of this rival plan until the *Monitor* was proved. Late in January, John Griswold wrote to Ericsson: "I cannot imagine that the 'twenty gunboat' conspirators have grounds for hope—Certainly not if the 'Monitor' is *demonstrated* first." When the bill finally passed, on 7 February, it allowed the secretary to have built "by contract or otherwise" twenty ironclad steam gunboats.[8]

This concession, plus the "demonstration" at Hampton Roads a month later, ended the Coles turret in the United States and severely reduced the eventual number of turreted vessels built at navy yards. Other than the never-completed *Kalamazoo* class, only four Civil War monitors were navy-built: *Miantonomoh*, *Monadnock*, *Tonawanda*, and *Agamenticus* (plus the converted frigate *Roanoke*). Advertisements for bids were in the newspapers on 20 February 1862, and prospective builders were given the department's specifications. Besides incorporating a rival turret design, the use of more than one turret was anathema to John Ericsson, who harped continually on maintaining a full-circle field of fire with the required single turret—regardless of how enormous the vessel or the guns used.

This chain of events also ended any ideas of obtaining warships and iron armor plating overseas. As early as May of 1861, the Laird firm of Great Britain had received an inquiry from Secretary Welles concerning the construction of gunboats. Laird recommended iron rather than wood for their hulls and offered to send estimates for their construction.[9] Welles's original letter has not been seen, however, and it is possible from the context of Laird's reply that Welles had merely inquired as to the relative merits of wood and iron hulls for warships. Later Welles denied approaching foreign sources for warships. In this case, Laird's offer to send estimates was simply good business practice.[10]

Much has been made of the efforts of a private citizen, John T. Howard, who visited England that summer and approached Laird's with a "memorandum" from the department concerning the construction of an ironclad. According to Baxter, this effort was more at the bidding of Assistant Secretary Fox than of Secretary Welles, and nothing came of it.[11]

After the formulation of the department's double-turret plan, Daniel B. Martin, an engineer with the department, was sent to England, France, and Belgium to determine whether armor plating and turrets could be supplied by European firms. He obtained prices but found that the manufacturers were preoccupied with filling orders from their home governments. Further, at least one British firm feared making any such agreement until the diplomatic situation between the United States and Britain was satisfactory. Lenthall ordered Martin to return to the United States on 15 February, and this was the last wartime departmental foray into foreign suppliers for American armored vessels. As Welles put it, "We would have had terrible indignation upon us had we gone abroad for vessels."[12]

The ink had yet to dry on the appropriation for twenty ironclads when the *Monitor* and *Merrimack* met on 9 March 1862. In the wake of this fight came intense clamor for ironclads and "monitor fever" set in. Welles responded with a request to increase the appropriation to $30 million and a board was appointed to study the ironclad proposals that continued to pour in. On this committee were John Lenthall, B. F. Isherwood, Edward Hartt, Daniel Martin, and Joseph Smith.

These proposals again ran the gamut of sophistication. Probably the oddest was submitted by a sailor who suggested a steam ram equipped with "saw and hammers." The latter were four sledge hammers on the bow, mounted to rotate fan-wise and "deliver . . . blows with the greatest force and accuracy, upon the hull of an enemy's vessel." While these were pounding away on the adversary, a circular saw, also mounted on the bow, would be slicing the vessel "to the water's edge in five or six minutes." Commodore Smith replied, with great tact, that the plan was not as good "as some others which have been submitted."[13]

More formally, there were responses to the department's advertisement, inviting bids based on the twin-Coles-turret plan for "harbor and coastal service." Twenty designs were submitted by nineteen would-be contractors. The majority submitted variations on the twin-turret theme, with differences in armor thickness, engine size, and other specifications. A few, however, introduced novelties—usually expensive ones.[14]

The most extravagant and costly plan was by A. D. Bishop of New York, whose "twin vessel" was to be an iron-hulled monster with each of its three 50-foot-diameter turrets housing no less than *six* 20-inch guns. It was to be 300 feet long and 64 feet wide, with catamaran hulls, two central paddle wheels, and a ram at each end. The configuration of the bow was to be such that it would "run over an enemy." All this and a $950,000 price tag made for a distinct lack of enthusiasm in the department.[15]

Among the other ideas were three vessels with water tanks to be filled to lower the ships' profile in combat, and one of these incorporated compressed air to facilitate the evacuation of the tanks. Other proposals included an armored loading tower between the turrets, steel and iron armor, "Husband's Patent Feathering Bucket Wheel," hot water–spewing "blow holes" in the deck, and a ram that could be hammered at the enemy "up to 20 times per minute."[16]

Though some of the contractors would be heard from again later in the war, only one of this batch was successful: G. W. Quintard. His proposal, at a price of $625,000, would be the basis for the iron-hulled *Onondaga*. This selection by the board was the subject of a minority report by Commodore Smith, who wrote that casemated vessels would carry more guns, both iron- and wooden-hulled vessels ought to be tried, and the monitor type was not suitable for coastal ocean service.[17]

(It should be noted that the 20 February advertisement also included solicitation for plans for iron, screw-propeller, "river and coast defense" ironclads of 6-foot draft: these will be addressed along with the other river vessels in chapter 8.)

At this point, 17 March, chief constructor Lenthall and Isherwood also submitted a letter outlining their suggestions for an ironclad navy. First they dealt with the problems inherent in obtaining iron plates of sufficient size for warship armor. They noted that private businesses had no need for such masses of iron; therefore there was little incentive for firms to make the capital investment necessary to produce it for the government's limited needs. They advocated the construction of a government facility for producing the iron necessary for "the largest size" man-of-war.[18]

The extent of their ambitions was then set forth: these iron-producing facilities would provide for the construction of more than mere harbor and coastal vessels. "Cruising vessels of iron for offensive" purposes were needed to prevent blockades, preserve the nation's ports, and operate on the open seas. These would be armored, suitable for rams, possess maximum steam power, and be "larger than

any . . . we now possess." Second would be a class of corvettes of similar characteristics but shallower draft.[19] These ideas remained unrealized for decades to come, as the nation concentrated on the domestic enemy and as the department declined into the postwar Dark Ages where the huge Civil War fleet deteriorated rapidly and new construction was out of the question.

The immediate aftermath of Hampton Roads brought to fruition vessels in two categories. First, Ericsson single-turret monitors of the *Passaic* class, which will be addressed in the next chapter, and second, alternate plans involving multiturrets: the *Roanoke*, *Onondaga*, and the four double-turret navy-built monitors (*Miantonomoh*, *Monadnock*, *Tonawanda*, and *Agamenticus*). Additionally there were the *Keokuk* (a holdover from the 1861 contractees) and the *E. A. Stevens* (also known as the *Naugatuck*). The latter was the attempt by the Stevens family to revive the hopes for their battery.

Roanoke

Ten days after the converted Union steam frigate *Merrimack* engaged Ericsson's *Monitor*, B. F. Isherwood and John Lenthall wrote Secretary Welles advocating the conversion of the *Merrimack*'s sister ship *Roanoke* into a "seagoing" ironclad. The advantages: conversion would be both cheaper and faster than new construction.[20] Comparing the river-class vessels with the other major vessels available made the choice obvious. Lenthall had already dealt with a hypothetical conversion of one of the *Iroquois* class (see chapter 2) and found it unsatisfactory. The *Hartford*-class vessels, as they were, carried the largest battery possible and still be able to meet draft limitations in Southern ports; they were, therefore, exceedingly useful in their present role.

Lithograph of the Roanoke *(1863) showing her relatively high freeboard. Though flawed in design, she was for many years the world's only triple-turret vessel. (Mariners Museum, Newport News, Va., courtesy Naval Historical Center)*

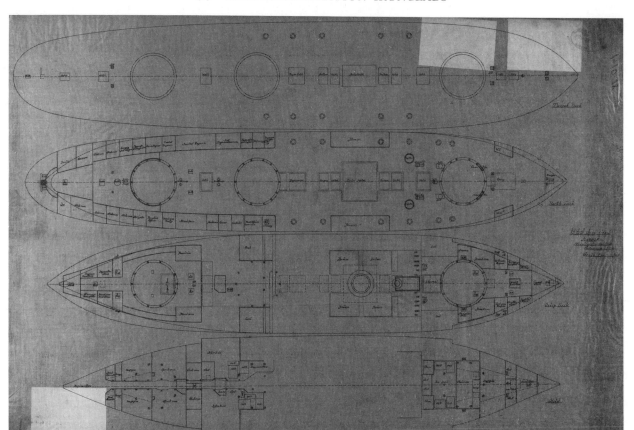

Deck plans of the converted ironclad Roanoke, *1872. No other plans of this conversion have been found. The location of the turrets can be seen as well as the circle of vertical timbers under each, carrying the weight through each deck to the vessel's wooden bottom. (NARS Plan 1-10-18, National Archives)*

By contrast, the river-class vessels were far too deep for harbor work and would otherwise ride out the war in support roles.

The original plan for the *Roanoke* called for cutting the frigate down to the "top of the gun deck plank," plating the sides and deck, and mounting no less than four Coles towers on her, with eight 12- or 15-inch guns. The turret deck would be 6 feet above the waterline, making her not quite a monitor. The only other modifications, other than additional support for the turrets, were the elimination of the hoisting screw and reduction of its diameter and the addition of a ram. Side plating was to be 6 inches maximum, reduced to 4 1/2 inches below the waterline to its lower edge (about 4 feet below water). Deck armor was to be 2 1/4 inches. An auxiliary engine was to provide ventilation and power to revolve the turrets. The estimated cost was $495,000; time to completion: 3 1/2 months.[21]

In April, a contract was let to Novelty Iron Works for the plating and other metal work. The razing of the frigate had already begun at Brooklyn Navy Yard. From the contract and other sources a relatively coherent description of the vessel can be assembled. The sole existing plan of the converted

Roanoke shows her decks and is dated 1872: no building draft has been found.

The contract reveals that the deck plating was reduced to 1 1/2 inches, though still in two layers. A layer of felt steeped in pitch was interspersed between the wood and iron, to allow leeway for the working of the ship. Wooden planking was laid over the plates. The contract allowed two alternatives for the side plating: 4 1/2-inch solid forged iron plates, or six 1-inch layers, depending on availability. In the former instance, it would be reduced to 3 1/2 inches below the waterline. The vessel's ends were to have five 1-inch layers. The side plating used was 4 1/2 inches in thickness, around 24 inches wide, and ranged in length from over 11 feet to 22 feet, with the 22-foot plates weighing over 4 tons.[22]

These plates were obtained "raw" from various firms in Massachusetts, New York, and Pennsylvania and were bent at Novelty Works to match the curves of the vessel's hull, a process described as "tedious and troublesome" by a contemporary reporter. First they were heated white hot in an oven, then transferred by overhead crane to a press, the bed of which was made with a series of "bolster blocks" adjustable to match the curvature of the ship's side. About thirty minutes of pressure in the press sufficed to shape the iron for use.[23]

The contract backpedaled from the four turrets originally envisioned, calling for three, all "precisely the same" as those of the *Monitor*. Removal of one turret was apparently the chosen alternative to reducing plating or taking off another deck—both suggested by Lenthall to decrease her draft. Below the turrets, "affixed to the ceiling of the main deck" were circles of 12-inch-square oak supported by stanchions. A circle of ten stanchions supported each turret, and the plans show stanchions on each successive deck—down into the hold itself. Each turret shaft rested on an "immense cast iron step," probably on the berth deck. As with the other Ericsson designs, the turrets were raised for turning. The weight of the turrets, when not in use, was carried to the bottom of the vessel.[24]

The three Ericsson turrets were constructed of [15]/[16]-inch or 1-inch thick plates, totaling 11 inches. This was in accordance with the turrets of the *Passaic* class—3 inches more than those of the original *Monitor*. Each original flat plate was 9 feet by 40 inches and bent cold in a hydraulic press.[25]

The gun ports were drilled out after the second assembly, using a borer made for the purpose. The first boring was 15 inches in diameter. Top and bottom holes were drilled first, then a third eliminated the remaining center section.[26]

Though the contract called for pilothouses at each end of the turret deck, illustrations indicate she received *Passaic*-class type structures: cylindrical enclosures atop the forward two turrets. The turrets were operated by an oscillating steam engine, whereas the pilothouses remained stationary.[27]

The final significant modification to the old *Roanoke* was a ram. This was placed at the 20-foot draft line and shaped like a "huge ax." It was formed by two thicknesses of 4[1]/[2]-inch plate, making a 9-inch "blade." Its length is not known, but it was formed from the 22-foot-long plates and was presumably one course in height: 24 inches.[28] Given the momentum and mass of the *Roanoke*—regardless of her speed—this would have been a formidable weapon. Little else in the ship was changed during this metamorphosis. The frigate's original motive power remained: a pair of trunk engines, 79[1]/[2]-inch diameter by 36-inch stroke, with only sufficient power to justify calling the original vessel an *auxiliary* steam frigate. The boilers, four in number, were also original Martin water-tube installations. A fifth boiler was added to operate her turrets, and auxiliary engines were introduced for turrets, steering, and ventilation. Her engines remained exactly as originally built in 1855, rated at 950 horsepower. Her dimensions were 278 feet on the turret deck, not including the ram (262 feet 10 inches between perpendiculars—unchanged from the original vessel), by 53 feet 3 inches extreme (including armor)

beam, with depth of hold of 26 feet 2[1]/[2] inches.[29]

Though the modifications—turrets, armor, and so on—were not minor, it appears that very little of the actual hull of the original frigate was changed to compensate for the new strains being placed thereon. A rough figure of 1,000 tons of iron was added in armored deck, sides, and turrets. By way of compensation, her battery was reduced from forty-four to six guns, saving in excess of 100 tons, and her top hamper and sides above the gun deck had been removed. Each turret (without guns), however, weighed something on the order of 125 tons, placing an aggregate weight, with guns, of over 450 tons on the bottom of the vessel—by way of the stanchions running from beneath the turrets. In actuality it is unlikely that these supports were sufficient for the purpose, with the result being immense torquelike strains upon the already flexible wooden hull.

Hopes that the new *Roanoke* would be a quick-fix ironclad were dashed primarily by the difficulty in obtaining plating of the required thickness, plus the "tedious and troublesome" bending process. No description has been found of mounting the side plates: manhandling tons of iron dangling from overhead cranes was no doubt fraught with its share of danger for the workmen.

She was finally completed and commissioned on 29 June 1863, with a complement of 347 men. Her guns were one 15-inch and one 150-pounder in the forward turret, a 15-incher and an 11-incher in the middle turret, and a 150-pounder and an 11-inch Dahlgren in the after turret. Despite attempts by local politicians to keep her as a harbor battery in New York, she made passage to Hampton Roads to join the blockading squadron.

The *Roanoke* was an impressive vessel, at least in theory, bringing anxious responses from across the Atlantic. Capt. Cowper Coles wrote a letter to the London *Times* in October 1863, decrying Britain's broadside ironclads such as the *Warrior*, with their 68-pounders and rifled 110-pounders, which guns were "professedly inferior" to the 15-inch Dahlgrens. "It strikes me that this is a very serious matter," he wrote, that Britain had not a trial gun and "not a ship afloat that can carry it." He continued: "The Americans have thoroughly accepted the necessity of having these heavy guns and of having ships of special construction to carry them."[30]

Coles was referring primarily to the 15-inch gun and the turret system. The *Roanoke* itself proved far from successful. The passage to Hampton Roads from New York marked one of the two sea sorties in the vessel's career. Her commanding officer, B. F. Sands, wrote the report that destroyed any idea of using her on the open seas. With a heavy swell from the south her rolling was so great that it would "preclude the possibility of fighting her guns at sea, and I was obliged to secure them by bracing them with pieces of timber to prevent their 'fetching away.'" He concluded that she was not "adapted to fighting a battle at sea on account of her rolling, rendering her guns unserviceable, and exposing her to shot below her iron plating, yet she has proved herself capable of being safely and readily transported from harbor to harbor."[31] She was not significantly slower in this form than she had been as an auxiliary steamer: she reached a maximum of 8½ knots on the passage south, averaging around 7.[32]

The mighty *Roanoke* remained a station ship for the duration of the war, with her great draft preventing her going "but a mile or two above Newport News."[33] In exercising her "great guns" her turrets were not particularly efficient, with the after turret requiring nearly five minutes for a 360-degree turn. As she vegetated as a station flagship, her hull began to show the strain: by war's end "pumping ship" was a per-watch routine, with her seams allowing over a foot and a half of water in a day.[34]

She returned under her own power to New York in April 1865 and was decommissioned on 20 June. Apparently some hull repairs were accomplished after the war, because she remained as a rusting relic until sold for scrap in 1883. Though a failure, the *Roanoke*, along with the British turret ironclad *Prince Albert*, foreshadowed the modern all-big-gun battleship: with all major guns in centerline turrets and a practical amount of freeboard for ocean cruising. To contemporaries, however, the vessel fulfilled Assistant Secretary Fox's notation on the department's 1862 conversion plan: "I am afraid she will be useless."[35]

Onondaga

G. W. Quintard's proposal from early 1862 was one of the few that adhered closely to the department's advertised plan and therefore might be considered the first monitor designed by the navy. The Quintard vessel, named *Onondaga,* was iron hulled, however, not the specified wood.

Unlike Ericsson's "upper" and "lower" hull monitor arrangement, with its overhanging shelf, the Quintard hull was conventional: iron hull frames as well as deck beams forming a single "box." Her hull form was decidedly shipshape, unlike the angular box of the first monitor. The side armor was attached directly to the sides rather than resting on an exterior shelf.

Angle iron, 6 inches by 3 inches, formed the vessel's hull frames. The deck beams were of ¾-inch iron, 16½ inches in depth and up to 180 inches long—the longest that could be rolled at the time. Hull plates were ¾- to 1-inch thick and up to 90 inches long.[36]

The armor for the two turrets was layered in ¹⁵/₁₆-inch plates, totaling 11 inches. These plates were about 30 inches wide by 108 inches long. Deck plating was two 1-inch layers.[37] After April 1863, a 5- by 15-inch glacis was added around the base of each turret, as additional protection for that vulnerable area.[38]

Quintard's original proposal called for an armored pilothouse placed atop the forward turret. This was an idea that was taken up by Ericsson for his later monitor designs. This structure on the *Onondaga* was given 11 inches of plating and rested

The Roanoke, *probably after her decommissioning (note the roofed-over turrets). As she is shown lightly laden, it is possible that the dark rectangular area forward of her stem is the axe-shaped ram, formed of two layers of 4½-inch iron plating. (Naval Historical Center)*

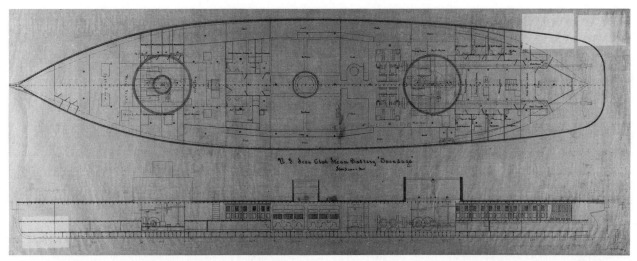

Inboard and deck plans of the Onondaga. *The first two-turret, twin-screw monitor, her hull was of conventional iron construction, without Ericsson's "upper" and "lower" hull dichotomy. (NARS Plan 1-9-38, National Archives)*

on a collar to allow it to remain stationary as the turret turned. It housed a steering wheel and engine room telegraph but, oddly enough, was isolated from the turret itself.[39]

Side plating was originally to have been solid plates $4^{1}/_{2}$ inches thick. These were in 27-inch strakes, up to 162 inches long. This simple plan was modified in April 1863, when she already had two-thirds of her armor mounted. Ericsson suggested that wood be used *inside* the side armor, because she would be under "extremely heavy fire." Though Ericsson may have been referring to his monitor's use of substantial timbering inside 5 inches of iron, the result on the *Onondaga* was somewhat ludicrous: 12 inches of wood was simply added to the sides of the existing armor belt, then sheathed with another 1-inch plate. Ericsson also suggested adding an angular piece below the projection, to "resist the sea."[40]

The motive power for the *Onondaga* was two pairs of horizontal back-acting cylinders, a pair for each screw, built at Quintard's Morgan Iron Works. The Quintard proposal called for only two 30- by 18-inch cylinders.[41] The size of the cylinders finally used is not known. Steam was developed in four vertical water-tube boilers as well as an auxiliary boiler located forward of the engines, and each turret was turned by a two-cylinder donkey engine. The screw propellers were 10 feet in diameter, turned by shafts approximately 65 feet long.[42] To protect the screws from underwater obstructions, a narrow band, or ring, of boiler iron was secured around the periphery of each.[43] These were apparently removed sometime during her career, since the French reports made on her after the vessel's sale fail to mention them.

Living areas in the vessel were all located on platform decks, with storage areas below. Officers' quar-

ters were aft, engineers and midshipmen amidships, and crew forward of the fore turret.[44]

Built at Continental Iron Works, the vessel was launched on 29 July 1863, and after countless delays, she was commissioned 24 March 1864. Work was slowed by the modifications introduced midconstruction, scarcity of labor, difficulty in obtaining materials, labor strikes, and the closing of the shop during the draft riots of 1863.[45]

As completed, she measured 226 feet overall by 51 feet 5 inches (including the additional wood and iron plating), with a depth of 12 feet 10 inches, and she carried a complement of 130 men.[46] Her battery was one 15-inch smoothbore and one 150-pounder rifle in each turret. The final cost to the government was $759,673.08, some $134,000 in excess of her contract.[47]

On trials, the vessel made 7 knots at sixty-six revolutions and her machinery was considered very satisfactory. She drew 12 feet—nearly a foot deeper than called for. Most of this was a result of the

Model of the Onondaga, *David Taylor Research Center. Her bow shows that the designer eliminated the Ericsson monitor overhang and the excessive armor shelf, or hip, of those vessels. (U.S. Navy)*

Wartime view of the Onondaga *on the James River. Her 15-inch guns played havoc with the* Virginia II *at Trent's Reach in 1865. Major distinguishing features were her rotund funnel, relatively small ventilation stack, slightly raised foredeck, and angular rather than curved rifle screens around the top of the turrets. (Naval Historical Center)*

additional 207,000 pounds of protection added to her sides and elsewhere.[48]

Her service record in the U.S. Navy was short and uncomplicated: a year on the James River as a deterrent to Confederate ironclads there. At this time she received one of the more unusual deck fixtures for a warship: an oil-burning locomotive headlight on her bow—in the event the rebels attacked at night.[49] She participated in actions at Dutch Gap and Trent's Reach. The latter was the last ironclad battle of the war, and *Onondaga*'s 15-inch solid shot punched a 2-foot-square hole through the side of the *Virginia II*—despite 5 or 6 inches of plating.[50]

At the close of hostilities, the *Onondaga* was returned to Quintard by act of Congress. Quintard, in turn, resold her to France, and a French report of 1870 reveals further details of the vessel.

In heavy seas on her transatlantic passage, her roll was about 4 to 5 degrees, pitching her screws out of the water—while her high-freeboard escorts were recording up to 20 degrees. Through this, habitability on board was "supportable," though the humidity was uncomfortable. Engine-room temperatures were excessive, and her steering was inadequate. She eventually received a larger rudder, French breech-loading guns, and sensible side plating consisting of teak and iron, with the latter outboard the former. Classed as a coast defense vessel, she was finally broken up around 1905.[51]

Monadnock Class

In July 1862, Lenthall directed that four two-turret monitors be laid down at the four major navy yards.[52] Welles described them as "similar" to the vessel under construction by Quintard.[53] These vessels and yards were *Agamenticus* (Kittery), *Monadnock* (Boston), *Miantonomoh* (Brooklyn), and *Tonawanda* (Philadelphia).

Before proceeding some comment ought to be made on the naming of these vessels, as well as others of the period. Welles apparently wished names that were unmistakably American, whereby the name alone would distinguish the vessel from those of other services—obviously, the British—which tended towards classical nomenclature. The result was names that one commentator called "unquestionably original, not to say aboriginal." This system was also contrary to law: Congress had directed previously that first-class vessels be named after states and second-class after rivers and principal towns. This practice resumed after the Civil War. During the conflict, however, the rush of new vessel construction found the department resorting to minor Indian tribes or Indian-derived geographical names: multisyllabic and as the commentator said, "only the cacaphonous ones" were left.[54] In the case of these monitors, Monadnock is a mountain in New Hampshire; Tonawanda, a lake in New York. Miantonomoh was a chief of the Narragansett tribe in the 1630s.[55] Agamenticus is a mountain near Kittery, Maine. (The names gave way to typical sailor corruptions: *Agamenticus*: Agy-meant-to-cuss; *Miantonomoh*, My-aunt-don't-know-me.[56])

Generally the four ships are classified by a division into at least two "classes," based on the two types of engines used (Ericsson and Isherwood). As will be seen, however, all four monitors were generally alike in their dimensions, armor, inboard and outboard arrangement, and, of course, battery.

As these were wooden-hulled ships, this general similarity seems sufficient to justify unifying the four under one designation (*Monadnock* was chosen because she was the first to be commissioned). If the classification of wooden ships was applied strictly, requiring practically identical vessels, the result would be few true "classes": only such things as the 90-day gunboats where the department supplied detailed plans to contractors would qualify.

Unfortunately, in wooden ships where local naval constructors could exercise much leeway in both the design and construction phases, this method is best only for identification and cannot be relied on in terms of performance, handling, and such aspects as durability and the quality of fastenings. The best example is the river-class frigates of the 1850s. Only two of the five (*Roanoke* and *Colorado*) were built to the same plan, and three different engine designs were used. Using strict criteria, they should have been designated four separate classes. As it is, the class designation is, and was, sufficient to place the vessels in useful administrative categories for personnel and ordnance purposes but veiled significant differences in performance and other aspects of the ships.

Though the four *Monadnock* class vessels were monitors, the department fell back on its time-honored methodology for the design of their wooden hulls: general dimensions and other criteria—including the directive to use Ericsson turrets—were provided to each yard's naval constructor, who proceeded to develop his own version of the vessel—for good or ill.

The four monitors were to draw 12 feet with the main deck 18 inches above the waterline. The wooden hull was to have 44 feet clear for the machinery, carry 300 tons of coal, and measure approximately 235 feet in length. The Ericsson turrets

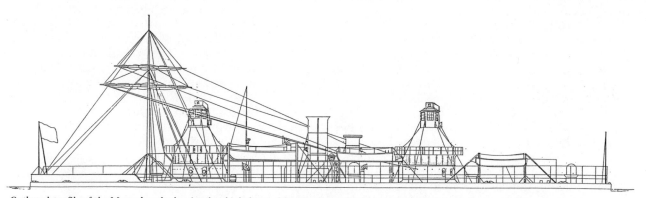

Outboard profile of the Monadnock *showing her high forward breakwater and postwar raised wooden pilothouses. The foremast and spars were first added on her passage around Cape Horn in 1865–66. (NARS Plan 136-9-51, National Archives)*

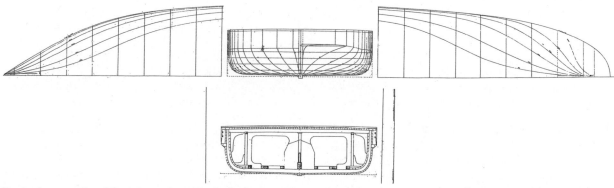

Lines and cross section of the Agamenticus. *Nominally the sister ship of the* Monadnock, *she was slightly deeper and her other dimensions also varied somewhat. She was also sharper forward. Note the vertical support timbers on the cross section. (NARS Plan 104-3-32, National Archives)*

were to take two 15-inch guns each and be protected by 11 inches of iron. The department expected 9 knots.[57]

The constructors at the yards responded with plans for such vessels, all of which varied somewhat in dimensions. Lenthall directed that all be 250 feet from the fore side of the rabbet of the stem to the aft side of the sternpost, with a 49-foot beam exclusive of the side armor, totaling 53 feet 8 inches over plating. From the side of the keel to the top of the deck, the vessels were to measure 15 feet.[58] Despite this directive, it will be seen that dimensional variations would persist.

Some have deduced that the vessels were simply the reemergence of the department's double-turret design of 1861. Existing plans and documents refute this, and in any case, the new design was significantly larger and was based on a much heavier battery. The four 15-inch guns weighed, in aggregate, over five times that of the two 11-inch guns of the department's design. Such differences make any resemblance between the two designs only superficial.

The *Monadnock*, designed by W. L. Hanscom, will be described first. With this vessel as a pattern, significant differences in the other three ships can then be outlined.

The *Monadnock* was 250 feet between perpendiculars and 259½ feet overall. Her breadth (molded) was 48½ feet and 52½ feet to the outside of the armor belt.[59]

The depth of the ship, for purposes of comparison, is here given as the measurement from the underside of the deck (top of the frames) to the bottom of the floor timbers at midships—in other words, from the top to the bottom of the hull framing, excluding the projection of the keel. This is a molded measurement: without hull or deck planking. In practice, the depth of hold measurement is from the bottom of the deck to the top of the floors. This measurement, however, is one that is associated with determining the interior hull capacity and therefore disregards the size of the floor timbers themselves, a dimension that can significantly alter the outside hull measurement. The hull framing of the *Monadnock*, as described above, measured 14½ feet at midships.[60]

As with the single-turret monitors, the side plating extended 5 feet from the deck to the bottom of the overhang. The plating was 1-inch layers, totaling 5 inches at the sheer and 3 inches at the lower edge. Two iron stringers, approximately 5 inches square, ran behind the plating at the bow, and the wooden backing measured 12 to 14 inches thick. Deck plating was two ³/₄-inch layers of iron, and the turrets were of ten (as opposed to the originally planned eleven) laminated 1-inch layers. Pilothouses were protected by 8 inches of iron.[61]

The wooden hull had a berth deck interrupted by engine and boiler spaces. There were no watertight bulkheads. Twelve-inch-square stanchions supported the majority of the deck beams. The stanchions in most cases were along the centerline, except where displaced by machinery, water tanks, and other apparatus. Plans for *Agamenticus* show second and third rows of stanchions supporting the beams 5 feet inboard of each side of the ship. Presumably *Monadnock* followed this pattern. Diagonal timbers over 1 foot square gave extra support beneath the turrets.[62]

As will be seen, the original Ericsson vessel was the only one of the monitors to dispense with traditional ship hull lines. Its successors retained rather flat floors and vertical sides. Among these four twin-turret vessels, fore and aft body lines differed considerably, reflecting their different designers. The *Monadnock* exhibited the fullest entrance lines, though she was sharp in the 2- and 4-foot waterlines. At the 10- and 12-foot lines she was comparable to the sloops of the Hartford class in her entrance angle.[63]

Both the *Monadnock* and *Agamenticus* received Ericsson-designed power plants, built by Morris and Towne of Philadelphia. Each vessel was powered by two Ericsson trunk engines, of 32-inch diameter by 22-inch stroke, with surface condensers.[64] Each drove a single four-bladed screw measuring about 10 feet in diameter. There were four boilers of the approved Martin vertical water-tube variety and several auxiliary engines for ventilation, pumps, and turret operation.[65]

The *Monadnock* was commissioned 4 October 1864. On her passage to Hampton Roads and back to New York she was under tow most of the time and met some rough weather. Without the tow, going into New York, she made 7 knots, and 8 or 9 was the maximum gotten out of her. In a fresh breeze the sea broke completely over the deck and drove her "pretty well into it" and curled "well up the turrets." Her commanding officer continued: "The ship behaved well, all things considered; the rolling however, was such as at times to cause anxiety for the boats. They broke completely over the vessel . . . occasionally threw spray inside [the turrets]." Admiral Porter noted that she was "the best monitor afloat, and can safely and expeditiously go anywhere, and in any weather."[66]

In May 1865 she went in convoy to Havana to confront the (former) Confederate ram *Stonewall*. She and the *Canonicus* created a minor sensation at that port, and comparisons made at the time favored the big monitor over the swifter but less well-armed *Stonewall*.[67]

The *Monadnock*'s ultimate test was her round-the-horn passage to San Francisco in 1865–66. She had been fitted with a 3½-foot-high wooden "breakwater" forward as well as high, many-windowed, wooden pilothouses. During the passage a jury-rigged foremast was erected, with course, topsail, and jib. The major problem of the passage was 120- to 140-degree temperatures in the fireroom as they approached the equator, prostrating sixteen crewmen. Incentive pay and additional ventilators helped alleviate this. The sailing rig was reported to add ½ knot to her speed, and the breakwater effectively prevented solid seas from battering the forward turret.[68]

In head seas with light bunkers, she worked longitudinally—"undulates with the waves"—because of the weight of the turrets on her ends. Her maximum speed without sail was 8 knots, but in terms of seakeeping, John Rodgers, who had commanded the expedition to the West Coast, was convinced she had met no weather that "seemed to touch the limit of her seagoing capacity." She had not been towed at any point and had stood up quite buoyantly and easily under high seas.[69]

The *Monadnock* was the only one of the class to see combat, participating in the two operations against Fort Fisher in 1864 and 1865. After her passage to San Francisco she was decommissioned at Mare Island on 30 June 1866. She was broken up in 1874 and a new iron vessel of the same name was begun.

Agamenticus

The *Agamenticus* was designed by Isaiah Hanscom, constructor at Kittery and brother of W. L. Hanscom at Boston. Her machinery was identical to that of the *Monadnock*. She was 251 feet between perpendiculars and 261 feet overall. Her molded beam was 48 feet, and total breadth over armor belt was 52 feet. The depth of her hull amidships was 15½ feet.[70] Note that none of these measurements match those of her sister ship. Also, there were slight differences in the location of the turrets, the shape of their rudders, and the height of the main ventilator (the *Monadnock*'s was shorter).[71]

The Terror *(formerly the* Agamenticus) *at Philadelphia, showing breakwater, raised pilothouse, and wheel forward of iron pilothouse. Besides providing improved vision, the raised pilothouses may have decreased compass variations because of the vessel's iron structure. (Naval Historical Center, Paul Silverstone Collection)*

The *Agamenticus* had substantially more timbering forward, no doubt in anticipation of ramming. Also, the forward hull lines were significantly sharper—by some 15 degrees at the planksheer—and showed more concavity in the lower lines.[72] Rather than a high bulwark on the planksheer forward, as in the *Monadnock*, the *Agamenticus* received a lower breakwater midway between stem and fore turret. Photographs indicate she received only one raised wooden pilothouse.

She was commissioned on 5 May 1865 and was preparing to do battle with the *Stonewall* when that vessel was reported crossing from Europe. Nothing came of this and she was decommissioned in September. She was renamed *Terror* in 1869 and put back in service in the North Atlantic Fleet. In 1872

The Agamenticus, *probably at Kittery, after the addition of the light hurricane deck. Awnings conceal pilothouses above the turrets. (Jim Dolph, Portsmouth Navy Yard)*

she was decommissioned and two years later was broken up. These monitors fell into the same category as most of the other wooden construction of the late war period: vessels built of unseasoned timber and therefore with short service lives. *Terror* was "rebuilt" beginning in the mid-1870s to reemerge as a new iron vessel, hull number BM4, with four 10-inch breech-loading rifles.

Miantonomoh and *Tonawanda*

The *Miantonomoh* and *Tonawanda* are generally set apart from the other pair by their Isherwood-designed engines. As with most steam engines designed by the chief steam engineer, these were back acting: rather than the piston rod cranking the propeller shaft directly, the piston rods were doubled and straddled the propeller shaft, with both operating a connecting rod that "returned" towards the cylinder to operate the shaft. The object of this seemingly extraneous motion was to allow a longer piston stroke, and thus larger capacity cylinders, within the confines of the warship's hull. In the case of the two monitors, these cylinders were 30 inches in diameter. The *Miantonomoh*'s were given a 27-inch stroke, whereas the *Tonawanda*'s stroke was 21 inches. The *Miantonomoh*'s engines were built at

Novelty Works of New York; the *Tonawanda*'s at the Merrick firm of Philadelphia. The vessels also used Martin boilers. The original contracts for the engines called for each to have a 21-inch stroke, but 6 inches was added to that of the *Miantonomoh* in March 1863.[73]

Again, there were significant hull differences between these two ships—greater differences than appeared between the other pair of twin-turret vessels. Both, however, had molded breadths of 49 feet; over the armor, 53 feet, 8 inches. The length between perpendiculars of the *Miantonomoh* was 250 feet; the *Tonawanda* was the longest of the four, at 256 feet.[74]

More significant differences were found in the depth dimensions and hull lines of the two. Although the *Miantonomoh* was the deepest of the four, at 16 feet from bottom to top of frames, the *Tonawanda* was the shallowest, at 14 feet.[75] This was a significant variation: something over 10 percent less depth on the *Tonawanda*, resulting in greater longitudinal strains exacerbated by her extra length.

Finally, the *Tonawanda* was the only one of the four to exhibit any deadrise. She was also a bit sharper in entrance lines than the *Miantonomoh*.[76]

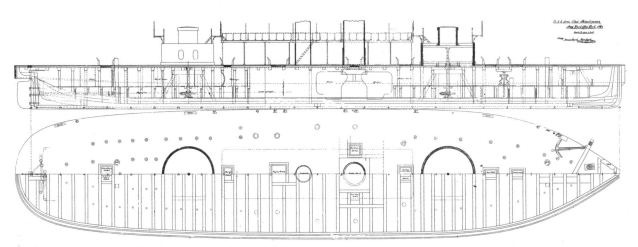

Inboard and deck plans of the Miantonomoh, *showing vertical timbering supporting most of the deck beams and diagonal braces beneath the turrets. (NARS Plan 2-11-51, U.S. Naval Institute)*

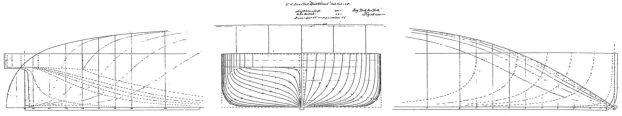

Lines of the Miantonomoh. *She was the deepest of the four vessels. She and the* Tonawanda *had Isherwood-designed back-acting engines rather than Ericsson power plants. (NARS Plan 2-11-53, National Archives)*

The Miantonomoh *(left) and* Terror *at Portland, Maine, 1870. Note the awnings surrounding the raised pilothouses. (The Peabody Museum of Salem)*

In general, if any of the four could be classed by itself, it would be the *Tonawanda*.

The career of the *Tonawanda* was the least active of the four: after commissioning 12 October 1865, she was a training ship at Annapolis until 1872. Rumor had it that her shallow hull was too weak for service on the line. Though detailed plans of the vessel have not been found, a photograph shows her two turrets much closer together than those of the other three—an attempt to counteract excessive weight on her ends, no doubt. Renamed *Amphitrite* in 1869, she was broken up in 1874 and a new vessel of the same name was begun.

The *Miantonomoh* was the sole American Civil War monitor to cross the Atlantic. In 1866, in a diplomatic mission to Russia, she was sent to Cronstadt, via Great Britain, accompanied by the *Augusta* and *Ashuelot*. Assistant Secretary Fox, always a friend of monitors, was the envoy and returned a glowing report on the vessel.

The passage across was uneventful: the weather was very good, with westerly winds. Fox made much of her moderate rolling: in the trough the maximum was 7 degrees to windward, 4 to leeward, whereas the side-wheeler *Augusta* reached 18 degrees, and the *Ashuelot,* 25 degrees. The conditions

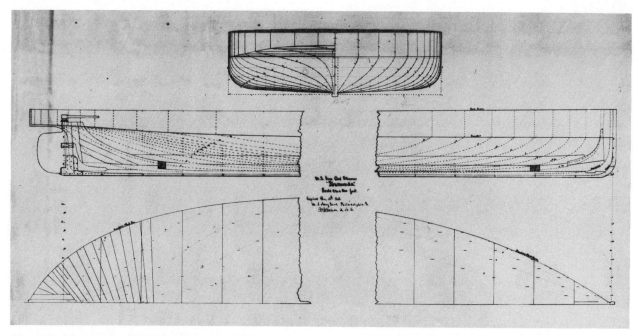

Lines of the Tonawanda. *She was the shallowest and longest of the four and experienced correspondingly greater longitudinal strains than the others of the class. She also exhibited some deadrise, which was unique to the group. (NARS Plan 77-3-17, National Archives)*

The Tonawanda. *This only known broadside view indicates her turrets were considerably closer together than those of the other double-turret vessels. Photo site is Annapolis, where she was a training vessel, 1870. (Naval Historical Center)*

The double-turret monitor Miantonomoh, *in a foreign port. Note the platforms around the turrets. Curved rifle screens also served to deflect seas away from the turret tops. The* Miantonomoh *made a unique monitor passage to Europe in the late 1860s. (Naval Historical Center)*

when these comparisons were made is not clear. The *Ashuelot*'s performance, however, could be expected from her flat-bottomed hull, and the *Augusta* was a relatively light-draft vessel for ocean navigation, having been a coastal merchant steamer before the war. In any case, the monitor's 7-degree roll was quite remarkable. Fox contended that her leeward guns could still be worked in such seas; and in head seas, the forward guns were still workable—protected by the breakwater on the foredeck. In the trough, however, her guns to windward would be flooded. He noted that the roll of the monitor was

less than that of a high freeboard vessel, simply because the water would pass over the monitor, rather than acting on the high sides of a conventional ship.[77]

The vessel created a sensation in Europe, and some have attempted to tie the great European naval arms race of the later part of the century to her visit.[78] After the European tour, she was recommissioned in 1869, then decommissioned in June 1870. There was some interest in giving her a full ship rig, with the mainmast measuring over 120 feet and 10-foot high bulwarks all round—resembling the ill-fated British *Captain*.[79] This was never done and she was broken up in 1874.

Generally the four vessels were considered successful—with the exception of the *Tonawanda*. Their cost had ranged from approximately $980,000 for the *Monadnock* to $1.3 million for the *Miantonomoh*, placing them among the most expensive vessels of the war—significantly more expensive than the *Onondaga*.[80]

Keokuk

The little *Keokuk* was, fortunately, one of a kind. C. W. Whitney's original proposal had been rejected in 1861, but he continued to correspond with the department on the project. In the aftermath of Hampton Roads, monitor enthusiasm spilled over and apparently aided the case of projects that incorporated any semblance of a turret, and by 18 March 1862, Whitney had a contract.

By that date, Whitney had also agreed to some modifications to the proposed vessel. Other than a change in the shape of the gun towers from diamond-shaped to circular, the only new elements were a shortening of the delivery time from 150 to 120 days, a penalty clause for each ½ knot below contract speed, and a "guarantee" that she would be "shot proof all over."[81]

Very generally, the *Keokuk*, originally named *Moodna*, resembled a twin-turret monitor but with inclined turret sides and turtle-backed deck. She measured 159 feet 6 inches overall, including ram, by 37 feet beam.[82] Both the hull and machinery were built by J. S. Underhill of New York.

The basic hull was formed of bar iron frames, 3/4 inch thick by 4 inches wide, with each frame including floors, sides, and deck beams. Plating was 7/16-inch boiler iron. Five keelsons were incorporated, as well as three watertight bulkheads. The latter were located 20 feet from the stem, 20 feet from the stern, and just forward of the boilers. Two side longitudinal bulkheads connected the forward and aft thwart bulkheads.[83]

The areas forward and abaft the end bulkheads were reserved for water tanks. In this case, these were to allow water ballast to be pumped in and out to trim the vessel—and bring her down an extra foot for a lower profile.[84]

Despite Whitney's claim that the vessel was "entirely" of iron, the armor system used was both iron and wood. Iron 1 inch by 4 inches was set "edgewise upon the outside skin of the boat & stationed 1 1/4 inches apart. The spaces between these bars to be filled solid with dry oak wood." Two layers of boiler iron formed the outer "skin" of this armor, and a third, the inner skin, with a total thickness of 5 3/4 inches. The armor extended about 3 feet below the waterline.[85]

The gun houses were armored in the same manner as the upper hull and were 20 feet in diameter at the bottom and 14 feet at the top. These were stationary structures, provided with three gun ports each, allowing the two 11-inch guns (one per tower) to fire forward, aft, and to the sides only. The ports

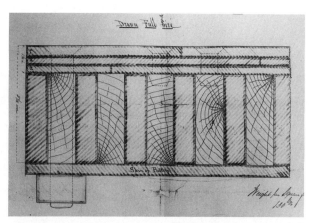

Plan for the armor plating of the Keokuk. The outside skin was made up of light layers of iron, covering alternating wood and iron "set edgewise" on the skin of the vessel. The total thickness, including inner skin, was 5 1/4 inches. Obviously, the interspersed wood weakened the armor significantly. (NARS Plan 80-11-28C, National Archives)

allowed the guns 8 degrees lateral movement and 10 degrees vertically. Though the contract called for engines to rotate the gun within the tower, there is no indication in available sources that such was the case.[86]

Whitney originally planned a pilothouse amidships, in the form of a truncated cone with the smokepipe passing through.[87] As completed, the *Keokuk* had the pilothouse on the aft side of the forward gun tower, leaving the smokepipe a separate entity amidships. The vessel also had a ram 5 feet long placed below the waterline.

The vessel's motive power was a design unique to the navy and one of the first to have four steam

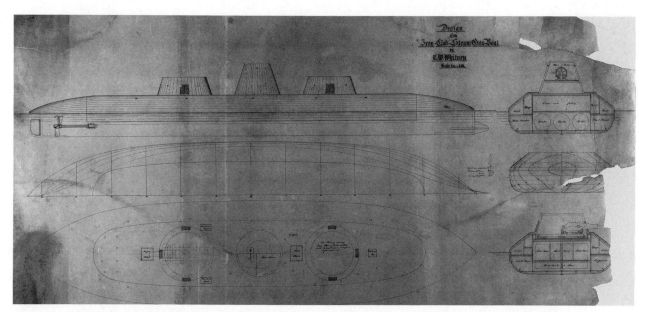

Whitney's original plan for the Moodna, *renamed the* Keokuk. *Note the ram and sharp forward lines. The midship pilothouse was originally intended to surround the funnel. (NARS Plan 107-15-23C, National Archives)*

cylinders. These were 23-inch bore by 20-inch stroke, with each pair independently operating one propeller shaft. The cylinders were vertical, operating "bell cranks" to translate the up-and-down motion of the piston rods to circular movements suitable to prop shafts. Three boilers were used and two 7-foot-diameter screws.[88]

The "boat," as Whitney referred to it, was launched 6 December 1862 and delivered 24 February 1863—considerably beyond the 120-day deadline. The delays were attributed to the "complicated forms" for the ironwork, a loss of ironworkers to other yards, and a "want of energy" on the part of some of her constructors. In particular, Mr. Wheeler, who superintended the machinery, was accused of showing little interest in the success of the vessel. She cost the government about $227,507.02, slightly above the contract price of $220,000, and was 172 tons heavier than originally planned, totaling 840 tons.[89]

In March 1863, the Keokuk made passage to Port Royal, with her commanding officer criticizing her draft, which, at 9 feet 3 inches was over a foot over contract, keeping her hawseholes underwater when under way. She was a deep, easy roller with a tendency to bury her head when going forward. He suggested the same type vessel twenty feet longer would be the "best" seagoing ironclad. She made 10 knots maximum.[90]

The career of the Keokuk was entirely Hobbesian: short and violent. On 7 April 1863, as part of the Union navy's first attack on Charleston, she was brought within 550 yards of Fort Moultrie, took over ninety shots—"was completely riddled," according to commander Rhind—and sank the next morning.[91] Despite numerous holes in hull and towers, no one was killed.

There will always be those who predict disaster, and in this case, Alban C. Stimers, steam engineer, had written Admiral Gregory, superintendent of ironclads, in September 1862 that the vessel should not be placed "within short range of heavy ordnance." Rhind himself had also expressed some doubts about the efficacy of the armor in his initial evaluation of the vessel, which he felt had been adequate "when she was first designed."[92] Later, Whitney persisted in defending the vessel, emphasizing her good qualities—good ventilation, seaworthiness, efficient machinery, and so on—but tacitly admitted that her armor plating was inadequate, saying that "a vessel of her dimensions would not support any more." Whitney also complained that

Highly decorative and detailed plan of the Keokuk. *See the annotated ribbons in the center, giving pertinent data on the vessel—including the date of her loss at Charleston. Fore and aft were watertight bulkheads, beyond which were water tanks for bringing the vessel down in combat. (Courtesy of The New-York Historical Society, New York City)*

the ship had been a "pecuniary" disaster: a $500-per-day late delivery fee, called for in the contract, had cost him over $100,000, even before she was completed.[93]

In a final footnote, the Keokuk's two 11-inch Dahlgrens were recovered by the Confederates from the wreck. These two guns were the heaviest ordnance defending the city, with the exception of two imported Blakely rifles. One of the Dahlgrens remains today at White Point Gardens, Charleston.[94]

E. A. Stevens (Naugatuck)

In the strictest sense, the little iron steamer *E. A. Stevens* is out of place in this volume. She was never a U.S. naval vessel, nor was she armored. As part of the U.S. Revenue Service, or Revenue Marine, however, she formed an integral part of the continuing saga of the gigantic Stevens battery.

Though a board had turned down Stevens's battery late in 1861 (as too deep, among other things), E. A. Stevens did not desist in his efforts. On 12 March 1862, the former coastal steamer *Naugatuck* was commissioned in the Revenue Service. She had been built in 1844 and acquired by the Stevens family, then modified to exhibit the salient characteristics of their battery, with an eye towards regaining the interest of the department.

She was 101 feet between perpendiculars and 20 feet in breadth, with iron hull, twin screws, and a normal draft of 5 feet. The hull was subdivided into engine space, crew space, and three flooding tanks: one forward, one aft, and a third, about 2 feet deep, between the upper and main decks. Flooding all tanks would take her down over 3 feet further, reducing her height significantly. This same semi-submersion was part of Stevens's plan for his battery but was not particularly well illustrated by the ex-*Naugatuck*—in view of the two boxy cabins exposed on deck, one a pilothouse, the other, officers' quarters.[95]

The only "armor" used was a heavy bulwark of white cedar, 20 inches thick by 4½ feet deep. This was given slanting sides and measured 1½ feet above the deck. This was intended to prove the resistance of slanting planes to shot and shell and provide extra buoyancy if needed.[96]

The second unique feature of the still-incomplete battery was to be her gun-loading arrangements: though the guns were exposed above the deck, they were to be loaded from below, by "aiming" each gun barrel down to align with an aperture in the deck, from whence a steam-driven rammer would introduce powder and a projectile into the weapon. In the case of the revenue steamer, a single 150-pounder Parrott rifle was mounted on the centerline about amidships and loaded through a slanting hole in the deck. No provision was made for training

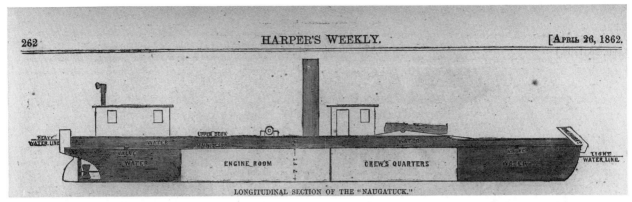

LONGITUDINAL SECTION OF THE "NAUGATUCK."

The U.S. Revenue Service steamer Naugatuck, *also known as the* E. A. Stevens, *or the Stevens battery. Longitudinal section from* Harper's Weekly *shows water tanks fore and aft and between the main and upper decks. Vessel was only 101 feet between the perpendiculars and 20-foot beam. (Naval Historical Center)*

the gun other than by turning the vessel itself. Rubber disc "springs" were mounted fore and aft of the trunnions to absorb the recoil and "bounce" the gun back into position after firing. For low-angle fire, a groove was cut forward across the deck to a gate at the bows to be opened for the purpose.[97]

Nothing is known about her power plant except that the screws were independent of each other, making her quite nimble: according to one report she could turn "end-for-end" in 15 seconds.[98] She had one boiler, and a donkey engine to operate her ballast pumps.[99]

The *E. A. Stevens's* active role in the Civil War was confined to a few weeks in May 1862, when she led an expedition up the James River. (Note that she was often referred to in action reports as the "Stevens Battery.") Along with the *Galena* and *Monitor,* she approached the batteries at Fort Darling. In this, her second combat, her Parrott rifle burst early on, leaving her with only a pair of 12-pounder howitzers. She later received a 42-pounder pivot gun, which burst during practice in 1863. The remainder of her career was that of a revenue steamer, stationed in North Carolina. It appears that she was broken up around 1871.[100]

The *E. A. Stevens* did not have the desired effect on the powers that be in the Navy Department. The Stevens battery remained unfinished beyond the end of the war, when yet another effort was made to obtain official sponsorship and funds for its completion. These events will be seen in chapter 11.

Contemporary model of the E. A. Stevens. *Shown are the location of the single gun, provision for loading it from below deck, and the thick bulwarks around the deck. Note the gutter provided for direct low-angle forward fire. Both her first and second guns burst, the first in action at Drewry's Bluff in 1862. (Naval Historical Center)*

CHAPTER 7

Ericsson Monitors:
Passaic and *Canonicus* Classes, *Dictator* and *Puritan*

To judge the impact of John Ericsson's *Monitor* on the U.S. Navy, a few statistics are in order. Including the original vessel, a total of sixty monitor-type vessels were begun during the Civil War years and thirty-seven of these were commissioned before the end of 1865. All but one of the total were low free-board ships (*Roanoke* was this exception, and she was the only attempt to convert a conventional vessel to a turreted ironclad). Of the sixty, only three used non-Ericsson turrets, and these were three of the four double-turreted *Milwaukee*s, which had a combination of one Ericsson and one Eads turret each.

For comparison, the nonturreted ironclads were a mixed bag, totaling about nineteen. Fifteen were river vessels, many of which were originally begun by the army. There were only two commissioned broadside vessels (*New Ironsides* and *Galena*). The huge *Dunderberg* was never commissioned and was originally to have had turrets. The *Keokuk* (and *E. A. Stevens*) were neither fish nor fowl—not fitting the "broadside" or "revolving turret" classifications.

The navy's dependence on John Ericsson for its Civil War ironclad program was overwhelming.

And there was no sign that the trend would have slackened had the war been prolonged. Indeed, the only ironclads retained for postwar service were the Ericsson turreted vessels. Consequently, for over twenty years—until the new navy came into being—the various permutations and revisions of the *Monitor* formed the basis of the navy's ironclad fleet. And, as will be seen, some of Ericsson's monitors were astoundingly long-lived: at least six were *commissioned* during the Spanish American War, and the last went out of service as late as 1908. These last vessels are not to be confused with the "rebuilt" new navy monitors, which were entirely new ships the last of which was disposed of in the 1920s.

Passaic Class

As has been seen, Ericsson was not reluctant to press for authorization to build more monitors and did not idly sit by while the Congress considered authorizing the construction of other ironclad ships, even as the original *Monitor* was under construction. After Hampton Roads, it was little more

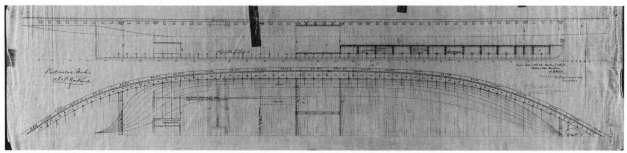

Lines of the Passaic-*class monitors, 1862. This design replaced the angular hull of the original* Monitor *with true ship lines and reduced the overhangs fore and aft. Fore-and-aft and transverse bulkheads are shown, forming a box to support the turret. (NARS Plan 1-11-21, National Archives)*

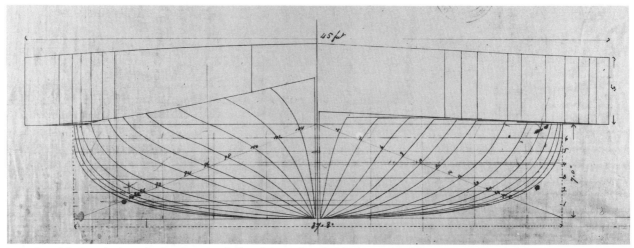

Body plan of the Passaic *class, showing the armor shelf carried over from the* Monitor *and hull lines. (Naval Historical Center)*

than a week before a somewhat panicked government accepted his offer to build six more vessels, ships that became the basis for the *Passaic* class.

On 17 March, Commodore Joseph Smith wrote Ericsson indicating the changes he wished to see in the new ships. These included thicker bottom plating, bigger guns, improved steering and pilothouse, and filling in the "jog" where the upper and lower hulls met. Ericsson replied two days later with his list of changes, among which was making the bottom of the ships "ordinary," with the lower part almost four feet wider with shiplike lines. The pilothouse was to be 6 feet in diameter and mounted above the turret, the stern was to be modified to reduce drag, and four bulkheads (two transverse and two longitudinal) were to be incorporated to support the area below the turret.[1]

A total of ten *Passaic*-class vessels were built, with overall dimensions 200 feet by 45 feet, compared to the 179 feet by 41 feet of the original ironclad. The "lower" vessel was 37 feet 8 inches in beam by 159 feet, stem to sternpost. These ships are generally characterized as mere improvements over the first monitor, incorporating suggestions resulting from the fight at Hampton Roads. Following this group, the *Canonicus* class are also seen as yet another incremental improvement, in this case incorporating the lessons of the attack on Charleston.

Close inspection of available plans and particularly building specifications, however, reveals that little more than the general above-water shape and interior arrangement remained unchanged from the famous progenitor.

The framing for the new vessels was on 18-inch centers, formed of 4- by 4-inch angles. These were 16 inches deep except for a dozen in the fore section, which were 48 inches deep, on which the berth deck was laid. The *Monitor*'s frames were 15 inches

deep and on 36-inch centers (with 3- by 3-inch angles interspersed midway between each frame).[2]

Further strength was provided by six athwartships bulkheads (at frames 1, 9, 51, 61, 69, and 100) fastened to both the ship's bottom and the deck beams. Those at frames 51 and 61 were tied to longitudinal bulkheads forming a box beneath the turret. Another pair of longitudinal bulkheads ran between frames 69 and 93. All bulkheads were of 1/2-inch or 5/16-inch iron, stiffened by vertical angle iron, usually set 36 inches apart. This contrasts to the *Monitor*'s three bulkheads: far forward and aft and at midships.[3]

Three rows of vertical stanchions were used in the forepart of the *Passaic*-class hulls, compared to the twin rows on the *Monitor*. Aft, in the later class, no stanchions were used and their purpose was served by the two longitudinal bulkheads.[4]

Ericsson characterized the new design as a substantial departure from the original: "These vessels will possess extraordinary strength, their bottoms being of greater stiffness than any of similar tonnage yet built." Ericsson continued: "The vessel's side near the bulwarks, will be fully twice as strong as in the *Monitor*."[5]

The armor system of the new vessels was little changed from the prototype monitor. The side armor of the *Passaic*s was slightly tapered from midships to ends, from 46 inches down to 32 inches wide. The inner portion of the protection was vertical 12- by 17-inch oak timbers bolted through the brackets supporting the shelf. Longitudinal timbers of widths varying with the taper of the shelf were then bolted to the vertical timbers. A planksheer measuring 18 inches by 7 inches completed the wooden portion of the protection. The iron armor was a repeat of the *Monitor*: 5 inches of 1-inch plating, with the outermost 60 inches top to bottom and the innermost, 30 inches; 1¼-inch bolts were driven through all but 4 inches of the entire bulwark, securing the outer plates.[6]

The deck beams were 12 inches square in the middle and 12 inches by 10 inches at the ends of the vessel. Wider beams were placed on each side of the smokepipe and by the watertight bulkheads. Deck plank was 7 inches thick by 8 inches wide, covered by two layers of iron, ½ inch each.[7]

The turret armor was increased from the *Monitor*'s 8 inches to 11 inches, with the internal dimension 21 feet (up from 20 feet, 2 inches). The turret was designed to accept 15-inch Dahlgren smoothbores.

A cylindrical pilothouse was placed in the center of the turret top, measuring 6 feet in internal diameter and mounted in such manner as to allow it to remain stationary while the turret itself rotated. Eight layers of 1-inch plates formed its walls. Two 1-inch layers formed its top, and peep holes were provided for a "clear view in all directions." A hatch provided access from the turret, when the latter was correctly aligned.[8]

A rather singular "accessory" designed for this as well as the *Canonicus* class was a copper binnacle about 5 feet high, mounted directly on *top* of the pilothouse. The compass, near the upper end, was read by means of mirrors from within the pilothouse.[9] No doubt this extremely vulnerable location was chosen as the least affected by the magnetism of the iron ship. Photos indicate that none of the combat monitors had this binnacle, for obvious reasons, but one can be seen on the *Camanche*, built on the West Coast.

The two-cylinder trunk engine was the same as that in the *Monitor*. New, however, was the introduction of Martin's patent water-tube boilers, two in number, with 3,600 feet of heating surface (up from the two fire-tube boilers in the *Monitor*, with 3,000

feet of heating surface). The *Passaics*' propellers were 3 feet larger in diameter, at 12 feet, and an "impregnable smoke pipe" was introduced, with its lower reaches composed of six layers of 1-inch plating, tapering to the top.[10]

Interior arrangements were very like the first monitor, with the exceptions created by the additional bulkheads. Ventilation was now provided by engines located below the turret rather than in the engine room. The blowers were to draw air down through the grating of the turret, in through the center chamber, and out through the boiler room and the remainder of the vessel.[11]

Ordnance for the new vessels was predicated on the performance of the *Monitor* at Hampton Roads, which, according to a letter from Fox to A. A. Harwood of the ordnance branch, proved that the 11-inch guns were "entirely inadequate." Though increased charges could be used in the 11-inchers, their endurance would suffer. What was needed was a larger caliber and "great initial velocity."[12] The 15-inch shell gun designed by John Dahlgren in 1862 was the answer. Interestingly, the procurement of a 15-inch Rodman (army pattern) had been in the works in June 1861. Objections were raised, however, concerning the range and weight of the weapon and the idea died within two weeks. Dahlgren's gun design, shorter and some four tons lighter than the Rodman, was ready in April 1862, but production was slow and the first was not tested until 11 October. In the end the *Passaic*-class vessels (except *Camanche*) received a combination of one 15-incher and one 11-inch Dahlgren. *Camanche*, completed after the war, received two of the 15s. In 1865, *Nahant*, *Montauk*, and *Catskill* received their second 15-incher.[13]

The contracts called for a completed vessel able to make 9 knots for twelve hours and carry coal for seven days steaming at that rate. Ericsson suggested

The USS Lehig (Passaic *class*). *This wartime photo shows the major differences between this class and the* Monitor: *the pilothouse atop the turret, conventional funnel, slight sheer, and ring, or glacis, around the base of the turret. The glacis was a lesson from the abortive attack at Charleston in April 1863. (U.S. Army Military History Institute)*

the names *Impenetrable, Penetrator, Paradox, Gauntlet, Palladium,* and *Agitator* for the ships but was over-ruled by the department, which designated them *Passaic, Montauk, Catskill* (early on called *Kaatskill*), *Patapsco, Lehigh,* and *Sangamon:* good American geographical features. Note that *Sangamon* was *Conestoga* until a name change was ordered in September 1862. Four others were later added to the class using the Ericsson design but not contracted through the inventor. These were named *Nahant, Weehawken, Nantucket,* and *Camanche* (an archaic spelling of the Indian tribe Comanche).

Externally, these monitors could be distinguished from the later *Canonicus* class by the smokepipe and ventilator. The ventilator was placed aft of the smokepipe on the *Passaics,* forward of it in the *Canonicus* class. The smokepipe itself was placed closer to the turret in the *Passaics* and was about half the diameter of that on the later ships. Both classes of monitors had a slight sheer.

Identification of the individual monitors was obviously problematic. The South Atlantic Blockading Squadron used both distinguishing pennants and paint variations for this purpose. A Confederate report after the first Charleston attack reported the colors of six monitors but without the corresponding names. Two were black, a third black except for a lead-colored top of smokepipe, a fourth black with white and green stack, one lead color, and one lead color with top of stack red with a black ring. Attempting to make positive identification today is complicated by black and white photography. Tentative identifications are: *Passaic,* black turret; *Patapsco,* lead color or black with red smokepipe top;

The Passaic-*class monitor* Catskill. *Note the peepholes in the pilothouse and turret base ring. A tell-tale difference between this and the* Canonicus *class is evident in the gun ports: on the left is the 15-inch Dahlgren smoothbore, which was too large to protrude through the port and therefore was fired inside the turret. On the right is the 11-inch Dahlgren. Another distinguishing feature of the* Passaic *class were the prominent rivet heads on the turret. The* Canonicus *class, and possibly the* Camanche, *had smooth-sided turrets. (U.S. Army Military History Institute)*

Catskill, light lead color turret; *Lehigh,* black; *Nahant,* possibly green turret and top of stack.[14]

The first of the class to be delivered was the *Passaic,* commissioned on 25 November 1862. The last East Coast vessel was *Lehigh,* commissioned 15 April 1863. The *Camanche* went into service 24 May 1865 on the Pacific Coast.

The *Camanche* was a response to the citizens on the West Coast concerned about possible Confederate depredations and clamoring for a formidable naval presence. Structurally there was only one significant difference in this vessel: she was given iron deck beams as a consequence of the "rapid decay" of wood in California.[15]

The actual construction of the *Camanche* was unique in U.S. Navy annals. She was contracted to Peter Donohue and James Ryan of San Francisco, and Francis Secor of New York, and built at Jersey City, New Jersey. When the components were completed, the contractor purchased the merchant vessel *Aquilla* to freight the knocked-down monitor to California. This was done in late spring 1863. The delays thus far (her contract due date was April 1863) were attributed to the "cannibalization" of various of her parts for use in the combat-zone monitors: parts of her engine replaced those that had failed in the *Weehawken* at Port Royal, for instance.[16]

The *Aquilla* sank at the pier after making her round-the-Horn passage, taking the monitor with her. Thus the re-assembled *Camanche,* probably the only U.S. naval vessel to be salvaged before she was launched, was not commissioned until 24 May 1865.

The first of the class, *Passaic,* had her trials in October and November 1862. She made $7^{1}/_{2}$ knots but foamed her boilers in the process.[17] Possibly more important was the testing of her 15-inch Dahlgren. She was the first vessel to mount this massive piece of ordnance: the tube alone weighed over 41,000 pounds, and it threw solid shot weighing 440 pounds or shells of 330 pounds. The size of the muzzle was such that it would not protrude through the turret ports, necessitating firing the gun entirely within the enclosure. Ericsson dealt with this by concocting a closetlike smoke box bolted to the interior of the turret, isolating the gun's muzzle. Also, a muzzle ring connected the gun with the turret side, to direct the concussion and smoke out of the vessel. The muzzle ring fractured in later trials. It was found that the ship's blowers were quite effective in clearing the smoke from the turret, and there seemed to be no strenuous objection to the concussion within the turret, so the "interior" 15-inch gun remained so in this class of vessels throughout the war.[18]

Probably one of the most critical statistics of these new vessels, and one whose effect on the entire course of the Civil War has yet to be studied, was their draft of water. The contracted draft was 11 feet, loaded. On 20 December 1862, S. P. Lee, commander of the North Atlantic Blockading Squadron, who was under orders to undertake a major operation against the defenses of Wilmington, North Carolina, wrote Secretary Welles reporting that the "unexpectedly deep load draft of the *Passaic* and *Montauk* . . . 11½ feet" was going to prove a problem for the expedition, which was to get under way as soon as sufficient vessels were available.[19] Later, a report that the *Passaic* drew 12 feet further cast doubts on the utility of these vessels in waters estimated at 9½ feet deep at high tide (New Inlet channel off Wilmington). The *Monitor* was reported at 10 feet, but her loss on 31 December left Lee with only the "deep" draft *Passaic* and *Montauk*. Within one week of the *Monitor*'s foundering, the department had canceled the Wilmington expedition and redirected the ironclads to the South Atlantic Blockading Squadron, setting the stage for the abortive April attack on Charleston.[20] Wilmington, by far the more strategic port, did not fall until 1865.

Even as the department pressed for lighter and lighter draft vessels, many continued to see performance at sea as important in the monitors. Certainly there was skepticism: one sailor wrote, "They might as well send a lot of men to sea in a wash tub."[21]

The first trial of the class at sea was not long in coming. Both *Weehawken* and *Nahant* encountered a gale on their passage to Hampton Roads in January 1863. Although *Nahant* retreated to the breakwater, Capt. John Rodgers rode it out, allowing the tug *Boardman* to "look out for her own safety." During the height of the storm thirty-foot waves "swept over us so violently that no one could go on deck" and the *Weehawken* leaked copiously, through the hawsehole, openings in the overhang, and at the base of the smokepipe. In contrast to the *Monitor* the hemp packing at the turret base was not a problem. Through the storm Rodgers reported her "easy, buoyant and indicative of thorough safety. . . . Her movements fill me with admiration. . . . The waves . . . swept harmlessly by."[22] In yet another gale off Hatteras on passage to Port Royal, Rodgers's admiration was not diminished. She continued to leak, but her hull "stood triumphantly" the tests of the sea. Rodgers's audacity in riding out the first storm was characterized by Fox in a letter to Ericsson as "the bravest act of the war": a compliment to Rodgers but not quite as complimentary to the Swede's vessel design.[23]

On the *Passaic*'s passage to Port Royal, Capt. Percival Drayton was less complimentary, making much of something Rodgers did not mention: the "terrific shock of the waves on her bow," blows that he feared would seriously strain the vessel and that he connected with leakage at the bow overhang. Captain Worden voiced the same concerns on the *Montauk* but did note her "easy" motions at sea.[24]

Anchor well of the Catskill. *It was placed forward, designed to allow raising the anchor from below deck. The hawse pipe was a point of considerable leakage in the early monitors. Photograph taken circa 1898—note the later type of ventilator in the background. (Naval Historical Center)*

The key test of the monitors, in this war, however, was in action. In early 1863, the *Montauk, Patapsco, Nahant,* and *Passaic* engaged batteries at Fort McAllister, Georgia. A few problems surfaced quickly. Shots striking the pilothouse wrenched off interior nuts, which became dangerous projectiles themselves. The gun ports had to be opened to reload the Dahlgrens, necessitating turning the turret from the target, then reaiming for the next discharges. Enemy gunners learned to wait for the turret to open to fire their own ordnance.[25]

The attack on Charleston on 7 April 1863 added no luster to the monitors' reputation. No less than seven *Passaic*-class vessels participated, along with the *Keokuk* and *New Ironsides*—the largest ironclad engagement to date.

A joint report outlined the vessels' shortcomings. Turrets were liable to jam if shots struck near the base or the base of the pilothouse. Flying boltheads made the pilothouse dangerous, if not untenable. Pilothouse plating was not strong enough—with shots bending in the plating and thus forcing the top off the structure. In general, it was felt that the close range required for the effectiveness of the slow-firing 15-inch gun significantly reduced the "impenetrability" of these monitors, and the monitors were not exceptionally manageable or fast (4 knots) in the currents of the harbor.[26]

The *Weehawken* provides an example: she was hit over fifty times, had her turret jammed for a time, had a ball through her deck, and two feet of her side plating was shot away, exposing the wood backing.[27] The *Nahant*, hit thirty-six times, had one man killed by a flying bolthead in the pilothouse, and one shot apparently broke every plate at the point of impact, nearly penetrating that structure. Her side plating was partially stripped from the wood in one place, and turret bolts were forced out and found lying on the deck. A shot to the top of the turret had broken every plate at point of impact, some completely in half. It was late the next day before workmen were able to turn her turret again. She had fired a total of fifteen rounds, seven of them 15-inch.[28]

Several other difficulties surrounded the guns and turrets of these vessels. The 15-inch guns, because of the visual interference of the smoke box, could only be aimed by way of the 11-inch gun. The aiming process itself was exceedingly awkward. The steam-powered turning mechanism required some jockeying in order for the turret to stop at a predetermined spot. If the turret overshot the mark, the engine would have to be reversed and a second try made. It was sometimes easier to continue the turn 360 degrees rather than attempt a reverse. The time required to fire the 15-incher was not speedy in any case: five to seven minutes minimum. The *Nahant* reported her maximum rate was 11 per hour for 1½ hours (vis à vis the 11-incher's 19 per hour). Her longest stint was eight hours in July 1864, firing fifty-three 15-inch projectiles—over 6 per hour.[29]

To obviate the need for opening the gun port to use the long-handled rammer and sponge, a "sectional" handle was devised, which was unfolded and "fed" into the gun muzzle within the turret—an innovative idea, but the process of unfolding and refolding the handle proved time-consuming and did nothing to improve the rate of fire.[30]

As the war progressed, other modifications were adopted to rectify the monitors' outstanding problems. To prevent enemy shot from jamming the turret, an iron base ring, or glacis, was retrofitted to each. This was 5 by 15 inches in cross section, bolted around the bottom. For the same purpose, a composition ring was placed at the bottom of the pilothouse. To prevent the loss of the pilothouse top, a sleeve was placed around the structure, extending some 9 inches over its top and curved inward. Finally, the leakage problem was addressed by incising a recess beneath the turret base and placing in it hemp packing covered with an iron ring.[31]

If the monitors' effectiveness against fortifications was questionable, the story was somewhat dif-

ferent in ship-to-ship encounters. On 17 June 1863, the *Weehawken* met the Confederate ironclad *Atlanta* in Wassaw Sound, Georgia. A total of five shots were fired to bring out the *Atlanta*'s white flag, with the first 15-inch cored shot penetrating 4 inches of iron and 18 inches of wood, "prostrating about 40 men by concussion." A second 15-inch projectile removed the top of her pilothouse. At three hundred yards the big Dahlgren had been a deadly effective worker.[32] Another encounter between the *Montauk* and the CSS *Nashville*, a commerce raider, was equally one-sided. It should be kept in mind that the original *raison d'être* for the monitors was as a counter to rebel ironclads—not the demolition of coastal fortifications.

Postwar Modifications

With longevity, the monitors accumulated modifications and accretions resulting in some cases in vessels hardly recognizable as monitors. Most of these changes were superficial, however, and did not involve major alterations in their general arrangements. By 1876, according to a rather optimistic annual report of the secretary, fourteen—including the eight surviving *Passaic*s—single-turret monitors had been so changed that "from being incapable of going or keeping to sea in rough weather and of very imperfect and unreliable arrangements for fighting purposes, [they] have been made perfectly sea-worthy, and of good facilities for working turrets and guns, and have been furnished with all modern improvements."[33]

The major change was raising the deck by some 15 inches. In the *Canonicus* class, their original depth was increased 18 inches late in the construction process in order to give them increased reserve buoyancy. Documents indicate the *Catskill* was raised 15 inches in 1874 and had her wood deck beams replaced with iron at the same time. A 3-inch wooden deck was laid over the armor deck.[34] Other changes were the inclusion of a steam windlass and hydraulic jacks for raising the turret. Plans for the *Montauk* and *Passaic* show similar changes.[35]

The major battery change was the addition of the second 15-inch gun.[36] The ports were enlarged, allowing the gun's muzzle to protrude from the turret.[37] Exterior alterations are obvious from the photography of the era, including a very tall engine

Inboard profile of the Montauk, *after a postwar rebuild that raised her deck 15 inches and replaced the wooden deck beams with iron. Fifteen-inch guns now protrude through the gun ports. The engine remains unchanged, but ventilation has been improved and a hurricane deck supports the boat davits. (NARS Plan 1-10-32, National Archives)*

Lines of the Montauk. *These remained essentially unchanged except for extra depth that resulted from raising the deck 15 inches. (NARS Plan 1-10-30, National Archives)*

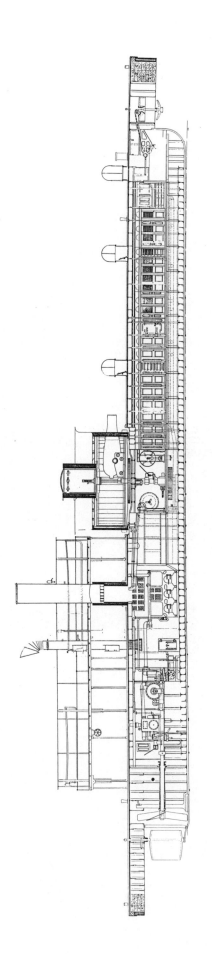
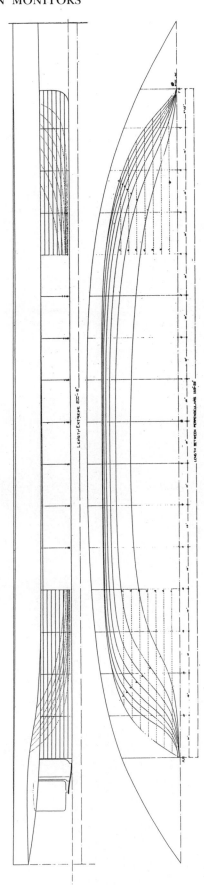
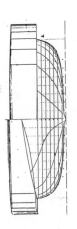

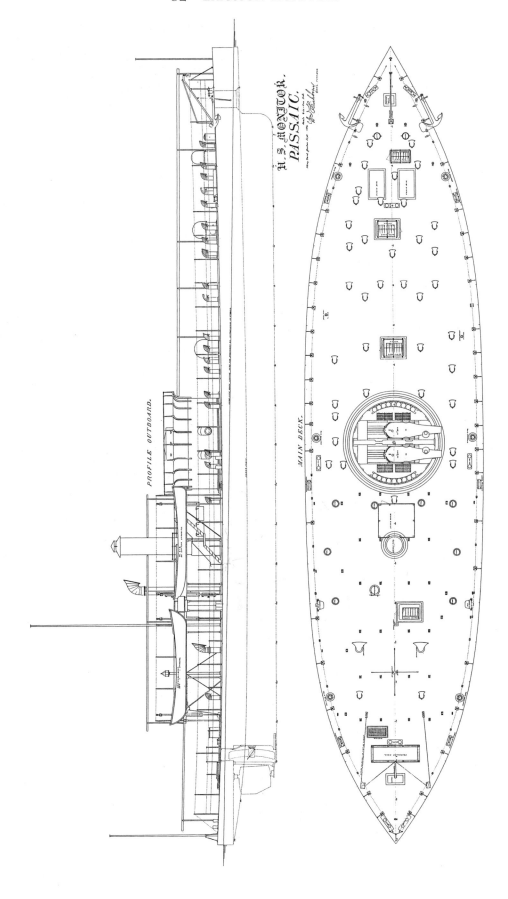

Commanding officer's cabin of the Catskill. *On the left is the windlass room bulkhead, with a watertight door in the center. The forward bulkhead measured some 14 feet and ran the width of the ship. The berth is angled along the curve of the vessel's side. The door leads to a private water closet. A relatively high ceiling—7¹/₂ feet—contributes to the roomy effect. Two black posts may be deck support stanchions. The photograph, part of a series of the vessel, was taken about the time of the Spanish American War. (Naval Historical Center)*

room ventilator and substantial hurricane deck aft. In particular, the *Passaic*'s once smooth foredeck was now studded with a field of over thirty vents, and the *Catskill* had an enclosed house on the hurricane deck. Many such changes were in connection with training rather than combat roles.

Only the *Camanche* avoided wartime combat service. She maintained a sedentary existence on the West Coast, including training duties, until sold in 1899.

Two did not survive the war. *Patapsco*, after service at Charleston and Fort McAllister, was sunk by a torpedo (mine) in January 1865. *Weehawken*

Profile and deck plan of the USS Passaic, *1896. This is the latest depiction of the class, including anchor crane and a host of ventilators. (NARS Plan 2-5-36, National Archives)*

foundered at her moorings in a storm off Charleston, 6 December 1863. An inquiry blamed the accident on the misplacement of ammunition too far forward, trimming her down by the head, which prevented leaking water from reaching her pumps aft until it was too late.

Only two saw service outside of the South Atlantic Blockading Squadron. *Lehigh* served on the James River in 1863 and 1865 (and was off Charleston in between these stints). *Sangamon* was a fixture on the James during the war. She was renamed *Jason* in 1869 and was one of the few to retain her new designator afterwards. She was in commission during the Spanish American War and sold in 1904. In the postwar years, *Lehigh* was a Naval Academy training vessel for a time in the 1870s, was commissioned in 1898, and sold in 1904.

Catskill served off Charleston, was part of the North Atlantic Squadron in the 1870s, and sold in

Turret chamber of the Catskill, *circa 1898. The quarter-geared mechanism to the left, probably hydraulically operated, was to jack up the turret for turning. (Naval Historical Center)*

1901. She was named *Goliath* for a short time in 1869. *Montauk* served in the South Atlantic Blockading Squadron and was laid up after the war, then was in "partial commission" in the 1870s. She was commissioned on the Delaware River in 1882, recommissioned 18 April 1898, and sold in 1904.

Nahant, Passaic, and *Nantucket* served in the operations off Charleston during the war. Only the latter was not commissioned in 1898. The *Passaic* was sold in 1899, *Nantucket* in 1900, *Nahant* in 1904. *Nahant* was the *Atlas,* and *Nantucket* was the *Medusa* for a short time in 1869; then they reverted to their original names.

Canonicus Class

These nine vessels were the ultimate development of the single-turret coastal monitor and were significantly improved over the *Passaic* class. When the contracts were parceled out, builders looked forward to simply repeating the construction of the *Passaics.* Combat experience and other factors, however, resulted in extensive midconstruction alterations, seriously slowing progress and escalating

The Jason (*formerly the* Sangamon), Passaic *class, 1898. This high-angle view clarifies the arrangement of the hurricane deck and shows the typical look of the class during the last years. The* Jason *was one of the last of the class: she was sold in 1904. (U.S. Naval Institute)*

costs—becoming government contractors' night-mares. Resulting claims for these cost overruns would rattle around Congress off and on into the next century.

These vessels were officially termed "Harbor and River Monitors" and were contracted early in September 1862—before the trials of any of the *Passaic*-class ships. The major improvement sought over the previous ships was in speed, to be achieved by lengthening and further refining the lines of the hull and increasing engine power.[38]

In mid-September 1862, just a week after letting the contracts, Alban Stimers, who supervised the construction of these ships in his role as general inspector of ironclads, wrote that the contractors were "so eager to get plans and lists of iron that they really retard me to some extent"; some had ordered iron "before they understood what was required." Even as he wrote, Ericsson and his men were still drawing plans. Later, contractors would complain that they had accepted the contracts under the impression that the vessels were simply slight improvements of the *Passaic*s. They indeed had not yet seen completed plans for the new class.[39]

An administrative note is pertinent here. Alban C. Stimers and Rear Adm. F. H. Gregory were filling newly created positions. Gregory, out of retirement, was the general superintendent of ironclads, based in Washington, with Stimers as his representative in New York. Stimers, whose office was next door to Ericsson's, formed the liaison between the inventor/designer and the ironclad contractors, receiving reports from local inspectors assigned to superintend the individual vessels. This ironclad office was independent of both the Bureau of Construction and Repair and the Bureau of Steam Engineering, which somewhat muddied the lines of responsibility.

With the iron monitors, the navy was presented with an entirely new phenomenon in warship construction. Contract work was not an innovation. In the era of wooden ships, however, contractors generally followed their own plans to meet rather general criteria set forth by the department. Never before the *Passaic* and *Canonicus* classes had builders been totally dependent on plans promulgated by the department. In iron construction, precise mechanical drawings were required for each part—from the nuts and bolts upward—for entire vessels. Thus the fulfillment of the contract was a function of both the department (to supply timely and accurate plans) and the builder (to interpret these correctly and build therefrom). The amount of paperwork that was generated by the need to coordinate builders with inspectors and designers and superintendents was daunting: shades of the modern age.

The first major change to the already in-process vessels occurred in December 1862, after Stimers recalculated the displacement of the vessels. The order went out to add 18 inches to their depth, an operation that required other changes: lengthening stem and sternposts, raising the armor shelf, adding another strake of side plating, and increasing the floor depth. The tops of the boilers were raised at the same time. Some of the vessels were farther along than others and required some dismantling of completed work to make the changes. The *Canonicus*, for instance, had to have her stern removed and replaced to incorporate this change.[40] To compensate for the extra weight, the side armor was also reduced in width, from 50 inches to 33 inches.[41] Because of the acute angle of the armor belt at the centerline fore and aft, reduction of the armor width also reduced the length from an original 235 feet to 224 feet.[42]

The next round of alterations was the result of the engagement at Charleston. These included those already mentioned for the *Passaic* class: a 5- by 15-inch iron band around the turret base, an increase in armor of the pilothouse from 8 to 10 inches, and a hemp-lined "gutter" at the turret base. Additionally, sponsons were added, forming a triangular filling from the side overhang to the side of the hull. This was to be of pine framed with 3/8-inch iron.[43]

The side armor of these vessels was modified to add iron stringers under the plating, running aft about 70 feet. On the *Mahopac, Manhattan,* and *Tecumseh*, these were in pairs, two inches apart, four measuring 12 by 7 inches and four 6 by 7 inches. These totaled over 90,000 pounds.[44]

Other differences between the *Passaic*s and the *Canonicus* class are quickly described. Two 15-inch guns were mounted, both of which had their muzzles turned down to allow them to be run out the gun ports. The engines were considerably larger: 48-inch diameter and 24-inch stroke.[45] Surface condensers were substituted for jet condensers. Stimers's patent fire-tube boilers were used, four in number, two of which were for the auxiliary engines: for turret machinery, blowers, and so on. The propellers were 14 feet rather than 12 feet in diameter. A tall permanent vent was provided between the turret and smokepipe. Turret armor was 10 inches thick rather than 11, and the deck plating was 1½ inches (planked over with oak). Probably for the first time in the U.S. Navy, bunks were provided for the crew.[46]

The first of the class in commission was the *Saugus*, on 7 April 1864; the last, *Tippecanoe*, was delivered 15 February 1866. As far as can be determined, none of these vessels were built to the originally specified length or breadth (235 feet by 46 feet, with 11 feet 10 inches depth of hold). *Catawba* and *Oneota* measured 225 feet in length, 43 feet 3 inches in breadth over the armor, and 13 feet 3 inches deep.[47] *Tippecanoe* was 224 feet 6 inches, by 43 feet

5 inches, by 13 feet 3 inches.[48] Postwar plans of *Canonicus* and *Manayunk* also show similar lengths (224 feet 6 inches for *Manayunk*, 224 feet for *Canonicus*).[49] There is sufficient evidence to indicate that the dimensions of all the vessels were affected equally by the many construction alterations.

Trials of the *Canonicus* were encouraging. She made 8 knots at lower pressure than designed. Her ventilation was called the "most successful improvement," giving an "abundant supply of fresh air to all parts of the vessel." Stimers reported that when he put his hat over a vent on the berth deck and released it, air would cause it to rise.[50]

At sea, the *Mahopac* reported 5½ knots in light winds and smooth conditions but "steered wild," with her commander blaming this on the "new fashioned rudder, hung on a pivot amidships, which is not approved."[51]

At the Battle of Mobile Bay, the commanding officer of the *Manhattan* reported the vessel steered "beautifully" and all her machinery worked "to a charm." Though struck in the pilothouse and turret, there were no jams. He complained only of the dense interior smoke from the 15-inch gun, which obscured steering. He reported the officers' and crew's quarters were "cool" and "comfortable" even after blower engines were stopped in late August.[52] This despite late summer Alabama heat.

The only other major engagement in which the vessels of this class participated was at Fort Fisher. Here *Canonicus* and *Mahopac* sustained relatively little damage, compared to the injuries to the *Passaic* class at Charleston. In these attacks, however, Confederate fire was not concentrated on the monitors as it had been at Charleston in 1863.

In their long postwar service, these vessels received some modifications similar to those of the

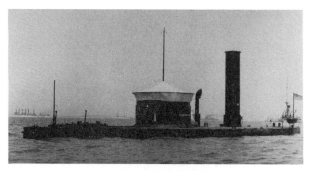

The Canonicus *at the Jamestown Exposition, 1907, looking much as she did during the Civil War. (U.S. Naval Institute)*

Passaic class. Hurricane decks appeared on the *Wyandotte* (former *Tippecanoe*), *Ajax* (former *Manayunk*), and *Manhattan. Canonicus* remained relatively untouched, and the status of *Saugus* and *Mahopac* is unknown.[53]

The *Catawba* and *Oneota* may have had a light deck in place when sold to Peru in 1868. An unusual addition to the *Catawba*, renamed *Atahualpa*, was a two-masted sailing rig, fore-and-aft type, added no doubt temporarily for the passage to the purchasing nation.

Five of this class saw Civil War combat. The *Tippecanoe* and *Manayunk* (as well as the two sold to Peru) were completed after the end of hostilities.

The *Canonicus* served in both the North and South Atlantic blockading squadrons, participating in actions at Trent's Reach and Fort Fisher. She was one of only two single-turret monitors (see *Saugus* below) to visit a foreign port and leave American coastal waters, visiting Havana in 1865 as part of a squadron to confront the Confederate ironclad *Stonewall*.[54] She was renamed *Scylla* in 1869, then reverted to the name *Canonicus*. In and out of commission in the 1870s, she was sold in 1908—the last single-turret monitor in the inventory.

The *Catawba* and *Oneota*, sold to Peru, both participated in the War of the Pacific, which began in 1879. The *Catawba* (*Atahualpa*) was scuttled and *Oneota* (now *Manco Capac*) was blown up to prevent capture by Chile. Both were built at Cincinnati.

The *Mahopac* was in the North Atlantic Squadron and on the James during the Civil War, participating in the attacks on Fort Fisher. She was temporarily renamed *Castor* in 1869, in commission in the late 1860s and early 1870s, and sold in 1902.

The *Manayunk*, completed after the end of the war, was laid up until 1867. Some of the delay in their completion was a result of the low stage of the Mississippi, which prevented their movement

The Saugus, Canonicus *class, probably at Trent's Reach on the James River, April 1865. This class saw an addition of another 25 feet to the length of the single-turret vessels and had increased engine power. A torpedo rake is mounted on the bow. The turret has a light stripe around the top of the turret itself as well as the rifle screen, and a stripe around the funnel. Black-and-white photography makes it unclear whether this was white, a light lead color, or another light hue altogether. (Naval Historical Center)*

General plan and lines of the Canonicus *class, sometimes referred to as the* Tippecanoe *class during the war. Note the much-reduced forward-and-aft overhang and the very sharp hull lines forward. (Naval Historical Center)*

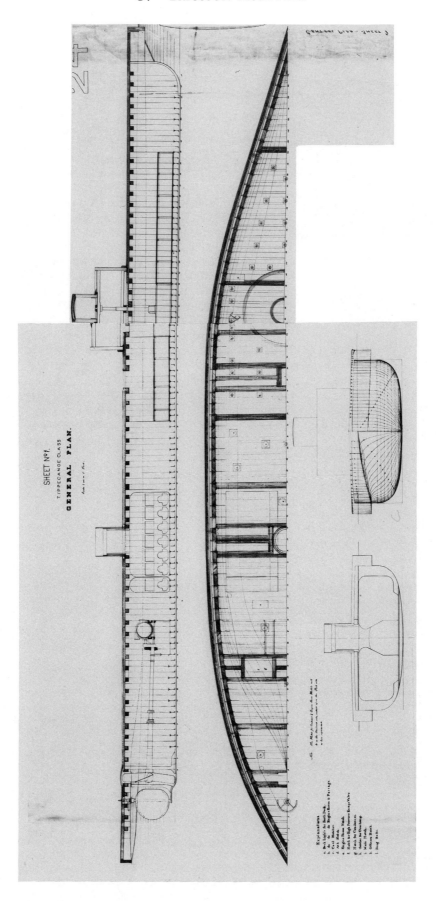

SHEET Nº1.
TIPPECANOE CLASS
GENERAL PLAN.

The Manhattan *(circa 1898) obtained all the modifications that the* Canonicus *missed, most noticeably an elaborate hurricane deck. This is an excellent view of the sharply pointed prow characteristic of this class. (U.S. Naval Institute)*

downriver from the builder in Cincinnati. She was renamed *Ajax* in 1869 and retained that designation until sold in 1899.

The *Manhattan* was one of two vessels to serve in the Gulf during the Civil War. At the Battle of Mobile Bay, she was instrumental in bringing the Confederate ram *Tennessee* to rout, expending a

few well-placed 15-inch projectiles into the rebel ironclad. Her temporary name in 1869 was *Neptune*, and she was sold in 1902.

The *Saugus* served in the North Atlantic Squadron, at Trent's Reach, Dutch Gap, and Fort Fisher. Renamed *Centaur* and reverting to *Saugus* in 1869, she was in service in the 1870s, steaming to the West Indies in one commission, and sold in 1891. She was the first of this class to be sold out (other than the *Oneota* and *Catawba*).

The *Tecumseh* was in the North Atlantic Squadron a short time before transferring to the West Gulf Squadron. She was the last vessel to join Farragut's squadron before the Battle of Mobile Bay. She was lost to a Confederate mine in that battle, going down in less than thirty seconds, with only 21 surviving of a crew of 114. She remains at the bottom of Mobile Bay in some thirty-five feet of water. In 1901 the navy gave up claim to the vessel, and in the 1970s there was a move afoot to raise her and build a bicentennial park around the ship. Nothing ever came of this, despite her relatively accessible location and what divers described as her "amazingly good condition."[55]

The *Tippecanoe*, built at Cincinnati (renamed *Vesuvius*, then *Wyandotte*) was first commissioned in 1876. She was a station ship at Washington, served in the war with Spain, and sold in 1899.

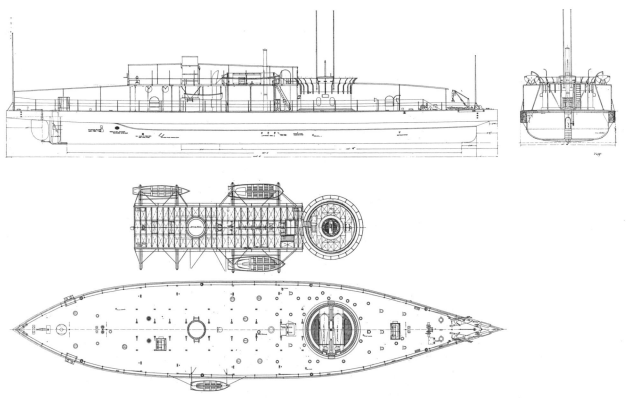

Deck and outboard plans of the Ajax *(formerly the* Manayunk*), 1890s. (NARS Plans 1-10-43, 1-10-46, National Archives)*

Dictator and *Puritan*

Given Ericsson's original concept of a slightly awash raft for his war vessels, it would seem that the terms *seagoing* and *monitor* would be mutually exclusive. The post–Hampton Roads "monitor fever" was such, however, that some basics were overlooked in the Navy Department, with the upshot being contracts with Ericsson for two vessels of the "big class": oceangoing warships on the monitor principle.

To be sure, the department was far from unanimous in its approval of the project. John Lenthall and B. F. Isherwood, two of a three-man board that studied Ericsson's design, registered their doubts, contending that the overhang would limit maximum speed and the low freeboard would be a significant drawback in many sea conditions. They also recommended iron deck beams rather than wood.[56] Joseph Smith, the third member of this board, complained that the vessel would be more appropriate for harbors than oceans and that three smaller-sized batteries could be had for its price.[57] These opinions seemed to have had no effect on the outcome.

The *Dictator* and *Puritan* (the former named by Ericsson, the latter a department name substituted for the designer's name *Protector*) would be huge: at over three thousand tons, they were more than four times the size of the *Monitor*. They would be the largest American iron naval vessels built to date and were more than half again the displacement of the largest American seagoing iron merchant ships built by that time.

Because the *Puritan* was never completed and there are few available plans of her as Ericsson designed her, emphasis here will be on the *Dictator*. As a seagoing vessel, the *Dictator*'s hull form diverged considerably from that of the coastal monitors. She was designed to draw 20 feet, leaving some 16 inches above water. Her length was 314 feet on deck with an extreme breadth over armor of 50 feet. With an eye towards great speed (16 knots was expected) she was "one of the sharpest vessels afloat." The entrance angle of the hull proper was a total of only about 28 degrees. Clipper ship architect Donald McKay described her hull as "beautiful as a woman's leg."[58] Her forward leanness was probably part of the reason Ericsson wrote in 1864 that he did not know how to estimate the tonnage, because of the hull's "peculiar" form.[59] The bilges were nearly circular, and the armor shelf/overhang measured 6 feet vertically and created a 4-foot hip at midships.[60]

In deference to the "universal clamor of naval officers," the forward overhang was significantly reduced by a protesting Ericsson, who was forced to create an alternate method of raising and protecting the anchors. Plans show the anchor with an attendant steam hoister located well aft of the stem.[61]

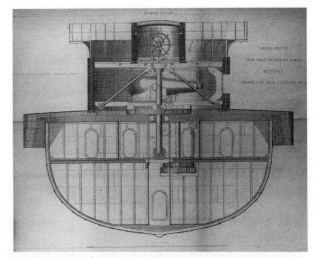

Cross section of the Dictator. *Turret armor included outer and inner cylinders of 1-inch layers, with 4¹/₂-inch iron slabs in between. Note the gun-port cover and traversing rails for 15-inch projectiles. (From* The Artizan, *1 October 1867; Naval Historical Center)*

The armor belt itself was vintage monitor: vertical and horizontal wood backing timbers, two armor stringers, and layers of 1-inch iron. In this case, the plates were six deep, bolted to the backing. There were no bolts through the entire belt, iron and wood.[62] Deck armor was 1¹/₂ inches.

The turret was 24 feet inside diameter, with armor plating 15 inches thick. Rather than laminated 1-inch layers throughout, there were six layers in an outer cylinder, four in an inner cylinder, with 4¹/₂-inch-thick segmental slabs between the cylinders. The superimposed pilothouse was 8 feet in interior diameter, with 12 inches of plating. Its top was composed of three 1-inch layers of iron, covered by 8 inches of wood and an outer plate of 1-inch iron.[63]

The hull itself was framed of double angle iron, 6- by 4- by ⁵/₈-inch on 18-inch centers, with a keel consisting of 1-inch plates, and hull plating measuring ¹³/₁₆-inch thick. Conventional iron hull construction was used, with iron frames and wooden deck beams forming the complete hull cross section. Iron trusses were used to strengthen the deck over the boilers. A "railway" was to carry coal through the watertight coal-bunker bulkhead to the boiler room. The wooden deck beams, 14 inches square, were to be *kyanized*—impregnated with a metallic solution to prevent decay. The *Dictator* was the first monitor whose original design included a grated hurricane deck abaft the turret.[64]

Motive power for the *Dictator* was a new variety of the Ericsson vibrating lever system, using vertical rather than horizontal cylinders. These were "kettle bottomed" and measured 100 inches in diameter by 48-inch stroke. No bedplates were used; rather, each cylinder was bolted to keelsons measuring 10

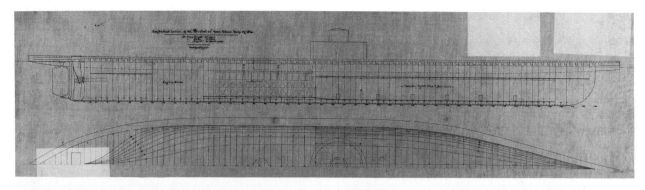

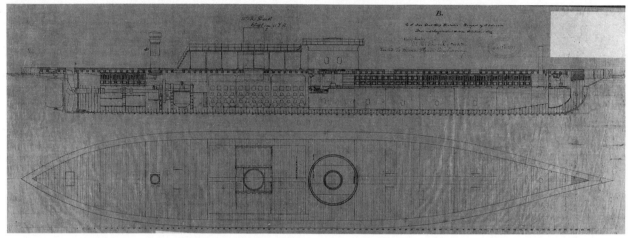

Lines and inboard plan of the Dictator. *With the* Puritan, *this was Ericsson's second seagoing monitor design. She was 314 feet on deck and 50 feet wide over the armor. Her forward overhang was greatly reduced and her anchor hoisting apparatus was moved farther aft. (NARS Bureau of Steam Engineering Plans, National Archives)*

feet deep and 24 inches wide. The two vibrating shafts ran fore and aft, operated by levers from the piston rods. Two additional levers operated the propeller shaft, located on a midship line nearly level with the tops of the cylinders. Again, because no bedplates were used, the vibrating shafts were mounted on the keelsons. The propeller shaft was 21 inches in diameter, and the cast iron prop was 21 1/2 feet in diameter. Six Martin water-tube boilers were used, with a single huge funnel about 12 feet in diameter.[65] The absence of engine bedplates has also been seen in the early design for the Stevens battery, where the hull framing did double duty as engine supports.

Two 15-inch guns were mounted in the turret and given recoil dampening by a series of discs adjusted by screws. Hand wheels ran the guns out for firing.[66]

The *Dictator* was launched on 26 December 1863, with Welles noting that he put "full confidence" in her as a fighting craft but not as a "cruiser."[67] Before commissioning, Ericsson proposed a sailing rig for the ship. This apparently was to be a single mast, over 100 feet high, with three yards, the largest a hefty 114 feet in length. John Lenthall was not impressed at all: he expressed his doubt that such

an enormous ship could be worked with one mast and commented that the introduction of a sailing rig would release the contractor from the contract speed obligation.[68]

Shortly before her commissioning, she "participated" in the election of 1864—by lying off the Battery, guns loaded with canister, to discourage street rioting.[69] After her commissioning (11 November 1864), problems continued to plague her. The stern overhang had settled, jamming the rudder post, and the experimental anchor hoister required over three hours to heave 40 fathoms of chain.[70] The former problem was rectified simply by extending wearing in the rudder until it could turn "passably," after which her commanding officer was favorably impressed by her steering and handling.[71]

It was planned that she would be ready for the attack on Fort Fisher in December 1864. Engine heating problems prevented this, however, and her engineer expressed his doubts that the bearing surface provided was sufficient for a main shaft of such a large dimension.[72]

Though ordered not to exceed 8 knots, the *Dictator* made passage south from New York. It was then found that her main journal brasses (bearing surfaces) were worn to the extent that she needed immediate repairs. New brasses did not improve the matter. A new shaft was installed and she was sent at slow speed back to New York. From July to September 1865, after further tinkering with her shaft and bearings, she cruised off New England and apparently never exceeded 10 knots.[73]

In postwar years she was commissioned twice before final decommissioning in 1877. Other flaws noted were her inability to use half of her grate surface, which limited her steaming capacity, and a severe limitation on the amount of coal and stores she could carry and still remain above water. The storage problem prevented any extended passages.[74]

The performance of the *Dictator* did not enhance Ericsson's reputation with John Rodgers, who, though convinced Ericsson was a genius, also termed him an "obstinate fool." Ericsson blamed the fiasco on the civilian heads of the navy bureaus, in particular B. F. Isherwood. Isherwood had forced on him larger boilers than he desired, Ericsson wrote, and, in general, they had placed requirements that had increased the design weight of the vessel by some 600,000 pounds. (Ericsson also wrote that he had successfully compensated for this additional weight burden.[75]) It seems, however, that the key problem with this big monitor was Ericsson's engine design. Its bearing heating problem was never adequately solved and she never approached her contract speed of 16 knots.

The never-completed *Puritan* would have been the largest of the Ericsson monitors, at 340 feet in length. Her hull was no more than a lengthened *Dictator* but was to have twin screws and two turrets. Ericsson objected to both of those features, insisting that the throw-weight of the guns be incorporated into one turret, sweeping the horizon and deemphasizing the steering advantages of twin screws.[76] By November 1865, the department had ordered the deletion of the second turret and called for two 20-inch smoothbores in the single turret.[77] This was

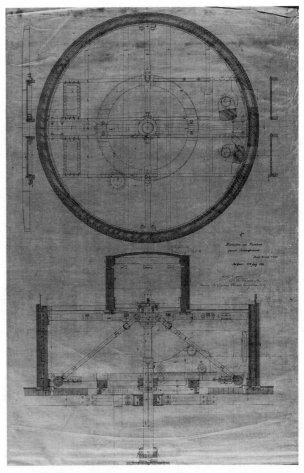

Turret arrangement of the Dictator *and* Puritan, *1863. Note the unusual armor: 1-inch layers outside and inside, with slabs of 4½-inch armor in between. (National Archives)*

over a year since the vessel's launch. Still incomplete when turned over to the navy, construction was suspended. The "rebuilt" *Puritan,* commissioned in the 1890s, was an entirely new vessel.

At this juncture, it is appropriate to evaluate the performance of the navy's monitors during the Civil

The only known broadside view of the Dictator, *circa 1865. The distinguishing feature is the tall ventilator abaft the funnel. (Courtesy of the New-York Historical Society)*

U.S. Navy ironclads at the close of the Civil War (right to left): the Saugus, Mahopac *(in background),* Sangamon, *captured Confederate ram* Atlanta, *and* Onondaga. *All were assigned to Trent's Reach, James River, in April 1865. (U.S. Army Military History Institute)*

War. First, however, certain nonissues must be put in their place. Regardless of the claims of men such as Fox and others, the true low-freeboard monitor as Ericsson envisioned it was not a legitimate ocean-going warship. The limited usefulness of such ships in the world's navies down to World War II should be sufficient proof of this.

The basic question becomes the practical one: Was the monitor system the proper, most efficient method of dealing with the Confederacy? Answering the question is hampered by the fact that, excepting the river flotilla, there was, for comparison's sake, only one legitimate broadside vessel in the inventory: *New Ironsides*, discussed in chapter 3.

The advantages of the monitor were these: all-round field of fire, low profile, ability to carry the 15-inch gun, and light draft. In operations against coastal fortifications, field of fire and low profile are luxuries. At Charleston, for instance, the vessels fired at anchor, and the low profile seems not to have prevented the disabling of a goodly number of monitor turrets in a fairly short time. The 15-inch gun, though firing the largest projectile on shipboard, had no particular range advantage and was at least twice as slow in rate of fire as the 11-inch gun.

The monitor was much more satisfactory in ship-to-ship actions, where movement and maneuver made the turret a distinct advantage and the low profile was of more practical consequence. Furthermore, the 15-inch gun was significantly more effective against the limited amount of armor and backing possible on the Confederate vessels than against the relatively unlimited protection possible in fortifications.

D. D. Porter had some pointed remarks on the type after the Fort Fisher expeditions:

These vessels have laid five days under a fire from Fort Fisher, anchored less than 800 yards off, and though fired at a great deal, they were seldom hit, and received no injury except to boats and light

matter about the decks, which were pretty well cut to pieces. Compared to the *Ironsides*, their fire is very slow, and not at all calculated to silence heavy batteries, which require a rapid and continuous fire to drive men from the guns; but they are famous coadjutors in a fight, and put in the heavy blows which tell on casemates and bombproofs. The smaller class of monitors, as at present constructed, will always require the aid of a steamer to tow them and take care of them.[78]

The admiral continued with positive comments on their ability to ride out rough weather—though not without considerable discomfort to the crews from leakage. He continued:

I have only to remark that the principle is a good one, if the vessels are all built like the *Monadnock*. The fire of these vessels, combined with the fire of such vessels as the *New Ironsides* and heavy frigates,

The prow of the Puritan, *Ericsson's largest monitor. She was 40 feet longer than the* Dictator *and was never completed. Ericsson argued for a single turret. The department argued for twin turrets but relented late in her construction. She was incomplete at war's end. (Naval Historical Center)*

is very effective, particularly against heavy plated vessels, bombproofs, and stone or brick walls. I have never yet seen a vessel that came up to my ideas of what is required for offensive operations as much as the *Ironsides*. She combines very many good qualities. The most important is the comfort with which the people on board of her live, though she would be no match for the *Monadnock* in a fight, the latter having more speed.

He concluded with a complaint about the slow clearing of smoke from the monitor turrets.[79]

In summary, the monitor-type vessel was necessary and well adapted to preventing the Confederate rams from breaking the blockade but was less successful in ship-versus-fortification roles—though the post-Charleston modifications seemed to have had significant positive results in increasing their protection under fire. It seems obvious, however, that success could have been had with broadside vessels, had the Navy Department exerted more energy in that direction.

As for any hypothetical match-up between a monitor and a vessel such as the *Warrior,* the former would have had few advantages. The penetrating power of the 11-inch and 15-inchers and the defensive strength of their armor would have been positive points. Their slowness, poor rate of fire, and problems using their ordnance in any kind of seaway would have severely limited their effectiveness against the fast, high-freeboard adversary.

The Chillicothe, *an inaccurate contemporary drawing. On the completed vessel, the paddle-wheel housing was much lower, compared to the hurricane deck. (Naval Historical Center)*

CHAPTER 8

Casemated River Ironclads and Rams, 1862–1865

In April 1862, a navy board reported on proposals submitted to the War Department for ironclad river vessels. The two main criteria were a draft of 3 to 5 feet and an emphasis on forward firepower. Contracts were to be awarded for a total of eight vessels: two to be built by Tomlinson and Hartupee, one by George Bestor, two by James Eads, and three by Joseph Brown and McCord. Eads's vessels were to have monitor-type turrets; the Tomlinson and Hartupee vessels were to be iron "as an experiment for river service." At the outset, these two were to be casemated but were completed with turrets. The Bestor vessel was the *Ozark*. Brown, of Cincinnati, was to construct three vessels, which became the *Chillicothe*, *Tuscumbia*, and *Indianola*. These three were the last Union-contracted casemated river ironclads of the war.[1]

In this chapter, the Brown vessels are presented, as well as three casemate-type riverboat conversions: *Choctaw*, *Lafayette*, and *Eastport*. Also included are the two last iterations of the ram principle, the *Avenger* and *Vindicator*. Save one—*Eastport*—all these vessels were begun under U.S. Army supervision. The *Eastport* was under construction by the Confederates when captured and turned over to the navy.

For the researcher, the western river vessels present considerable frustration: few documents or plans have been found, insufficient to give a complete picture of these unusual war boats. Indeed, no original complete detailed plans have been found for any of these vessels (except for the light-draft monitors). Oddly enough, plans for two converted vessels, the *Choctaw* and *Lafayette*, are more satisfactory than any drafts of the purpose-built boats.

Chillicothe, Tuscumbia, and *Indianola*

An early plan delineates Joseph Brown's general concept for all three of these boats: a wide riverboat hull, with only paddle boxes, funnels, and casemate above deck. To emphasize forward firepower, four guns were mounted in the athwartships casemate, with one additional weapon on each side (or "end" of the casemate). Below decks was an unusual power plant: four steam cylinders, two for the side paddle wheels and one each for the twin screws.[2] Given the extreme breadth and rather short length-to-breadth ratio, the independent engines, propellers, and paddle wheels were no doubt introduced to provide additional steering power, above and beyond the rudders.

Original plans for the *Chillicothe*, built at Cincinnati and armored by the firm of McCord and Junger, show a hull of 158 feet in length by 50 feet. The depth of hold was to be 4½ feet. Her contract shows a significant concern over the vessel's draft, with penalties for each inch of draft over 2 feet 11 inches. The government had the option to reject her if she drew over 3 feet 4 inches. This was to be the lightest-draft armored vessel built for the river fleet. The closest competition would have been the *Osage* and *Neosho*, turreted vessels with a contract draft of 3 feet 6 inches each.[3]

To deal with the longitudinal strains inherent in such a shallow hull, there were, in addition to the keel and two keelsons, three full-length bulkheads. On the centerline was a 2½-inch thick watertight bulkhead. On either side of this, according to the specifications, were "lattice bulkheads of 4 by 6 inch stuff, and arched to distribute the weight over the entire boat." The plans show these as diagonal cross

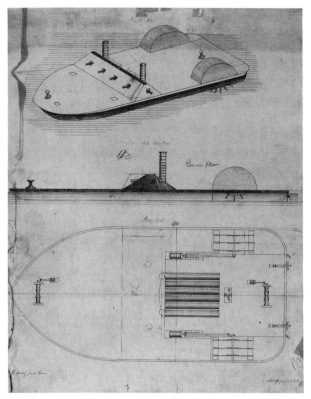

Joseph Brown's original concept for casemated river ironclads. On the back is written, "One boat 170 x 70, one boat 170 x 50." These dimensions correspond to the Tuscumbia, *which was over 70 feet in breadth, and the* Chillicothe *and* Indianola, *about 50 feet wide. Though all three used an athwartship slant-sided casemate, none carried four guns across. (NARS Plan 28-6-4Q, National Archives)*

braces the length of the vessel. The specifications also called for additional arches beneath the casemate: on the plan, a 32-foot arched timber is shown for this purpose.[4]

Two paddle wheels were to be in stern recesses measuring 15 feet in length, powered by high-

pressure cylinders measuring 23 inches by 4 feet. Three boilers were called for, each 40 inches in diameter and 28 feet long. There were to be two chimneys, 20 feet high, hinged close to the deck to allow clearing of overhead obstructions. Two steam capstans were provided. She was to maintain 4 miles per hour against a current of 2 miles per hour.[5]

The hull was to be oak and pine, with 9-inch-thick sides and frames 15 inches apart. There were no deck beams as such. Rather, the decks were simply 8-inch-square timbers laid athwartships, "bolted edgewise to each other and through the arch lattice bulkheads with 1 inch iron bolts." The deck was crowned 8 inches.[6]

Her battery consisted of two 11-inch Dahlgrens mounted to allow forward and side fields of fire. The casemate itself was 22 feet by 42 feet at its base, 7 feet high, framed with 12-inch-square pine, overlaid with 9 inches of the same wood.[7]

Casemated armor was to be 3 inches thick. The deck was to be given 1-inch plating; hull sides, 2 inches thick to 1 foot below the waterline. The bow was to have 2½ inches of iron, also extending below the waterline. Temporary cabins were to be constructed on deck.[8]

As completed the *Chillicothe* was somewhat different from her builder's specifications. Six feet had been added to her length, making a total of 164 feet. The dimension from bottom to top of the crown of the deck was now 8 feet—over 2 feet had been added. The paddle wheels were now moved forward some 18 feet. On her trial trip she attained 9 mph upstream, thus significantly exceeding her contract speed of 4 knots.[9]

It should be noted that the speed of these river vessels was in most cases given in miles per hour, rather than knots. On trials and in actual service, distances and times were based on runs between points along the river, therefore in statute miles. On contracts, many times the word *knots* has been

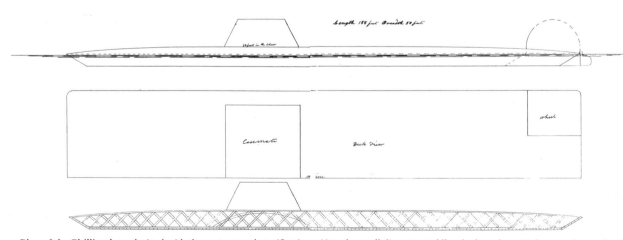

Plan of the Chillicothe *submitted with the contract and specifications. Note the small-diameter paddle wheels—about 15 feet—and exceedingly shallow hull. It was hoped she would not draw over 40 inches. Trusslike timbers were used to counteract longitudinal weakness. (National Archives)*

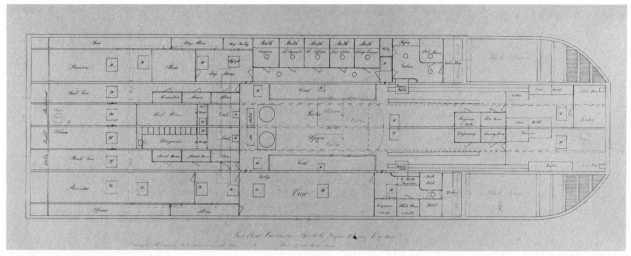

Deck plan of the Chillicothe, *showing her square scow bow. Dotted lines indicate the location of the gun casemate. The depth of hold was increased substantially during construction but the interior was cramped and poorly ventilated. (NARS Plan 28-6-1A, National Archives)*

deleted and replaced by the word *miles*. If the speeds of river and ocean vessels are compared, this distinction should be kept in mind: the speed in statute miles appears faster by over 10 percent.

A hurricane deck was soon added to the *Chillicothe*, extending from over the casemate to nearly abaft the wheel houses. A small cabin was built on deck, containing stores and pantry, but no doubt its most practical use was to swing the hammocks in warm weather. The steering wheel was located somewhat inconveniently for all involved: between the two guns in the casemate.[10] Below deck spaces were far from commodious, described as "small, uncomfortable [and] badly ventilated."[11] Crew quarters were amidships; officers to starboard, crew to port.[12] Given the vessel's light draft and single deck, living conditions were comparable to the monitors. Unlike the monitors, there was no provision for forced-air ventilation.

Once in service, the *Chillicothe*'s structural strength and ability to withstand shot were soon called into question. Within two months, the weakness inherent in her beamless decks became apparent: she had worked a ¹⁄₂-inch seam across the deck over the engines, and the contractor was jury rigging "iron straps fore and aft under the deck and bolted through it." Her commanding officer commented that she was a "scow, without knees or anything to strengthen her, and, I think, very weak."[13] The tendency for hogging in these vessels was phenomenal.

She also drew much criticism for her inability to resist shot. Her white pine casemate backing was repeatedly driven in, and the casemate's interior bolts proved to be "destructive to those on board."[14]

One freak incident did much to tarnish her fighting reputation. Early in 1863, on the Tallahatchie River, a Confederate shell impacted one of her 11-

inch shells at the moment of loading, exploding both projectiles. Fourteen were killed or wounded, and both port covers, each weighing 1,800 pounds, were thrown out by the blast.[15]

The *Chillicothe* participated in actions on the White River, Yazoo Pass, Tallahatchie River, and Red River during the Civil War. She was sold in November 1865 for $3,000 (her original cost had been $92,960). She lay on the riverbank near Cairo, Illinois, for years after the war, then was burned in 1872, in clearing for a railroad right-of-way.[16]

The *Tuscumbia* had the dubious distinction of being the widest U.S. Navy vessel built, up to the present century. She was referred to as the "broad giant" and was probably the maximum width possible in a flat-bottomed boat.

Her arrangement was intended to be similar to that of the *Chillicothe* but with a battery of three 11-inch Dahlgrens. To accommodate this firepower and casemate, she was 72 feet wide. Her length was 176 feet and depth about 7 feet. The casemate was

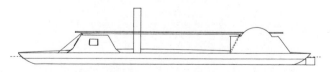

Outboard profile of the Chillicothe *as completed. Note the crown of the deck. The hog chain can be seen paralleling the hurricane deck, with a dotted line indicating the aft hog brace. A forward hog brace ran diagonally through the casemate. The lower edge of the armor is shown on the hull. (Drawing by author from NARS Plan 28-6-1B, National Archives)*

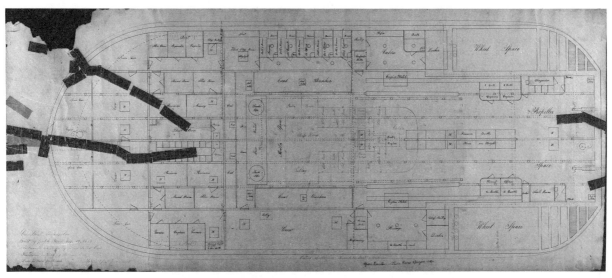

Deck plan of the Tuscumbia. *Over 79 feet in breadth, she required substantial turning power and had independently operating paddles and twin screws, in addition to twin rudders. Screw propellers were recessed under the stern. The general arrangement is similar to that of the* Chillicothe. *(NARS Plan 28-6-4M, National Archives)*

62 feet by 22 feet at deck level, with 12-inch-thick sides covered by 3 inches of iron. The deck was plated with 1 inch of iron. Around the hull was what the contractor referred to as a "fascia," 12 inches thick and 24 inches deep, extending below the waterline. This was beveled and covered with 2 inches of plating.[17] The hull had 8- by 10-inch floor timbers. The keel measured 15 by 30 inches, and there were two side and two knuckle keelsons. As with the *Chillicothe*, the arched decks were without beams, composed of 8- by 8-inch timbers attached to the fore and aft bulkheads.[18]

Below decks she was very much like the *Chillicothe* in the location of most compartments. She was fitted with two steam-operated capstans and a donkey engine. Her motive power was unlike any except the *Indianola:* four steam cylinders, two for the paddle

wheels and one for each 6-foot-diameter screw propeller. The side-wheel engines were 6 feet by 30 inches in diameter; the paddle engines, 20 by 20 inches.[19] The former were no doubt standard western rivers high-pressure engines, the latter, probably a beveled-geared installation (see *Marietta* and *Sandusky* in chapter 9 for a description of this type of engine).

It is not surprising that certain line officers looked askance at a boat of such dimensions mounting merely three guns. Late in 1862, over the objections of Joseph Brown, who rightly feared the consequences of additional weight on the ends of his vessels, D. D. Porter (brother of William D. "Dirty Bill" Porter) ordered the addition of a second casemate to her stern and saw to it that two 9-inch Dahlgrens were mounted thereon. (He similarly equipped the *Indianola* at the same time.[20])

With the second casemate, she was carrying some 480 tons of iron, including about 75 tons far aft. Casemate plating was similar to that of the *Chillicothe*, but the backing in the after casemate was 8 inches in thickness.[21]

To deal with both longitudinal and athwartship strains, the vessel was given both fore-and-aft and cross hog chains. Brown also placed bulkheads every 10 feet under the casemates, and (he said) substantial keelsons and timbering.[22]

The *Tuscumbia* was commissioned 12 March 1863 and was in action soon afterward. Within weeks Porter himself was complaining that the vessel depended "too much on hog chains . . . the cutting of one of which brings all the weight on her ends."[23] At Grand Gulf three of her four main hog chains were shot away and her stern dropped over 7

Bow view of the Tuscumbia, *obviously after some hard service. Three 11-inch Dahlgrens are in the forward casemate, plus two 9-inch guns in a stern casemate added later. (Naval Historical Center)*

inches. Even before this, her bottom had begun coming up in the middle and the deck had dropped 7 inches over the boiler spaces, pressures that resulted in a sprung bilge keelson.[24] More importantly, during the action her port wheel dropped down, disabling that engine and leaving the vessel at the mercy of the current—despite her props and second paddle wheel. Lenthall wrote subsequently that the wheel's dislocation was also attributable to the strains caused by the after casemate.[25]

In addition, a litany of other defects began to surface. There was no conventional support for the deck over the boilers; rather a bridge tree with chains was used to support the deck from above. The pitman boxes were exposed and not fastened to the backing properly. The decks were laid athwartships, without carlines and beams. The location of the shell room and magazine passages was dangerous: immediately aft of the midship gun port, and thus open to sparks. The hog chains, at 20 feet, were too high and exposed.[26]

The fastening of the armor plating caused the most consternation. Four-inch drift bolts had been used, which tended to be "drawn out" by shot. Porter wrote that every shot that "hits starts a plate and in some instances jarred out the bolts in the adjacent plates." Her commanding officer was particularly incensed by the "outrageous manner in which this ship has been put together," noting that one shot to the pilothouse loosened every bolt, timber, and plate in that structure.[27]

After Grand Gulf, where she had taken eighty-one hits and dropped out of the action, the *Tuscumbia* took part in the bombardment of Vicksburg. She was then taken in hand for a deserved refit and was out of action from August 1863 to May 1864. She saw no further major action, was decommissioned in February 1865, and sold that November.

The Tuscumbia. *Because of her width, she had both longitudinal and thwartship hog chains. The sagging of the forward end of her hurricane deck, however, is noticeable in this image. (Naval Historical Center)*

She brought $3,000: she had cost the government over $229,000.[28]

Regarding all three of these vessels, Admiral Porter wrote a semblance of an apology:

> If they did not come up to the Monitors in invulnerability, they accomplished all that was required of them at the time, viz: the capture of the enemy's stronghold. The builders never claimed that they should be considered more than *temporary* expedients with which to harass the enemy; and taken in that sense, they certainly may be considered very good vessels, and have fairly repaid all the money spent on them, taking into consideration the work they have done.[29]

D. D. Porter, of course, was known for stretching points.

Stern view of the Indianola *under construction, showing screw propellers and recess for paddle wheels. Her scowlike hull lines are obvious here. (U.S. Naval Institute)*

The third of this trio was the *Indianola*, a vessel that at different times in her short career caused trepidation for both sides. In size and layout *Indianola* resembled the *Chillicothe*. She had exactly the same casemate design, with twin 11-inch guns and an aft casemate, or bulwark, with two 9-inchers, but she was slightly larger, at 175 feet by 52 feet.

Her power plant was much like that of the *Tuscumbia*: two paddle wheels and twin screws. The former were powered by two 24- by 72-inch cylinders, the latter by 18- by 28-inch engines. The paddle-wheel cylinders were inclined to lower them into the hold. There were two four-bladed, 6-foot-diameter screw propellers and five boilers amidships.[30]

The single major distinguishing feature of the *Indianola* was her deck cabin. If an existing engraving is accurate, rather than a simple hurricane deck, she sported a complete riverboatlike two-story structure, extending from the casemate and pilot-house aft to the paddle housings. She had 3 inches of casemate armor over 12-inch backing, 2 inches of plating on the "fascia" around the hull, a prominent ram, and carried in her commodious interior a complement of 144. The hull framing, timbering, and deck were similar to that of the *Tuscumbia*.[31]

While a-building in Cincinnati, the vessel was commandeered by the local army commander (Lew Wallace) to add her guns to defend the city from an expected attack by Confederates under E. Kirby Smith.[32] This did not materialize and the *Indianola*

Starboard view of the Indianola. *The screw engines were of the beveled-geared type, and the gears themselves might well be those seen here on deck, yet to be installed. This image was originally captioned "Wreck of the* Indianola," *but it appears to be a construction photograph. (Naval Historical Center)*

was returned to the builders. Though incomplete, she was considered in commission as early as 4 September 1862.

Her first combat occurred 13 February 1863, when she ran the batteries at Vicksburg to blockade—detached—the mouth of the Red River. Less than two weeks later she was attacked by two rebel rams. In a running fight at close quarters the *Indianola* was rammed seven times, forced aground, and surrendered.

The Confederates, elated at capturing such a powerful, and nearly new, prize, began repairs. D. D. Porter, not to be toyed with, then floated his

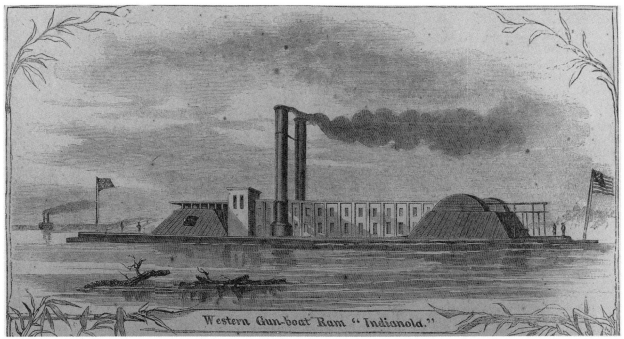

An engraving of the Indianola *from* Harper's Weekly, *showing a rather elaborate two-deck cabin. When plans were made to rebuild the ship late in the war, the two decks were retained. (Naval Historical Center)*

famous dummy ironclad ram downriver—panicking the Confederates, who hurriedly blew up the *Indianola*.

The story was not yet over, however: an inspection by the recaptors showed her hull and engines intact and portions of the casemate still on deck.[33] Plans were made to reconstruct her at Mound City along the lines of the city class: with a full-length casemate and eight broadside- and three forward-firing guns (plus a second-story cabin).[34] Nothing came of this and she was sold for $3,000 on 29 November 1865.

The *Indianola* had cost the government about $182,000. The total for all three vessels built by Joseph Brown was in excess of $500,000. To add perspective, especially in view of Admiral D. D. Porter's comments, it could be observed that the least expensive *Passaic*-class monitor cost $408,000. Therefore, though the *Chillicothe* might have been the only "success" of the three (she served out the war at least, without a major rebuild), as primitive ironclads these scows-of-war were at least cost effective.

Lafayette, Choctaw, and Eastport

If any man gained a reputation as a rebuilder of western river ironclads, it was W. D. Porter. In April 1862, as his greatly enlarged *Essex* was nearing completion, Porter purchased the side-wheel steamer *Aleck Scott* (sometimes rendered *Alick Scott*) for $8,500.[35] This vessel had been built in 1848 at Saint Louis and was one of the larger and well-known riverboats of the time. At one point her assistant pilot was Samuel Clemens—later calling himself Mark Twain.[36]

Given the size of the original boat, 296 by 44 feet, it is no wonder that the resulting ironclad was one of the biggest things on the rivers. The somewhat grotesque, snail-like shape of the final vessel was directly related to the original vessel and Porter's rebuilding rationale. In contrast to the tinclads, where the cabin structure was essentially closed in and plated, Porter, on the *Aleck Scott* (renamed *Fort Henry* in army service, then *Lafayette* in the navy), excised the entire tiered superstructure, including the wide overhanging main deck. All that remained above water was the shallow hull itself (something like 20 feet narrower than the main deck had been) and the paddle boxes and funnels. Porter then built compartmentation into the hull and constructed a full-length casemate on the main deck, 30 inches thick at the ends and 21 inches along the sides.[37]

The engines' cylinders (standard river installations) were 26 inches in diameter with 10-foot stroke, driving paddle wheels 34 feet in diameter. Six boilers were used, including one for auxiliary equipment (two donkey engines for pumping ship, and so on). Stores and mazazines were below deck, with quarters amidships and between the paddle boxes.[38]

There is some uncertainty concerning her armor. Porter had used a layer of india rubber under the plating of the *Essex*, and D. D. Porter wrote in 1864 that both *Lafayette* and *Choctaw* were built of "heavy frames, covered on the outside with gutta-percha, and then with a light thickness of iron." Despite W. D.'s report that 1 inch of iron backed by rubber

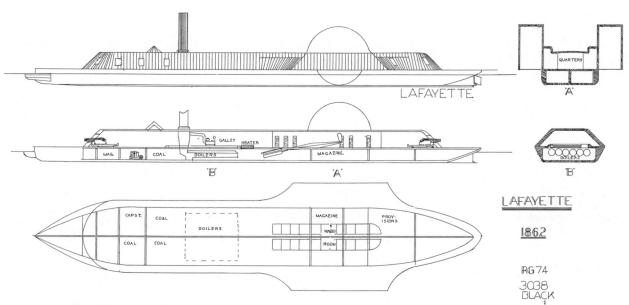

W. D. Porter's original plan for the Lafayette, *converted from the river steamer* Aleck Scott. *Over 290 feet long, the* Lafayette *was the longest ironclad on the rivers. Unlike the tinclads, the* Aleck Scott *was stripped down to the hull, then rebuilt with heavy timbers and iron plating. A major change from this plan was eliminating the cone-shaped pilothouse. (Tracing by author of NARS RG 74, Black Series, 3438, National Archives)*

The Lafayette, *shown in service on the western rivers. (Naval Historical Center)*

was as effective as five inches of iron, D. D.'s comment was that it was "not of the slightest use; on the contrary, it was a detriment, and aided very much in destroying the vessels by rot."[39] (It appears that the terms used for this material—gutta-percha or india rubber—were interchangeable.)

The thickness of the iron plating was reported as $2\frac{1}{2}$ inches and the thickness of the rubber as 2 inches. Admiral (D. D.) Porter wrote that the vessel was a "mass of iron" and was "ironed in places where a shot would not likely hit once in a century."[40] This may have been in reference to the "arched decks" for which there was a special bending frame made, costing $10,000. It appears that the armor in this case included the tops of the casemate between the paddle housings.[41]

The gun battery originally planned for the *Lafayette* was two 11-inch guns forward, two 9-inch guns broadside, and two 100-pounder rifles aft. Up to February 1863, she had an additional two 9-inchers, removed by order of D. D. Porter.[42] The removal was no doubt prompted by the fact that she had no clearance for her wheels, because of her excessive "mass of iron."[43]

She was commissioned in the navy 27 February 1863. Though classified by the army as an ironclad ram because of the substantial projection on her stem, she was exceedingly slow. Her overweight condition was attributed to the "impracticable" plans made by W. D. Porter and included, in addition to her armor, such things as an extra wheel house (weighing "some tons") and an "enormous" bell.[44] She attained a maximum of 4 knots.[45]

Her dimensions require some explanation. Annotations on Porter's plans indicate a length of 300 feet, but actual measurement yields 292 feet, including ram. Her width is generally given as 45 feet. This, however, is also the figure given in *Way's Packet Directory,* which is based on the hull alone, without paddle housings (or deck overhang). Measurement of the vessel's plans yields 45 feet measured at the hull and casemate, with the paddle

housings adding some 10 feet on each side, totaling 66 feet.[46] Photos of the vessel confirm the fact that her wheel housings extended substantially from her sides.

She was not impervious to shot. Passing the Vicksburg batteries at close range, at one point nearly running into the bank under the guns, her side casemates were penetrated by 100-pounder shot, and 32-pounder projectiles broke plating.[47] Later at Grand Gulf, shots penetrated the paddle-housing casemating and the iron plating, lodging in the wood backing.[48] It seems that her very size was an asset in combat: she could attract a lot of projectiles but there were few truly critical areas where a few incoming shot could disable her. In a casemate over 200 feet long, the only vital areas were at the boilers and cylinders, and all of the former and most of the latter were below the deck. Her paddle wheels were so enormous that individual shots simply broke a few of the radial arms. Had her rudder been disabled, she could be steered by the independent engines and paddles.

Her career began with the passage of the Vicksburg batteries in 1863, then included the attack at Grand Gulf and the Red River expedition. She was decommissioned 23 July 1865 and sold in March 1866.

The *Choctaw*'s design and construction closely followed the pattern of the *Lafayette*. She had been another side-wheel steamer, built at New Albany, Indiana, in 1855, and running the New Orleans–Saint Louis route before purchase by the War Department Quartermaster Corps in late 1862.

William D. Porter's design differed significantly from that of the *Lafayette*. Rather than a full-length gun battery casemate, there was a stationary "turret" (Porter's terminology) forward, containing two guns, with ports forward and on the sides. Engines and boilers were between turret and paddle housings, and quarters for officers and crew were between the housings. There was no casemate abaft

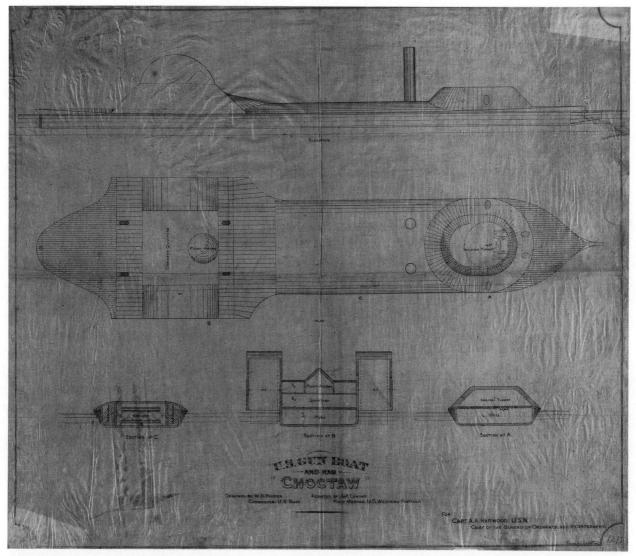

Original plan for the ironclad ram Choctaw, *the only ironclad designed to carry two 12-inch mortars. Built with similar construction methods as the* Lafayette, *this vessel was distinguished by having two distinct casemates, one forward and one aft, between the paddle housings. The* Lafayette *was originally planned to carry guns on two decks. (Tracing by author of NARS Plan RG 74, Red Series, 1213, National Archives)*

the paddle wheels, but there were two decks between the wheels, the lower for quarters and guns, and the upper for the pilothouse and—originally—additional guns.[49] The most unusual feature of the armament was apparently never used: "heavy platforms amidships for two twelve-inch mortars."[50]

Photos and documents indicate many changes from the original plan. D. D. Porter feared she would have the same overloading problem as the *Lafayette* and ordered S. L. Phelps, superintending her completion, to remove as much iron as possible from her ("except her casemates"). Phelps suggested adding sponsons to her sides to bring her up and removing the "fancy arched deck." There are no plans to show exactly what changes were

incorporated. From photographs, it appears that the second floor was removed and a small deckhouse built in its place. The pilothouse was moved forward of the wheel housings. Porter complained that her guards were underwater and hoped that Phelps could remedy this.[51] Photos indicate he did not.

As with the *Lafayette*, gutta-percha, or india rubber, was used beneath the iron. The thickness of the iron has been reported as 1 inch. Her wood backing appears to have been about that of the *Lafayette:* over 30 inches in the casemate.[52]

The engines of the *Choctaw* were 23 inches by 8 feet, with five boilers. The original vessel measured 38 feet across the hull (without paddle housings). Some 3 feet of wood was added to the sides of

The unmistakable profile of the Choctaw, *off Vicksburg. The only known victim of the ship's
ram was a navy tug that was caught by the current and impaled, then sank immediately.
(Naval Historical Center)*

her hull for protection or increased displacement,
making her 45 feet wide without her guards. Total
breadth with paddle housings was 69 feet. She was
270 feet long with her ram.[53]

Her battery varied during the course of the war.
Early on she had three 9-inch Dahlgrens, two 30-
and two 24-pounders. Later, a 100-pounder rifle
was added. At one point two of the 9-inchers were
removed, then replaced.[54] There is no evidence that
the two 12-inch mortars were mounted.

The new *Choctaw* was slow but dangerous, making
2 knots upstream. Her ram proved lethal, but for
the wrong victim. Before she went into combat,
the current caught the little tug *Lily*, 50 tons, and
impaled her on the *Choctaw*'s ram (*Choctaw* was anchored at the time), sinking the tug instantly.[55]

Her armor and backing were on a par with the
Lafayette's. At Droomgould's Bluff, in May 1863,
she took forty-six hits, some from 10-inch projectiles. Both iron and wood were penetrated, but total
casualties amounted to two men bruised. Her tow-
ering funnels caught eleven projectiles.[56]

The *Choctaw* participated in the action against
Hayne's (Droomgould's) Bluff, operations against

Yazoo City, and the Red River expedition. She was
decommissioned 22 July 1865 and sold in 1866.

The *Eastport* falls into a unique category: a commercial riverboat in the process of conversion by the
Confederates when captured by Union forces in
February 1862. She had been built at New Albany,
Indiana, in 1852 with two engines (26 inches by 9
feet) and five boilers. She was 280 feet by 43 feet
(hull measurement without guards).

The initial reports at time of capture indicated
her machinery was complete and of "first quality"
materials. She had oak hull planking and bulkheads
and her casemate timbers were complete. Her hull
was "beautifully modelled" and in excellent condition. S. L. Phelps and A. H. Foote recommended
she be completed, and she was taken to Mound City
for that purpose.[57] It was estimated that $56,000
was needed to convert her into a ram.[58] No original
plans have been found for the completed vessel.

In appearance the vessel was similar to the *Lafayette*, with long casemates extending aft beyond the
prominent paddle housings. No original plans have
been found of the vessel, therefore little is known

The Eastport. *High hopes were held for this captured vessel, but she was found too lightly built to carry her original battery. Her career was cut short when she grounded in the Red River expedition in 1864. (Arkansas History Commission)*

about her armor plating or internal arrangements. When turned over to the navy she was armed with six 9-inch guns and two 100-pounder rifles, a weight that, with her armor, strained her bottom, causing D. D. Porter to direct that she be lightened and reduced to four 9-inchers to prevent her bending "double" again.[59]

After lightening, she was considered "much improved in every way." She carried four 9-inch smoothbores, two 100- and two 50-pounder rifles for the balance of her career. She participated in the Red River expedition, including the capture of Fort DeRussy, then struck a mine on 15 April 1864, below Grand Ecore, Louisiana. S. L. Phelps ran her aground and worked for six days to get her under way and contain the leak. Once moving, she grounded eight times in the falling river. Finally, she could not be gotten off and Phelps was ordered to destroy her to prevent her falling into Confederate hands. On 26 April she was abandoned and blown up.

Avenger and *Vindicator*

Given the tendency of river combat to close quarters and the generally weak construction of most converted riverboats, plus "practical demonstrations" such as the battle of Memphis and the loss of the *Indianola,* it is not surprising that the "ram principle" was not abandoned as the war drew on. In October 1863, D. D. Porter wrote: "What we need now is fast rams, there is nothing like ramming."[60]

In 1863, the army began two purpose-built rams, *Vindicator* and *Avenger,* at the firm of Hill and Payneau, New Albany, Indiana, for the ram fleet under General Ellet. These were turned over in November to the navy, with Porter commenting: "I think the Navy can attend to the ram business. . . . I can have them made good vessels that will ram anything that comes this way, whether French or English or Rebel."[61]

S. L. Breese visited the construction site of the vessels and described some of their salient features. These included boilers and engines in the hold, with the boilers in pairs, capable of independent operation. As with the earlier rams, a huge fore-and-aft bulkhead divided the hold in two and ran its length. The hull form reflected the ideas of a Mr. Germaine, with extremely pointed bow and a hexagonal cross section, having its side points at the waterline. Germaine declared he could build a vessel to attain 50 mph, a claim that caused Breese much skepticism but did not deter him from recommending the vessels to Porter, and did not interfere with the continuation of the Ram Brigade.[62]

The *Avenger,* which was commissioned 29 February 1864, was described as a "great success" by Porter. She could make, Porter claimed, 12 mph upstream, 21 mph downstream, or "about 18 miles per hour."[63] The *Official Records* state a more leisurely maximum of 12 mph. She was 180 feet long and

The ram Vindicator, *built under the auspices of the army and later taken over by the navy. Vessels of this class were not armored and only lightly armed, and they achieved astonishing speeds. Note the narrow ram bow. (Naval Historical Center)*

41.5 feet wide, with two cylinders, each 28 inches by 90 inches. Her battery was generally a single 100-pounder rifle and upwards of four 24-pounders.[64]

The *Vindicator* Porter expected to be even faster. She was 210 feet in length and 41.5 feet wide, with cylinders measuring 28 inches by 7 feet. Her main armament was also a single 100-pounder rifle, with scattered 24-pounders. The *Official Records* credits her with 12 mph upstream.[65] On her trial trip in September 1864, she ran twenty-three miles upstream against a $3^1/_2$ mph current in one hour forty minutes—about $13^1/_2$ mph. Downstream she made the run in one hour eleven minutes, achieving an astounding 20 mph.[66]

She participated in the Yazoo River campaign and in the hair-raising chase of the CSS *William H. Webb* on 24 April 1865, as that vessel attempted to escape to the sea.

Avenger and *Vindicator* were sold in November 1865, despite S. P. Lee's suggestion that they would be useful as defenders for the Gulf ports.[67]

Also labeled the Vindicator, *this may be the* Avenger. *Notice the much shorter ram bow and some variations on paddle-wheel housings. (Naval Historical Center)*

CHAPTER 9

—◆•••—

Turret River Ironclads

The remainder of the vessels built for Civil War river service dispensed with the casemate in favor of the turret system. Nine were authorized by the end of April 1862, placing them chronologically with the *Passaic*-class monitors. Though in most cases using Ericsson turrets, their general design did not originate with that inventor. In 1863, twenty-three of the light-draft monitors were begun, to an original design by John Ericsson. These will be addressed in context with the other late war vessels in chapter 10.

The 9 April report that authorized the *Chillicothe* and others called for five additional vessels. Two, *Marietta* and *Sandusky,* built by Tomlinson and Hartupee of Pittsburgh, were to be iron and were originally to have had casemates. Very early in the contract process this was changed to require a single turret.[1] *Ozark,* built by George Bestor of Peoria, Illinois, at Mound City, was a one-off single-turret, wooden screw-propelled vessel, often attributed to James B. Eads. Eads was responsible for the *Osage* and *Neosho,* the navy's only turreted paddle-wheel vessels.

Osage and *Neosho*

These two vessels, along with the *Chillicothe,* were the smallest and lightest-draft ironclads of the war. The particular combination of turret and paddle wheels was unusual, necessitated by the shallow upper reaches of many southern rivers. The use of the recessed wheel placed that obstacle to the turret's arc of fire as far aft as possible.

The earliest plans of the vessel show some features dropped from the final boats. The turret is shown with slanting sides and with the guns on a platform to be lowered into the hold for loading. This was peculiar to Eads's turret design but was replaced on these vessels by Ericsson's more conventional turret. Rather than using normal exposed

funnels, Eads planned to run the pipes aft through the hull, thence upward and out on either side of the paddle wheel.[2]

The vessels were 160 feet in length and 45 feet wide, with armored deck and paddle housing. The deck was given a substantial crown, sufficient to allow standing height in the boiler room and quarters, most of which were along the centerline of the vessel.[3] In lieu of keelsons, these hulls were given fore and aft bulkheads to avert hogging.[4] To maintain the shallow draft, they were lightly armored. The Ericsson turret's wall was 6 inches thick (less than any of the coastal monitors), and they were designed to have 1½ inches of plating over 2 inches of pine on the convex deck. It is assumed that these dimensions applied also to the paddle housings.[5]

The single paddle wheel, recessed in the stern, was about 18 feet in diameter, driven by twin cylinders 22 inches in diameter with a stroke of 6 feet. Four high-pressure boilers were provided, each 40 inches in diameter and 16 feet long. An auxiliary engine supplied water to the boilers, pumped the bilges (and so on), and a second operated blowers for ventilation and draft for the boilers.[6]

The original specifications give directions for finishing this machinery, complete with paint colors. Such detail is rarely found. The cylinders and valve chests were to be cased in black walnut (lagging to reduce condensation), and steam pipes were to be felted, covered in canvas, and painted chrome green. The initial coat for machinery was brown zinc; then chrome green was applied after installation. Line shafting was to be done in white lead and oil, and boiler fronts, lampblack.[7] Much emphasis was placed in the quality of finish, particularly of the numerous brass fittings, oilers, flanges, and other design details that abounded on these engines, so the conscientious engineer always had much to keep sparkling in his engine room. It is surprising to the

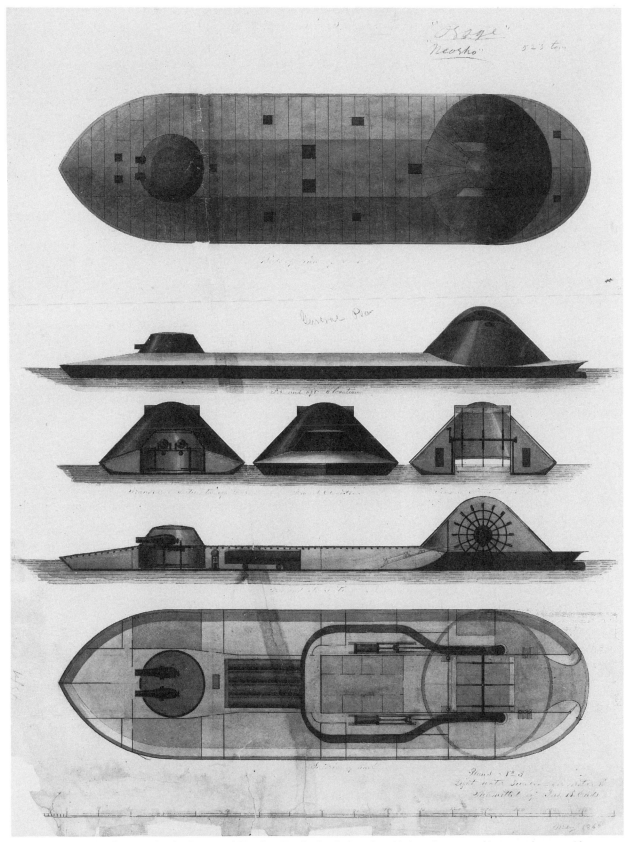

James B. Eads's original concept for the Osage and Neosho. Hand-colored plans show his intentions to use his patented turret with an elevator platform for guns. Funnels were to be replaced by pipes running the exhaust back and out through the top of the paddle-wheel housing. (NARS Plan 28-6-4G, National Archives)

The Osage, *showing changes from the original: the use of a conventional funnel and a cylindrical Ericsson turret. As was usual on the river vessels, a cabin was built on the wide armored deck, plus an elevated pilothouse. These were among the lightest-armored and lightest-draft government-built ironclads. (Naval Historical Center)*

modern reader the amount of attention details of finish were given in this era—even in wartime when such things usually bow to expediency.

Neosho was commissioned 13 May and *Osage,* 10 July 1863, and modifications were soon made to the vessels. They initially drew less water than the contract required, allowing another 1/2 inch of plating to be added to their decks. Extra armor was added to the pilothouses, an iron bulkhead was added forward of their boilers, and a "bulwark"—breakwater—was added on the bows.[8] On the *Osage,* the iron deck over the aft part of the wheel recess was removed, and a section of the lower aft part of the wheelhouse was eliminated, both in order to improve her speed.[9]

As can be seen by comparing photographs with the early plans, other modifications were made. A deck house was built forward of the funnel, as well as another under a hurricane deck forward of the paddle housing. A pilothouse was superimposed atop the after house.

Neosho and *Osage* proved useful vessels, and fairly speedy, credited with 12 mph. Their stern wheel arrangement resulted in some control problems in strong currents, in one instance resulting in a serious collision with a tree overhanging the riverbank.[10] Their light armor made them less desirable for actions against heavy batteries, but their light draft enabled them to go further up rivers in support roles than most other armored vessels.[11]

The operation of *Neosho*'s turret drew this description:

[The turret] worked admirably: revolves in thirteen seconds and can be made to revolve so slowly that you can scarcely perceive the motion; can be trained upon an object anywhere within 24 points, found no difficulty in stopping her on any object . . . and even when revolving fast I could stop her so that the slightest turn either way would bring the guns to bear where I wished.[12]

Both vessels participated in the Red River campaign, with the *Osage* involved in one of the more unusual engagements of the war: Near Blair's Landing, Louisiana, she was attacked by two brigades of Confederate cavalry with fieldpieces. With assistance from the *Lexington,* the *Osage* fought off an estimated 2,500 rebels and drove them back in "great confusion." Seven were wounded on the ironclad. There was some indication that an infusion of "Louisiana Rum" may have come into play in precipitating this strange episode on the part of the Confederate forces.

The *Neosho* participated in the Red River expedition and operations on the Cumberland River. She was decommissioned 23 July 1865 and sold in 1873. While laid up at Mound City, she received two name changes, *Vixen* and *Osceola,* in 1869.

The *Osage* fought on the Black and Ouachita rivers, then was part of the abortive Red River campaign. In June 1864, she went hard aground on a knoll amidships. Her ends dropped, splitting her fore and aft bulkheads some 4 inches at the top and her hull plates to the turn of the bilge. Three months later, she was straight again, waiting for the waters to rise and for workers to repair the damage. Despite her problems, her commanding officer considered her safe. Back in service, she struck a mine on the Blakely River in Alabama in March 1865, ending her career. She was raised and sold in 1867.

Ozark

The contract for the *Ozark* called for a draft of 4 feet 9 inches and two 11-inch guns. She was to have a complement of 120 men and stow provisions for twenty days and one hundred tons of coal. She was to steam 9 mph at 140 pounds pressure and make a satisfactory 72-hour trial.[13]

Speed notations are actually rarely encountered in these vessels' deck logs, unless it is specifically a speed trial. The standard log entry was pounds steam pressure and revolutions per minute. These two figures would even then be insufficient to calculate vessel speed, because the speed of the current (always a very significant factor on these rivers) was rarely given. Indeed, speed was much less important on the rivers, particularly in view of the primary function of these vessels: support of army operations. Therefore, except in the rare instance where a force rode the rails (or in cavalry operations), a vessel would need only to match the speed of the march to accomplish the goal.

The hull of the *Ozark* was subcontracted to the firm of Hambleton and Collier of Mound City, Illinois. Machinery was by Charles McCord of Saint Louis. The dimensions of the vessel were 180 feet by 50 feet, with 7 feet 4 inches depth of hold. Her sides angled out from the bilges and she had a pointed bow. At the stern, a run of some 25 feet was introduced to allow "free flow of water" to the propellers.[14]

Her hull structure was centered around a keel piece and four keelsons. The centerline timber was

4 inches by 14 inches and the others, 4 inches by 12 inches. Bilge strakes were 4 1/2 inches by 14 inches. There were three fore and aft and three athwartship watertight bulkheads, all spiked to stanchions and up to 2 inches thick. The floor and side timbers were 8 inches by 7 inches on 20-inch centers. Both bolts and spikes were used, and 3-foot scarfs between side and bottom timbers. Gun deck beams were 8 inches by 8 inches, and 12 inches by 12 inches under the turret. Support for the turret was to be "arched frames" or additional bulkheads.[15] No "as built" plans exist, therefore it is not known which alternative was used.

The armor plating on her deck was 1 inch in thickness. On the sides at the bow (the first 40 feet), two layers of 1 1/4-inch iron were used, extending 1 foot below the waterline. Aft of the 40-foot line, the two layers were 1 1/8 inch each. Armor on the Ericsson turret totaled 6 inches of plating. On deck were light pine officers' cabins, a low bulwark, and a hurricane deck.[16]

The *Ozark*, *Marietta*, *Sandusky*, and *Milwaukee* class boasted quadruple screw propellers. If they had not been specialized river craft, this might have been considered quite a technological advance. In actuality, these were fairly primitive installations.

The engines of the *Ozark*, *Marietta*, and *Sandusky* were identical. Each pair of cylinders operated twin propellers by way of mitered mortise gears and a single athwartship shaft for each pair of cylinders. Each propeller shaft was 6 inches in diameter and was fitted with a mortise wheel approximately 4 feet in diameter. Wheel teeth were of wood. The cylinders were 15 inches in diameter with a 24-inch stroke. The props were 7 feet, four-bladed, and cast iron, running in lignum vitae bearings. Each pair of props was independent of the other set. Four boilers some 26 feet long were used, and three rud-

The screw-propelled ironclad Ozark *early in her career. The innovative four-propeller boat was to carry two 11-inch guns in the turret. Note the light bulwark around the stern and water closets. (Naval Historical Center)*

The Ozark, *a later photograph, showing additional guns on deck: 9-inchers aft, on each side of the cabin and forward nearly to the stem. Note that the stern bulwark has been removed. Additionally, the vessel was to carry an experimental "submarine gun" of questionable efficacy. (Naval Historical Center)*

ders, one on the centerline and the others outboard of each pair of propellers.[17]

The *Ozark* was selected to be the test bed for a "submarine battery" invented by First Assistant Engineer James W. Whittaker. Though a detailed description of this battery has not been found, correspondence indicates it was to be a standard shell gun mounted in the hold, firing a projectile through a "conductor pipe" through the side of the hull below the waterline. (By contrast, Robert Fulton's 1813 "submarine gun" was to be fired underwater, *outside* the vessel's hull.) The government was to furnish the 9-inch gun. Work on this primitive version of the torpedo was discontinued in January 1863, about a month before the *Ozark*'s launch, because of cost overruns.[18] It was unlikely, however, that the round, relatively slow 9-inch projectile would have made significant headway against the river water.

The vessel was commissioned on 18 February 1864, though not without significant alterations at the request of the navy. On a trial run in September 1863, various defects were noted, including excessive working of the hull and engine frames, an unsatisfactory reversing gear, loose beveled gear teeth, and leaking boilers. She was accepted by the navy with her bottom stiffened by keelsons between the engines, added stringers on the deck beams, increased engine fastenings, new reversing gear, and additional hatches over the engine spaces for better ventilation. She ran 6 mph, with a maximum of 9 mph, at 2.1 tons of coal per hour and 79½ rpm. Coal consumption was excessive: more than that of a river-class steam frigate.[19]

The battery of the vessel was originally two 11-

inch Dahlgrens in the turret, and she had a bulwark around the stern made up of "heavy timber" and 1-inch iron plating. By July 1864, four additional weapons had been added: three 9-inch and one 10-inch smoothbores. Photos show all four on deck and in the open (one on either side of the cabin, one forward, and another directly aft) and no bulwark in sight. This change can be tied to her draft astern on trials in October 1863, when she drew 4 feet 10 inches forward and 5 feet 8 inches aft.[20]

Admiral D. D. Porter had nothing positive to say about the *Ozark*, complaining for the most part about her structural weakness, particularly beneath the turret. He characterized her as "very unwieldy" and "unmanageable." Engineer J. W. King commented that "a fleet of such vessels would ruin the nation." When it came time for the department to pay Bestor's contract price, however, John Lenthall recommended: "Pay the man if the vessel is performing as he said." It seems also that carrying four more guns than the contract called for said something positive about her sturdiness.[21] Furthermore, "unwieldy and unmanageable" were terms associated with the majority of the barge-bottomed river ironclads.

The vessel was involved in only one major campaign, that on the Red River in 1864. Coming over the rapids in Alexandria, Louisiana, she grounded with the impatient admiral on board. Against the advice of the engineer, who considered them knocked out of line and unsafe, Porter ordered the engines started, breaking the teeth of one of the mortise wheels. Repaired, she remained in service until decommissioned on 24 July 1865. She was sold 29 November 1865.

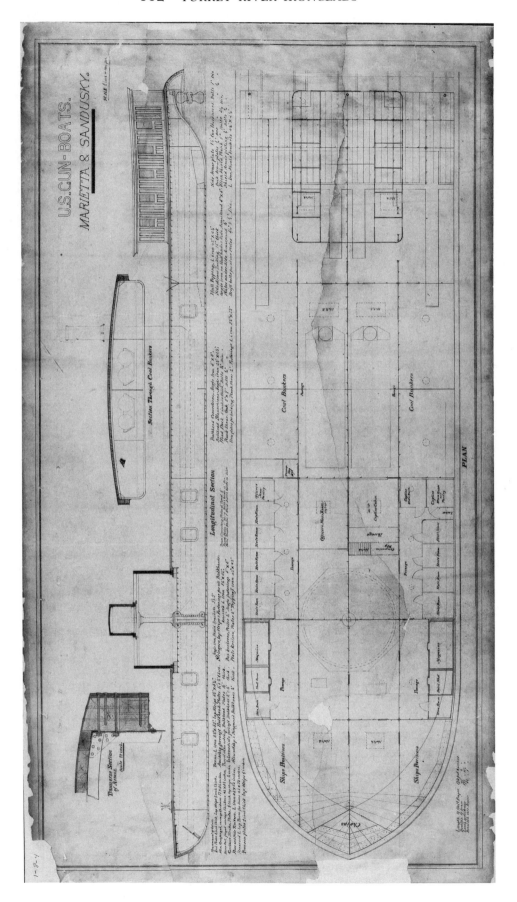

U.S.GUN-BOATS.
MARIETTA & SANDUSKY.

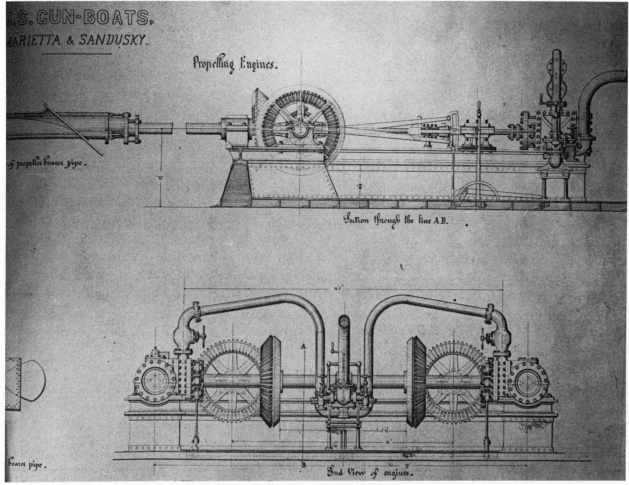

Engines of the Marietta *and* Sandusky. *Note the mitered- or beveled-geared machinery with each pair of cylinders powering two propellers. Some gear teeth were of wood, and gears were about 4 feet in diameter. (NARS Plan 1-8-7, National Archives)*

Marietta and *Sandusky*

These two vessels were not delivered to the navy until 26 May 1866: over three years after the contracted due date, and a year after the end of hostilities. Their story is a convoluted one of early contract and midconstruction alterations. Rather than an in-depth discussion of these proceedings, the original specifications and contract will be described, then compared to what is known of the completed vessel.

The contract, with Joseph Tomlinson, Andrew Hartupee, and Samuel Morrow (Hartupee and Company), dated 16 May 1862, called for each vessel to carry two 11-inch guns, a complement of one hundred men, stores for twenty days, and eighty tons of coal. The vessels were to draw 5 feet.[22]

The Marietta *and* Sandusky. *These ironclad vessels were not completed until after the war's end. Construction was delayed by many changes in plans. (NARS Plan 1-8-4, National Archives)*

Even before the contract was signed, a letter from the contractors signified trouble to come: "The calculations, estimates, and specifications for these boats were made by us in a few hours, hastily, and we fear, imperfectly . . . placing the weight and specifications of a larger boat for the price of a smaller one." What followed was a list of changes made by the department, which included cabin and furnishings, as well as increased speed and coal capacity. All this on a draft less than 4 feet 9 inches. The department apparently relented on the draft requirement, allowing 5 feet. The firm set forth a price of $193,250 for each vessel.[23]

Specifications were for a vessel 170 feet long and 50 feet wide, with a depth of hold of $6^{1}/_{2}$ feet and a revolving turret. The hull was to be of iron.[24] The firm, based in Pittsburgh, was an early builder of iron vessels, having constructed the navy's first such ship in the 1840s: the paddle sloop *Michigan.*

The hull was to be modeled for the first 30 feet, and "thence scow shape." The framing was to be T-iron, spaced 16 inches, center to center, with

5/16-inch hull plating. A 2-foot wide keel piece was to be of 1/2-inch iron, and bilge pieces were to rivet to both floor and side frames. A center fore and aft bulkhead was to be 1/4-inch iron, riveted to the deck beams and keel. One of three cross-bulkheads was to be located under the turret. Further turret support was to be in the form of "arched diagonal frames." Deck beams were to be L-iron, with diagonal bracing to the sides.[25]

The Ericsson-type turret was to be 22 feet in its outside diameter, protected by six layers of 1-inch plating. A 3-inch wood deck was to be plated with 3/4-inch iron. The bow and sides, to 1 foot below the waterline, were to have 2 1/2 inches of plating, in two equal layers. This was to be increased over the boilers. Five or six temporary cabins were to be constructed on deck.[26]

The machinery was, according to the specifications, identical to that of the *Ozark:* four cylinders, 15 by 24 inches each, with four propellers operated by mortise wheels. Each pair of boilers operated a pair of cylinders and propellers. Though the boats were greatly modified, the machinery remained relatively unchanged throughout the process.[27]

By delivery date, the vessels were substantially different. This was in part a result of the "very general" specifications provided by the contractor and the fact that the department did not oversee the construction in detail.[28]

When it came time to pay the contractors, a hearing was held to determine payment levels. These changes were taken into account, among others: the bow was modeled for 40 feet rather than 30 feet, and the bilges were rounded rather than squared. Substantial sheer had been added at bow and stern. An 18,000-pound armored shield had been added to protect the propellers, and the number of deck cabins increased from five or six to ten.[29] The pilot-house was now atop the turret. In the hull, two extra fore and aft bulkheads had been added, as well as three more cross bulkheads and one diagonal bulkhead. Side armor had been bolstered by adding a timber backing measuring 15 inches thick. The total cost for changes for both vessels was something over $74,000.[30]

The completed vessels were 173 feet 11 1/2 inches in length, by 52-foot 1-inch beam, both dimensions including armor. On trials, in still water, the *Sandusky* made 7 mph at 105 pounds pressure, "wide open." She obeyed the helm "readily," turning 180 degrees in 3 minutes 40 seconds. The vessel drew 4 feet 2 inches forward and 4 inches more at the stern, considerably less than required. The *Marietta* was slightly faster, at 7 1/2 mph.[31]

Total cost to the government was $235,039.57 each. After the initial hearing there apparently was no further dispute about payment. The contractors' explanations for the delays were the many changes involved, as well as labor strikes during the war. Both vessels were laid up at Mound City on delivery and never commissioned. *Marietta* was renamed *Circe* and *Sandusky, Minerva,* for a short time in 1869 (15 June to 10 August). They were sold on 12 April 1873.

Milwaukee Class

With these vessels, James B. Eads convinced the department to allow the use of his own patented turret. Three of the four boats received Eads's forward turrets, with the other turrets built following the standard Ericsson pattern.

The vessels originated with Welles directing Commodore Smith to recommend four more river ironclads, not to exceed 6-foot draft, to carry not two but four 11-inch guns.[32] Given the difficulty with which light draft was obtained in vessels carrying only two of the 11-inchers, this was a formidable order for any builder.

With the influence of Frank P. Blair, Jr., representative from Missouri, Eads obtained a contract to build four twin-turreted boats. Building time was to be six months, with a penalty for each week's delay on each vessel.[33]

The contracts required each vessel to attain 9 knots (not miles per hour) with a complement of 120 men, stores for twenty days, and coal bunkerage for 150 tons. These iron-hulled monitors were described as "For Western Rivers and Gulf of Mexico"—a somewhat different category than the earlier river ironclads.[34]

The four vessels were the *Milwaukee, Winnebago, Chickasaw,* and *Kickapoo.* The first two were built by Eads, the third by Thomas Gaylord in Cincinnati, and the *Kickapoo* by G. B. Allen of Saint Louis. All four were nearly identical, with the obvious exception of the *Chickasaw,* which had two Ericsson turrets.

Specifications called for vessels 220 feet long by 56 feet wide, with depth of hold measuring 8 1/2 feet. The hull plating was 3/8-inch thick, with a central keel plate 5/8 of an inch; 7- by 3/8-inch angle iron made up the floors, and the hull sides were made of 6- by 3/8-inch angle iron. Floors were on 12-inch centers; sides, 24-inch centers. Deck beams were T-iron, 4 inches by 4 inches by 3/8 inch. There were two fore and aft and six cross bulkheads, all of 3/8-inch plating. Extra bulkheads were placed under the Ericsson turrets. Aft, bulkheads were arranged to allow water to be pumped in, to depress the stern.[35]

The sides were first laid with pine planking in two layers totaling 15 inches thick, stem to stern. A 1/4-inch flange was riveted to the hull and extended out to cover the bottom of the wood planking. The iron armor was three layers of 1-inch plates. These were 3 1/2 feet wide except at the bows, where the

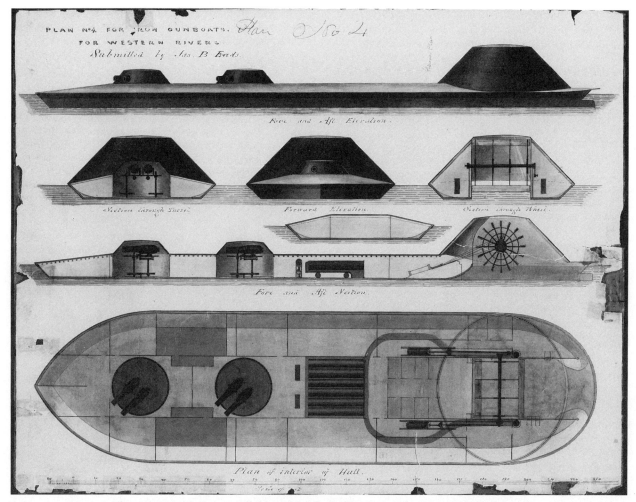

Eads's proposal for a double-turret river ironclad, propelled by paddle wheels. This may have been the genesis for the later Milwaukee-*class vessels and shows the same hull cross section. Dimensions of the completed vessels were somewhat less. (NARS Plan 28-6-4L, National Archives)*

width was increased in accordance with the sheer. The deck, with its substantial crown, was to receive 3/4-inch plating. This was increased by another 3/4-inch layer on the *Milwaukee* and *Winnebago*.[36] The pilothouse was of 3-inch-thick iron. The Ericsson turrets were to have 8 inches of plating.[37]

The machinery was another four-propeller installation, complete with pairs of cylinders on transverse main shafts, with bevelled gears, along the lines of the machinery in the *Ozark, Marietta,* and *Sandusky.* In this case, the cylinders were 26 inches in diameter, with a stroke of 24 inches, operating 6 1/2-foot mortise gears with hickory teeth. The propeller-shaft gear teeth were iron, and the wheel diameter was 4 feet 8 inches. The propellers were 7 1/2 feet in diameter, with each pair of propellers independent of the other set. There were seven

boilers in three sets: the center group was to have three; the others, two each. Each set of boilers was independent of the others. Auxiliary engines were provided for pumps and blowers.[38]

The Eads turret itself was a marvel of the times and far more complex than Ericsson's. First, rather than rotating on a central axis or pivot point, the Eads turret introduced a Coles-like ball-bearing system on the perimeter of the rotating cylinder. This allowed wider weight distribution than the Ericsson method. Second, the turret cylinder extended downward to the bottom of the vessel, with the entire structure revolving. Third, the weapons were mounted on a elevatorlike platform, which allowed the guns to be lowered into the hold for loading. A second advantage of the movable platform was its use in elevating the guns for firing, making greater angles (20 degrees elevation as opposed to about 10 for the monitors) possible without increasing the size of the gun port.[39]

The power of steam was harnessed for nearly every phase of the turret's operation. The elevator was a steam cylinder, which itself was mounted on ball bearings, or "spheres," to rotate with the outer shell. The guns were run out by steam cylinders, which were then refilled with sufficient steam to absorb recoil and limit gun travel. The gun port covers were operated by a combination of steam cylinders and counterweights, all arranged to open automatically as the guns were run out, and close as the recoil brought the muzzle into the turret. A total of six men formed the turret crew: one engi-

neer, two gun captains, and three loaders.[40] All in all, for 1864, this was a technological *tour de force*.

The exposed portion of the turret was armored with eight layers of 1-inch iron. Eads's method of bolting the laminations was also unique. The inner two layers were riveted together, and the outer layers were attached by tapered screw-bolts that were tapped directly into the inner layers' iron, eliminating the need for interior bolt heads, which tended to shear off when struck from the outside. Below deck, the turret wall was 1-inch iron, with apertures through which the guns were loaded.[41]

The first of the class commissioned was the *Winnebago*, on 27 April 1864, followed on 14 May by the *Chickasaw*, on 8 July by the *Kickapoo*, and 27

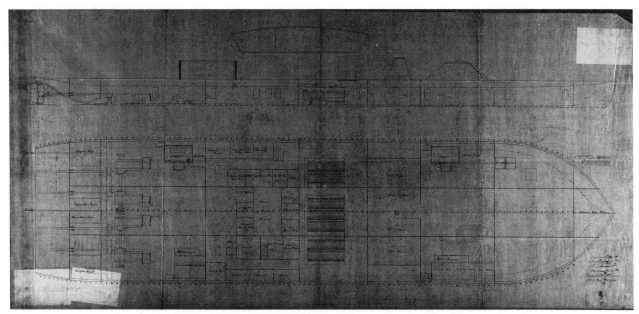

General plan of the Milwaukee class. James Buchanan Eads's most innovative design included quadruple screws and Eads's turret. As with most of the river ironclads, the deck showed considerable camber, necessary to allow sufficient room below deck and retain light draft. No detailed as-built plans have been found. (NARS Plan Alphabetical File: Kickapoo, National Archives)

One of best images of the Milwaukee-class ships, showing a relatively uncluttered upper deck and slightly different fore-and-aft turrets: Ericsson type aft and Eads type forward. (Library, U.S. Military Academy, Orlando Poe Collection)

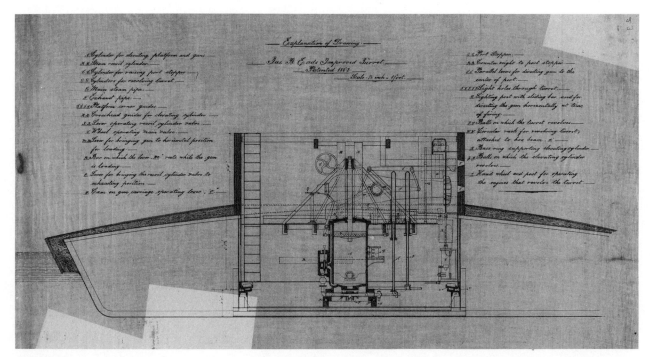

Requiring three men to operate it, the Eads turret used steam for rotation, raising and lowering guns for loading, running guns out, and absorbing recoil. Both the platform and turret rotated and loading was performed below deck. It was used only on Milwaukee-*class vessels. (NARS Plan 80-8-23, National Archives)*

August by the *Milwaukee.* The total cost for the government was approximately $390,000 each.

The performance of the Eads turret was first noted on the *Winnebago* in early March. Stimers reported he and one other crewman operated the turret, with good results both of the rotation and recoil mechanism. Eads wrote that the guns (presumably on the same vessel) were fired at a target $^{3}/_{4}$ mile away, sighting between the guns "like a double barrel shot gun." Both were fired at once, one scoring a bull's-eye, the other nine feet to the side.[42]

The vessels' steaming performance also brought satisfactory reports. An early trial of the *Winnebago* yielded 9 mph, and the *Kickapoo* showed "remarkable speed for a shoal water ironclad" (according to Eads, who also claimed she did 12 mph). The *Chickasaw* exceeded her contract speed in her seventy-two-hour trial run.[43]

Though D. D. Porter claimed that the vessels would "break to pieces in the least swell," two (*Winnebago* and *Chickasaw*) were sent from the Mississippi to Farragut at Mobile, in preparation for the operation against that place. The *Chickasaw* experienced difficulty with her steering gear and apparently came down under tow. The *Winnebago,* dispensing with the tow, "performed very well," according to Farragut, despite some rough seas.[44] Her commanding officer disagreed, considering her strength sufficient for rivers "but not for sea."[45]

Later, H. K. Thatcher wrote Welles that none of the Eads turreted monitors would make passage to Chesapeake Bay, because their frames were weak.[46]

After the Battle of Mobile Bay, her commanding officer offered further complaints on the *Winnebago.* She took nineteen hits, three of which though fired nearly horizontally did significant damage to the deck, convincing him that she would not withstand plunging fire. He disliked the stern overhang and propellers, claiming she would be faster with some modifications to these. He gave the Eads turret good marks for the recoil and hoisting mechanisms but considered the rotating engines too light for the purpose: the turret had not been in good working order since he took command in June, with a tendency to jam while rotating. In the battle, however, the Ericsson turret broke down after passing Fort Morgan. On a minor note, the Eads turret had loopholes, something the Ericsson turret did not.[47]

The *Chickasaw,* following the *Winnebago* at Mobile Bay, took several hits, nearly severing her funnel and one penetrating the deck on the starboard bow. No casualties were reported.[48]

The service careers of the four *Milwaukee*-class ironclads were brief. At Mobile Bay, the *Chickasaw* was instrumental in bringing ram *Tennessee* to bay, harrying her from astern and cutting her rudder chains with 11-inch projectiles at point-blank range. Subsequently she bombarded Fort Morgan. She was decommissioned in July 1865, renamed *Samson* in 1869, reverted to *Chickasaw*, then was sold in September 1874. In 1881 she was converted to side wheels and made into a railroad ferry named *Gouldsboro*. She was finally scrapped in 1944.

Winnebago, after operations in Mobile Bay, was part of the West Gulf Blockading Squadron. Decommissioned in September 1865, she was sold in 1874. In 1869, she was temporarily renamed *Tornado*. *Kickapoo* was part of the West Gulf Squadron and saw no significant action. Decommissioned in July 1865, she was also sold in 1874. She was renamed *Cyclops*, then *Kewaydin*, in 1869.

The *Milwaukee* saw service on the gulf and associated rivers, hitting a torpedo on 28 March 1865 in the Blakely River. The torpedo holed the vessel's stern, which sank quickly, leaving the forward part of the vessel afloat for another hour. There were no casualties. She was raised in 1868 and it is said that part of her iron was used in the Eads bridge at Saint Louis.

Though Eads and Assistant Secretary Fox proposed oceangoing vessels using the Eads turret, nothing came of these ideas.[49] No similar turrets were ever used on American naval vessels.

The USS Milwaukee, *veteran of Mobile Bay, with awnings and torpedo rake rigged out. (Naval Historical Center)*

CHAPTER 10

The Final
Civil War Ironclads,
1864–1867

These twenty-five vessels are a mixed bag: "ocean going" twin-turret monitors, light-draft monitors, and the broadside ironclad *Dunderberg*. They represent extremes of various sorts. The *Dunderberg,* if she had been commissioned, would have been the navy's largest broadside ironclad, and the vessel was the largest wooden steamer built in this country. The *Kalamazoo*-class twin-turret monitors were to have been the largest navy-designed monitors. The twenty *Casco*-class light-draft monitors were a less positive milestone: the failure of an entire class of warships. Only four of the vessels presented here were commissioned before the Confederate capitulation in April of 1865.

The Light-Draft Monitors

In August 1862, Assistant Secretary Fox suggested to Ericsson that monitors of 6-foot draft would be useful for river work. With no mention of remuneration, Ericsson submitted a general plan for such vessels in October, essentially donating the work to the navy for their use.[1]

Ericsson's original plan is long lost, which is unfortunate, because his written specifications present a rather curious description, using terminology that leaves some questions unanswered. The iron hull was to consist of an "oval cistern" with dead flat bottom and perpendicular sides. This hull was to be "encased" in a "raft of solid timber the external part of which was shaped to resemble an ordinary vessel with easy lines. The raft or wooden casing which formed the bow extended 20 feet beyond the forward part of the iron hull." The stern projection was 32 feet. Deck beams were 15-inch oak, forming an unbroken roof over the iron hull. Deck plating was to run longitudinally in two layers, each $1/2$ inch thick. The sides and bottom were to be strengthened by angle iron 18 inches apart.[2]

The propellers were decidedly unusual: twin 9-foot props, with the port prop 2 feet *aft* of the other and the shafts as close as the blades of the opposite prop would allow. To compensate for the wake generated by the starboard prop, the port blades would have 15 degrees more pitch. Two direct-acting, high-pressure engines (30-inch by 30-inch cylinders) were used, each operating one propeller shaft. Spur gears were then used to couple the shafts. These factors made these vessels distinctly different from the other monitor classes, except for the turret and its machinery—which were to be "precisely" like that of the *Passaic* class.[3]

At this juncture, the inspector of ironclads, Alban C. Stimers, entered the picture, and eventually, so did a host of alterations, materially changing the ships and resulting in their uselessness to the navy. Before delving into these, it may be well to elaborate on other factors not directly related to the design of these vessels that colored these proceedings.

The controversy over the vessels came about as a result of their failure, with blame thrown about thick and fast. As it happened, the navy was at the time drifting into other disputes based on more fundamental considerations. The rise of the steam engineers as a group was throwing promotion and seniority systems into disarray, with line officers not easily sharing their ancient prerogatives with "mere mechanics" who wished officerlike status commensurate with their duties (and often education). A second argument of the times concerned the role and efficiency of ironclads, and in particular, monitors. As has been seen, the broadside ironclad people, who were in a distinct minority, felt the low-freeboard monitors were not suited for the cruising, oceangoing navy—and they were right.

Third, there was the subject of Benjamin F. Isherwood, chief of the Bureau of Construction and

Repair. A clique of highly placed individuals, including David Dixon Porter and a number of steam engineers, disagreed entirely with Isherwood's basic steam engineering premises, feeling that he overloaded his designs with boiler power far beyond the capacity of the engines to work off the steam developed. The end result, they said, was relatively slow, overweight vessels. Furthermore, they accused Isherwood of "empire building" within the Bureau of Steam Engineering.

This background is given against which to judge the light-draft controversy. The positions of some of the players can be highlighted as follows. John Ericsson felt put upon by the Bureau of Steam Engineering, especially by Isherwood, claiming that he and Lenthall had dragged their feet and attempted to obstruct the Ericsson monitor program in favor of their own designs—both for vessels and machinery. D. D. Porter, always a vocal and influential opponent, came into the picture also arrayed against Isherwood—ostensibly because of the engineering controversy but more likely as a result of the line-staff question (particularly when Isherwood began angling for rear admiral). The *Army and Navy Journal,* which began publication in midwar, became virtually a house organ for Porter, against Isherwood. Ericsson had little to fear from the journal: its editor was William Conant Church, who happened to be Ericsson's brother-in-law. Within the engineer ranks, Isaac Newton, Stimers, and others were pro-Ericsson, promonitor, and anti-Isherwood. Another factor that may have polarized feelings was Stimers's action after the first attack against Charleston in April 1863. He held, in public print, that the monitors were quite capable of renewing the fight on the following day—directly contradicting Admiral DuPont, bringing upon himself a court martial at the hands of DuPont. Here again, monitor and antimonitor forces clashed.

In any case, it appears that there was more at stake in the light-draft monitor imbroglio than a simple engineering miscalculation. There were forces at work of much more import.

Alban C. Stimers was given the task of filling in the details in Ericsson's generalized plans. Given an office next to Ericsson's, it was expected that he would consult regularly with that gentleman. Further, he was directed by Fox to seek the advice of Lenthall and Isherwood. Stimers was to mediate any disagreements between the departments and Ericsson on features of the vessels.[4] The issue of how much control the bureau heads had over Stimers is another one of debate. Stimers was essentially independent, and that is reflected in the correspondence of the bureaus: there is very little communication found between Stimers and either Isherwood or Lenthall. There was certainly no ongoing dialogue over the light-draft vessels.

Isherwood later claimed he did not know even the number of light-draft vessels being constructed.[5]

Stimers visited Isherwood, who, according to Stimers, suggested the following substantial changes: enlarging the boilers, reducing cylinder size, separating the propellers and eliminating the overlapping blades, making the engines totally independent, and adopting a variety of the beveled geared arrangement used on western river ironclads. In the end, all of the above were done, with the exception of the beveled geared engines.[6]

In studying the testimony of the various participants, there are obvious contradictions. Isherwood said that Stimers brought the Ericsson plans with him, and the interview was short and informal. Stimers claimed that Isherwood had had the plans beforehand and had been more specific in his criticisms, including insisting on an 18-inch cylinder diameter rather than 30 inches. Isherwood made no mention of cylinder size in later testimony. On the boiler question, Ericsson later objected to the new boilers but assumed or was told that they had been designed by Isherwood. In fact, they were designed and patented by Stimers.[7]

At any rate, the final cylinders were 22 inches in diameter, 30-inch stroke. There were no beveled gears; rather, two athwartship direct-acting cylinders were used, angled slightly upward toward the center of the vessel. Each cylinder, as well as its propeller, was independent, though a single condenser was placed aft of the engines. The two propellers were 9 feet in diameter, separated in the normal fashion. (Any overlap would have militated against steering by independent propellers.) The two boilers were each 25 feet long and 10 feet wide, with firerooms arranged between them.[8]

At this point in the design process, Adm. Joseph Smith, of the Bureau of Yards and Docks, suggested the incorporation of water tanks and pumps to depress the vessel further when going into combat. This idea was quite the fashion, apparently, having been used on the *E. A. Stevens* and considered for the *Keokuk* and the *Milwaukee*-class. A further advantage was suggested: expelling the water to raise the vessel when she ran aground. (Though logic retorts that the vessel may not have run aground had she not been further submerged in the first place.) In any case, Stimers dutifully drew in a water compartment some 2 feet wide and over 6 feet deep, completely surrounding the perimeter of the iron vessel. Two steam pumps, one on each side, served

General plan of the light-draft monitors. Ericsson's original design has not been found and Alban Stimers's lithographs of his plans abound. At 225 feet in length, these were the size of the Canonicus *class—not small vessels. Cross sections show water tanks and piping between the side armor casing and the side of the iron hull. (National Archives)*

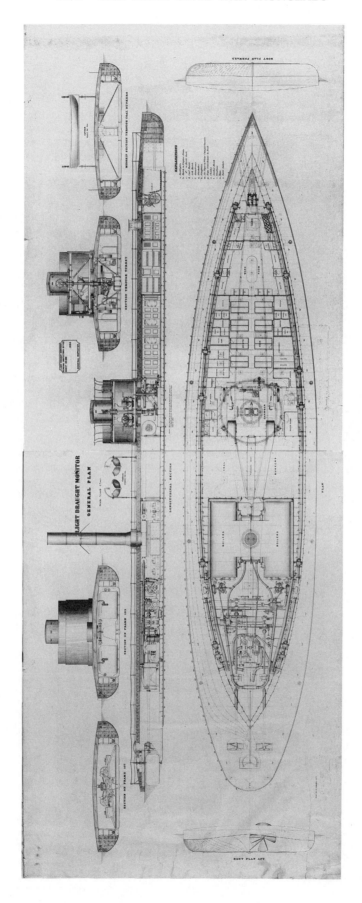

to fill and evacuate these tanks. The water compartments effectively separated the wooden side protection (over 4 feet wide on each side of the ship) from the inner iron vessel. The side casing was attached only by the deck beams and tank crosspieces.[9]

These were the major alterations made before the vessels were let out for contract in the spring of 1863. It is still not clear how extensively the bureau heads evaluated the plans as modified by Stimers. Lenthall indicated that his review of them was decidedly cursory, and Isherwood said he was not consulted at all.[10] Given the minimal role these bureaus had in the other contract monitors, this is really not surprising. The department, however, approved Stimers's plan over Ericsson's original.

Ericsson himself was outraged at the changes made to his monitors. He wrote in February 1864 that his original premises had "all been lost": These had been simplicity of construction and impregnability. The water compartments he called "useless," altering the draft by only 6 inches. The reduction in side thickness to incorporate the tanks seriously reduced the vessels' impregnability to shot. The increased breadth at the stern, a result of increasing the distance between propellers, would reduce maneuverability. The width of the boilers would make supporting the deck more difficult. Finally, the double sides resulting from the water tanks and pumping mechanism added to the complication of construction.[11] The inventor's pique was such that he avoided association with the project as much as possible.[12]

The first of the vessels to approach completion was the *Chimo*, launched 5 May 1864. Her launch draft was 5 feet 8 inches, without turret. Admiral Gregory wrote: "It will be impossible for her to float." W. L. Hanscom, naval constructor, examined her at the time of her trial run and found the top of her plating about 2³/₈ inches out of the water. Though she had turret, guns, and pilothouse, there was no ammunition and she was twenty tons short of her coal capacity. He estimated at full load she would have been 3 inches below the water, leaving only the top of her tortoiseshell deck above water. He stated at the hearings on the subject: "Rather a small margin for a man to go to sea with." She had been designed to have 15 inches freeboard, to the top of the side plating.[13] Somewhat ironically, the next question put to Hanscom concerned the water-tank system intended to "sink the vessel down." In these vessels, he said, "It was entirely unnecessary."[14]

The *Tunxis*, launched in June, was 1¹/₂ inches out of the water, with half her coal on board. Ericsson recommended "discipline" for Stimers, who seemed to look at the situation with unseemly "levity," claiming that "he had nothing to do with it."[15] Given the gravity of the situation, construction of the remaining light-draft monitors was suspended, and

engineer Stimers lost his job. A committee was formed to determine some remedy that would render the vessels useful.

Two approaches were employed. Five of the vessels—*Chimo, Casco, Modoc, Napa,* and *Naubuc*—were completed without turrets. They were then called torpedo vessels and each was armed with an 11-inch gun entirely exposed on the foredeck, as well as a spar torpedo. The water-pumping mechanism and piping were deleted as well as the armored funnel.[16] This was the inexpensive option and produced distinctly slow "torpedo" vessels with no protection for their gun crews.[17]

The remaining fifteen vessels had their upper decks raised 22 inches. This of course involved all bulkheads, braces and stanchions, and any other structural components affected by the elevation of the deck.[18] Other alterations included modifications in the stern lines to allow freer flow of water to the propellers, and stiffening plates for the frames.[19]

These vessels measured 225 feet to 225 feet 8 inches in length, by 45 to 45 feet 6 inches. Their depth was 6¹/₂ feet for the torpedo vessels and 8 feet 4 inches for the modified turret vessels. Displacement was 1,175 tons. Armor for the sides was 3 inches backed by some 4 feet of wood and the turrets were of 8 inches of plating. In consequence of the Charleston operations, the pilothouses were of 10 inches of iron, and the turrets were given 5- by 15-inch base rings. All the turreted vessels received two 11-inch guns, except *Etlah* and *Tunxis*, which had one 11-inch and one 150-pounder each. Three—*Casco, Napa,* and *Naubuc*—had one 11-inch gun in addition to the spar torpedo. On the *Chimo*, the gun was a 150-pounder. The *Modoc* received no gun whatever, only a torpedo apparatus.

Each vessel was to carry a complement of sixty-nine men. Quarters were forward of the turret. Bunks were provided for enlisted personnel, located between the ward room and turret.

The *Etlah*, completed with turret and raised deck, logged 5⁸/₁₀ mph and steered easily. In reverse, however, the rudder tended to jam athwartships until the vessel stopped. Her commanding officer was impressed with the care given her hull work and the operation of the turret. Her draft was 8 feet amidships, leaving over 12 inches freeboard at the top of the plating. The guns could be run in and out with two men and recoil was 32 inches. The *Shiloh* also approached 6 mph in still water and handled equally well, though with the same rudder defect.[20]

The final cost for these vessels, which were contracted for an average of $400,000 each, ranged from approximately $513,000 to $648,000. The latter figure was for the *Modoc*, one of the single-gun torpedo ships; the former was for the *Tunxis*, which had her turret in place when the order went out to raise her deck.[21] With such moneys spent and so

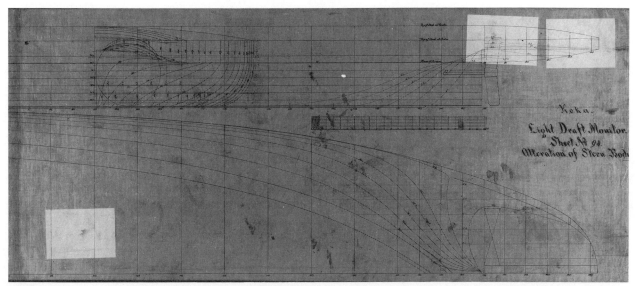

Plan for alterations in the Koka's stern body. The first light draft had 3 inches of freeboard—without ammunition or coal. One upshot was adding 18 inches to the hull, with the results shown here. (NARS Plan 1-7-6, National Archives)

The light-draft torpedo boat, former monitor, Casco, 1865. A torpedo-removal rake apparatus can be seen forward. Although others of the class rectified Stimers's design with higher decks and the retention of the turret, several had the turret removed and a single 11-inch gun mounted on the open foredeck. Still with minimal freeboard, the Casco and sister vessels had serious leakage problems. (Naval Historical Center)

little in return, it is surprising that the department was not the scene of a major personnel upheaval, with wholesale firings and the like. Stimers seems to have been the sole high-ranking casualty, and he was merely reassigned to rebuild the machinery of the old Wabash.

Hearings in 1864 illuminated the specific miscalculation that caused the failure of the light-draft vessels. According to Stimers, Theodore Allen, a young draftsman and former apprentice at Novelty Iron Works, had made the fatal mistake. Stimers, however, did not check the man's work; instead, he simply carried the figures to Lenthall. Here, the two men's testimony disagreed, with Lenthall indicating that Stimers did not mention the source of the figures and had at least implied that he himself (Stimers) had done them. Stimers, on the contrary, stated that he specifically mentioned the source of the figures: "a young second assistant engineer," indicating thereby that some rechecking might be in order. Stimers dismissed his own negligence simply: "I had no time to make the calculations myself."[22]

Some have spread the blame further: to Isherwood and Lenthall for failing to supervise in detail; to Fox for allowing Stimers too free a hand.[23] It appears that Admiral Gregory was not tainted by the scandal, however. This may have been because he was generally accepted as a figurehead for the ironclad organization, with Stimers as the working head.[24] Therefore, the seeds of the disaster may be traced to the organizational anomalies that cropped up in the massive wartime programs.

In the end, though, Stimers had little support. Isherwood suspected him of angling to supplant him as head of the Bureau of Steam Engineering, probably a reasonable possibility if the light drafts had proved successful.[25] Admiral Gregory had had to restrain Stimers earlier for authorizing substantial constructional changes without his approval (in areas other than the light drafts), and Ericsson had had similar problems with him.[26] In defense of Stimers, it must be stated that he was exceptionally busy: in February 1863, in the midst of preparing his plans for the light drafts, he was dispatched to Charleston with orders to prepare the ironclads there for the upcoming operation.[27] This duty, in addition to supervising the various inspectors of ironclads a-building around the country, certainly was sufficient to overwork any individual.

Little can be said of the operational careers of the light-draft vessels, most of which were exceedingly brief. Some idea of their weaknesses can be seen from the deck logs of two, the *Casco* and *Chimo*, both of which were completed as torpedo vessels. The *Casco*, under tow from Boston to New York, had her forward section "nearly constantly under water" even in light breezes and leaked with a vengeance. Her maximum speed was 7 knots. At one point the tow vessel, concerned for her safety, signaled "Are you leaking?" and received the sarcastic reply "Not more than usual."[28]

The *Chimo* went to sea in January 1865 and met a stiff gale, with hair-raising results. With the seas "sweeping completely over her" she leaked copiously from chain gutters, hawse pipes, and the forward plating. Water rose over cabin and anchor room decks, and the wardroom pumps were inoperable. With "all hands bailing with buckets," the boats were prepared for abandoning ship.[29] Both ship and men survived but the incident did nothing to elevate the reputation of these vessels.

The list of name changes for the light-draft monitors is literally longer than an account of their careers. Four (*Casco*, *Chimo*, *Naubuc*, and *Tunxis*) were commissioned before Appomattox. The latter was apparently then taken in hand and had the turret removed and deck raised. *Casco* served on the James River as a torpedo vessel and was decommissioned 10 June 1865. *Naubuc* was in commission from 27 March to 27 June 1865; *Chimo*, from 20 January to 24 June. All the remaining ships were laid up on completion. All were sold and/or broken up by late 1875.

The secretary of the navy in 1869, Adolph A. Borie, ordered wholesale name changes to naval warships, replacing Secretary Welles's favorite (though often strange) American Indian designations with those of classical gods and literary characters. The changes were ordered 15 June and rescinded 10 August 1869. A few vessels retained their new names. Note also that the *Suncook* was sometimes called *Simcook*. The following are the light-draft name changes:

Casco	*Hero* (not rechanged)
Chimo	*Orion* (then *Piscataqua*)
Cohoes	*Charybdis*
Etlah	*Hecate*
Klamath	*Harpy*
Koka	*Argos*
Modoc	*Achilles*
Napa	*Nemesis*
Naubuc	*Gorgon* (then *Minnetonka*)
Nausett	*Aetna*
Shawnee	*Eolus*
Shiloh	*Iris* (not rechanged)
Squando	*Erebus* (then *Algoma*)
Suncook	*Spitfire*
Tunxis	*Hydra* (then *Otsego*)
Umpqua	*Fury*
Wassuc	*Stromboli*
Waxsaw	*Niobe* (not rechanged)
Yazoo	*Tartar*
Yuma	*Tempest*

Kalamazoo Class

In April 1863, Lenthall directed the naval constructor at New York to design an ironclad vessel, to be of wood, with deck 3 feet above water, to carry two turrets. The side armor was to be 10 inches thick, with 12 to 15 inches of wood backing and 6 feet in depth, extending 3 feet below the waterline. Deck armor was to be 3 inches, with wood planking beneath and above. The vessel was to be capable of steaming one week at full power and would carry sixty days' provisions, at 15 feet draft. It was expected to have "sufficient speed" to make good use of a ram bow.[30]

The four vessels that were begun subsequently were described by the secretary of the navy in December 1864 as enlarged versions of the *Miantonomoh* with greater speed and "adapted to coast service."[31] They would have been the navy's closest approximation of an oceangoing turreted ironclad, had they been completed.

Plans for the *Kalamazoo* class, designed by B. F. Delano, show a hull 332 feet 5 inches between perpendiculars, and total breadth of 57 feet. The breadth included 21 inches overhang on each side. Side plating was two layers of 3-inch iron, backed by 21 inches of wood. This double layer was 6 feet in depth, with the outer layer extending 1½ feet farther below the waterline. The deck armor was 3 inches thick, over 6 inches of wood, with another 3 inches of planking above.[32]

These were the largest hulls built in a U.S. navy yard to that time. The *Wampanoag*-class fast cruisers, which were built contemporaneously, were 335 feet between perpendiculars but at least 10 feet narrower, as befitting their speed requirement. Neither were those vessels expected to carry the weights proposed for these ironclads: both armor and turrets, along with four 15-inch Dahlgren shell guns. Turret armor was to be 15 inches thick. They were to displace some 5,600 tons.

To support this weight on a wooden hull, extraordinary means were taken. In addition to the center keelson measuring some 2½ feet deep, there was introduced a longitudinal member on the centerline, 18 inches in depth by 15 inches wide, with 8-foot scarfs, supporting the deck. The deck beams were 15 inches square, 4 feet between centers, except under the turret, where they were 3 feet asunder. This was not all: between each deck beam were 12- by 12-inch timbers, making a completely solid "under-deck."[33]

Artist's conception of the Kalamazoo *class at sea. Note the twin funnels. Work was suspended at the end of the war and none of this class was completed. (Naval Historical Center)*

Connecting the keelson and the under-deck longitudinal timbers were iron braces. Vertical stanchions of 6-inch-square wrought iron were placed every 12 feet, attached by iron knees to the longitudinal timbers. Bolts some 2 feet long were used to attach the knees. Running diagonally from stanchion to stanchion were 4- by 5-inch wrought iron braces. Additional diagonal braces ran athwartships from the frames to the deck beams, but the number of these is not known.[34] The only other known vessel with similar iron bracing was the cruiser *Idaho*, built by Henry Steers about this same time.[35]

The engines for these ships were designed by John Baird of New York and cost $580,000 to $590,000 each and consisted of four direct-acting horizontal cylinders, two for each 15-foot propeller.[36] Cylinders were 46½-inch diameter, by 50-inch stroke. There were eight horizontal tubular boilers, each with six furnaces. The two funnels were each 10½ feet in outside diameter.[37]

On 17 November 1865, construction was suspended on all four vessels: *Kalamazoo* at Brooklyn, *Passaconaway* at Kittery, *Quinsigamond* at Boston, and *Shackamaxon* at Philadelphia. No substantial

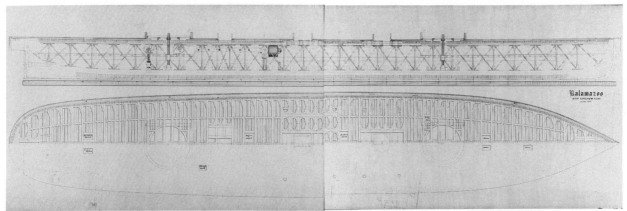

Inboard profile of the Kalamazoo *class. To support 6 inches of side armor and four 15-inch turrets, a longitudinal centerline structural member run beneath the deck and iron stanchions and diagonal braces were incorporated to stabilize the wooden hull. (NARS Plan 2-2-9, National Archives)*

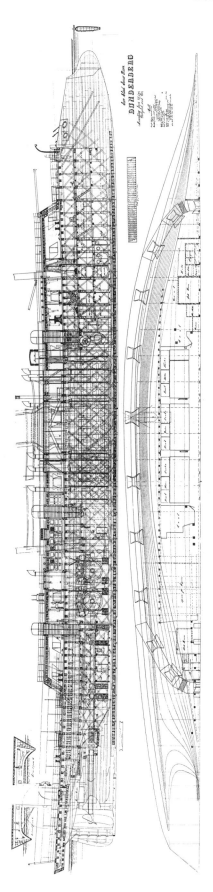

work was subsequently done on the ships, though Admiral Porter ordered the *Colossus* (former *Kalamazoo*) altered to carry ten large broadside guns, with ship rig and iron masts, in accordance with plans by Lenthall.[38] The idea was not carried out. *Shackamaxon* (renamed *Hecla*, then *Nebraska* in 1869) was broken up in 1874. *Colossus*, *Passaconaway* (later *Thunderer*, then *Massachusetts*), and *Quinsigamond* (later *Hercules*, then *Oregon*) were broken up in 1884. The prognosis for their actual service was in any case clouded by the quick onset of rot in their unseasoned timber, putting them in the same short-lived category as most of the late war naval construction, such as the *Contoocook* and *Guerriere* classes, most of which were out of service by the mid-1870s.

Dunderberg

The genesis of the *Dunderberg* came in mid-1862, when, as Gideon Welles put it, the United States was in danger of a "foreign war." The *Dictator* and *Puritan* had been begun, but these were not considered capable of cruising. Rather, they were to break a blockade of our coastline. Welles recalled that Admiral Smith urged two seagoing vessels, and Fox, four. Welles opted for two and proceeded to select a builder. One was to have been built by Cramp of Philadelphia, the other was the *Dunderberg*, constructed by William Webb at New York. Welles gave "crowded conditions" as the reason the vessel was built outside the navy yards.[39]

The specifications for the vessel, as originally conceived, called for a 368-foot hull, including a huge ram, with a beam of 68 feet, including armor. Two turrets as well as a casemate were planned, carrying four 15-inch and eight 11-inch guns, with the main deck 5½ feet above water, on a draft of 20 feet 6 inches.[40] She was to have a single screw, engines with two 90-inch diameter cylinders, and reach 15 knots. The contract was let in July 1862, and she was laid down in November.[41]

In the process of construction, modifications were made. The major alteration was the deletion of the turrets. As early as October 1863, Webb was contemplating the removal of the aft turret, citing the problems in supporting them atop the casemate.[42] In September 1864, he requested permission to remove both turrets. To compensate for this, the casemate was extended 26 feet at the sides and 17 feet 6 inches at the centerline. Four additional 11-inch guns were to be mounted in the casemate, with the whole extension costing some $20,000.[43] The

Lines and inboard profile of William Webb's Dunderberg. *The hull consisted of masses of solid wood, 368 feet long, including the ram. Iron hull strapping can be seen forming a latticelike basket to prevent hogging. Note the extremely pointed ram and the timbers solidifying the ram's connection with the hull. (Smithsonian Institution)*

removal of the turrets solved the nagging problem of masts and shrouds, which would have interfered seriously with their fields of fire.

Construction itself was a protracted process. War-time shortages and workers' strikes made progress slow. Then in July 1863 came the New York draft riots, halting the work. Webb feared the rioters were determined to "destroy the *Dunderberg*" and the military was called in to guard the yard.[44]

The vessel was launched 22 July 1865 and was arguably one of the most formidable ironclads in existence— certainly the most powerful in terms of firepower in the U.S. Navy.

The hull of the ship was unique, consisting of two portions: an inner hull of frames and planking, and an outer wood and iron armored "casing," which, according to Webb, "must be destroyed before the inner vessel can be reached."[45]

The inner hull was flat bottomed with angular bilges, sloping sides, and "extremely sharp ends." The frames were sided 15 to 18 inches and molded 17 inches. The keel was 18 inches by 30 inches, and four keelsons were somewhat larger than even these substantial measurements. The frames were set hard against each other with "no openings" between timbers. Seven-inch planking covered the whole. Diagonal braces were let into the frames forming a "basket" of strap iron, each measuring 4½ inches by ¾ inch, running from the bottom to a head strap immediately below the main deck.[46] Such strapping was standard practice in larger wooden vessels.

The outside vessel, or casing, was the wood and iron armor: at the bottom it was 2 feet thick and at main deck level it was about 5 feet of pine "logging." Outside of this was 3½ inches of iron, thinning to 2½ inches at the ends of the ship. The ram bow extended 32 feet forward and was 20 feet wide at its aft end. It was formed of "large white oak logs,

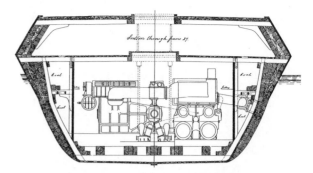

Cross section of the Dunderberg, *at the engines. Wood armor backing was about 5 feet thick at the main deck level, with 3½-inch plating; the casemate had 4½-inch solid plates. The back-acting engines had a 100-inch cylinder diameter. (Smithsonian Institution)*

running fore and aft . . . extending into the vessel," with a 12-foot cast iron beak.[47]

The casemate was supported by 12- by 12-inch deck beams, and had three 1-foot layers of timber backing for a single layer of 4½-inch iron. Main deck armor was said to be 4½ inches; casemate deck, 3½ inches of iron over 12 inches of wood. The two-piece port shutters were of 4½-inch iron, operated by levers within the casemate. Three watertight bulkheads were placed forward between the boilers and the ram. In addition to main and casemate decks, she had berth and orlop decks, both interrupted by the machinery.[48]

The hull dimensions were 377 feet 4 inches overall. The molded breadth of the inner vessel was 59 feet 7 inches; the breadth to the outside of the plating was 72 feet 10 inches. The depth of hold was 22 feet 7½ inches and casemate inclination, 60 degrees.[49]

Two back-acting cylinders were planned, with 90-inch diameter and 45-inch stroke, built by John

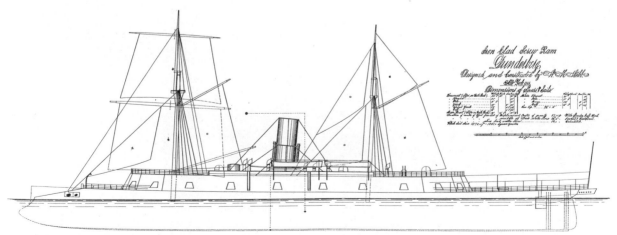

Outboard profile of the Dunderberg. *She was originally to have two turrets atop the casemate. Webb deleted them for weight considerations in 1864. She was active during the Franco-Prussian War and sold out of the French fleet in 1872. (From enlargement of drawing in William Webb,* Plans of Wooden Vessels, *New York, 1866, Smithsonian Institution)*

Roach of Philadelphia. The diameter was later increased to 100 inches. Thomas Main and Erastus Smith designed the engines, based on those Main had designed for the steam sloop *Iroquois* in 1858. There were six boilers, with double furnaces, allowing two sets of grates, one above the other, similar to those of the *Dictator*.[50] Two auxiliary boilers were provided. The screw propeller was 21 feet in diameter.[51]

After her completion, the *Dunderberg* was tried on at least two occasions before her sale to the French: in September 1866, and February 1867. In the first instance no speed run was attempted but she made 10 knots at 41 rpm, without journal heating or stoppage. She steered easily and in a light swell, rolled easily and slowly.[52]

In an ordnance trial, she carried four 11-inch and two 15-inch guns. The latter could be elevated

Stern view of the Rochambeau *(formerly the* Dunderberg*), at Cherbourg. In trials before her sale to France, she had been the only broadside ironclad to carry the 15-inch Dahlgren gun. The French found her speedy but very wet. (The Peabody Museum of Salem)*

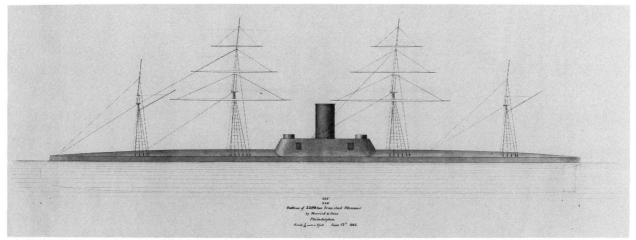

Seagoing ironclad proposed by William Cramp, 1863. Despite indications to the contrary, this 3,500-ton ship was apparently never laid down. The casemate was to hold four 15-inch guns on rotating platforms, to fire through two ports each. (NARS Plan 80-9-1A, National Archives)

8^{1}/$_{2}$ degrees and depressed 5 degrees, with a field of fire of 30 degrees. The 11-inchers could be trained 28 degrees. In this instance the larger guns were in broadside, the fifth port from the front of the casemate. The 15-inch guns were worked "with ease and facility" and recoiled from one to six feet.[53]

The disposition of this powerful vessel now became a problem. She had cost over $1 million—one of the ten most expensive vessels of the wartime construction programs. Webb was anxious to sell her to a foreign power, but there was resistance in the cabinet. Secretary of War Stanton went on record as opposing such a sale: her "name," he said, "was worth more than a million dollars to us."[54] In any case, on 2 March 1867, by act of Congress, she was returned to Webb. Webb sold her to France in June. Considering that her building had been in response to the threat of foreign war, this was somewhat ironic.

The French found her to be very wet. However, she made 15 knots—before any extensive rebuilding.[55] Generally, it appears that she would have been one of the few American ironclads to meet the majority of the contract specifications. She was sold out in 1872.

The 3,500-Ton Ironclad

The history of this never-built vessel is somewhat murky. As was stated above, Welles had made the decision to build two oceangoing ironclads. The second was to have been a 7,000-ton vessel, an advertisement for which was published in October 1862. Proposals were to include an iron hull, iron spars, and wire rigging. But all the proposals that came in were too expensive, and the tonnage was halved for a second round of bids.[56]

Seven designs were studied, including proposals from Merrick, Secor, Rowland, and the firm of Reaney and Archbold, ranging in cost from $1.9 to $2.5 million. All were over 300 feet in length, on drafts of 18 to 25 feet.[57]

According to the 1863 Secretary of the Navy's report, one contract was let.[58] The *Army and Navy Journal* (though not necessarily a reliable source) reported that such a vessel was under construction at Cramp's yard in Philadelphia, and detailed specifications with plans have been found.[59]

The vessel was to have been 340 feet overall, with a 54-foot beam, a depth of 21 feet, very low freeboard, and arched decks fore and aft. Plating on the sides was to have been 4^{1}/$_{2}$ inches with substantial oak backing. Four 50-by-30-inch cylinders were to drive two 14-foot propellers. The four 15-inch guns were in a central casemate, mounted on iron turntables turned by vertical shafts.[60]

The contract itself has yet to surface, and the 1864 Secretary's report denied that Congress had appropriated money for such a vessel.[61] Possibly the vessel was a subtle fiction—directed toward present and potential adversaries. It made for some rather interesting proposals and plans, however, many of which remain as curiosities in the National Archives.

The USS Miantonomoh *in the 1890s. Over the next decades, the vessel was completed with 10-inch breech-loading rifles and compound armor. She had the least superstructure of these new vessels. (U.S. Naval Institute)*

CHAPTER 11

The Postwar Years: Ironclads in Eclipse

At the close of the Civil War, the U.S. Navy found itself with the largest fleet it would have until World War II: in excess of five hundred vessels. Its ironclad fleet was the largest in existence, at least in number of vessels. An aggregate of eighty-four iron-plated ships were built or were a-building during the conflict, including the Stevens battery. Of this total, forty-nine were commissioned before Appomattox. Incomplete vessels included the *Puritan*- and *Kalamazoo*-class monitors, as well as most of the light drafts. Though any comparison with European blue-water fleets would be difficult, from a domestic, practical point of view, the ironclads had contributed significantly to the Union victory, both in the coastal war and the western campaigns.

With the end of the conflict and the evaporation of the short-lived French adventure in Mexico, a drawdown in forces was inevitable. Literally hundreds of vessels were sold and rows of inert, shingle-roofed monitors were a common sight at the navy yards. Except for the *Virginius* affair in the 1870s, the postwar decades presented the navy with little reason to prepare for foreign conflicts, and Con-

gress with even less incentive to fund new vessel construction. What little funds were forthcoming were sliced thinly among the least expensive ships possible: conventional cruisers little different from the likes of the prewar *Kearsarge*.

Ironclads, which were expensive to operate and maintain and most of which carried no sailing rig, were obviously useless in a cruising navy. Furthermore, the accidental destruction of the *New Ironsides* and the sale of the *Dunderberg* deprived the service of its only two rigged armored ships. Even so, it would have been politically unwise to dismantle the ironclad fleet entirely.

Even as the major European powers continued their upwardly spiraling naval arms race, with its attendant technology, the U.S. Navy was limited by fiscal constraints to rebuilding the Civil War–generation vessels and concocting paper schemes for armored vessels that would never darken a shiphouse. This stasis would continue until the early 1880s.

Before a survey of the developments within the navy in the postwar years, the Stevens battery must be dealt with—finally. The project languished after

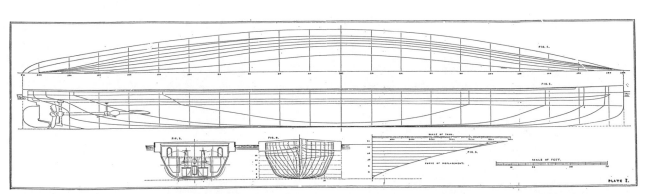

Lines and section of the Stevens battery, published in 1874 as part of the prospectus for the sale of the still-incomplete vessel. The extremely sharp hull was 401 feet long and 54 feet across the armor—a size not to be seen in the U.S. Navy for another decade. (From a booklet, "The Stevens Ironclad Battery," D. Van Nostrand, 1874)

The Stevens battery as a monitor. This engraving is nearly identical to a contemporary illustration of the Dictator. *No decision on casemate versus turret was ever made, and the forty-year project ended with the scrapping of the huge hull. (Naval Historical Center)*

the less than stellar performance of the little *E. A. Stevens* in 1862, but the huge unfinished hull of the ship represented a fortune invested and was by this time sufficiently along in its construction to be expensive even to dismantle.

In 1868, Edwin Stevens passed away, bequeathing the hull and plans to the state of New Jersey, along with $1 million to complete the project. The state appointed former Gen. George B. McClellan (who had commanded the Army of the Potomac during the short career of the *E. A. Stevens* on the James River) to supervise the construction.[1]

With the assistance of former navy steam engineer Isaac Newton, construction resumed but on a much modified plan intended to incorporate the newest technology. Accordingly, it was decided to include "an inner skin, transverse watertight bulkheads, watertight coal bunkers, to build new engines, and then prepare the ship for transformation either into an iron-clad of the 'Monitor' type, having very high speed, carrying a powerful armament within a turret of extraordinary thickness, and capable of acting efficiently as a 'Steam Ram,' or into a broadside iron-clad."[2]

Work continued into 1870, using up the bequeathed funds but leaving the vessel still incomplete. The state then took a hand and after producing a booklet extolling the expected virtues of the vessel, placed it up for sale.

She was to become a monitor. Indeed, the illustration used to show the completed ship at sea was virtually identical to that of the *Dictator*. The hull was 401 feet overall, by 54 feet over the armor. She was 24 feet in depth to the main deck with an expected draft of 22 feet. The hull was exceedingly sharp forward and fine aft, with a length to breadth ratio of 8.666 to 1. Her inner hull was up to 22

inches from the outer, and seven watertight bulkheads were incorporated, in addition to extra bulkheads for strength at the ends. It was claimed that 32 feet could be torn from her bow without mortal danger to the ship.[3]

The engines were of the return connecting rod, or back-acting, type, using four 72-inch cylinders operating on a 45-inch stroke. There were four piston rods per cylinder, surface condensers, and two 18-foot propellers. Ten boilers were to supply steam and occupied over 80 feet of hull space. It was expected that this power plant would develop over 5,600 horsepower, resulting in a speed of 15¾ knots.[4]

All of the above appeared quite satisfactory and seemed to promise great things. The fate of the vessel was determined, however, by the list of incomplete items: "No steps have yet been taken in the construction of either armor or armament," read the state report. A monitorlike armored side projection was proposed, with 44 inches of wood and 10 inches of iron, surrounding most of the hull. The turret was to be 16 to 18 inches thick, carrying two 20-inch smoothbores or 12-inch rifles. Other hull work yet to be done included all joiner work, rudder, hatches, ventilating pipes, deck beam supports, magazines, and so on. The list of engine and boiler needs was also significant: it appeared that only the basic cylinders and frames were complete, with boilers installed but unconnected. Despite this, the report blithely projected three months to complete her sufficiently to steam without armor and armament, at a cost of $100,000; complete with armature and guns, $450,000.[5]

The incomplete and ridiculously expensive Stevens battery was sold for scrap in the 1880s and dismantled where she lay. The total amount spent was a *minimum* of $2.2 million, including the estimated spending given by Stevens in 1862 and the million of the bequest. Not included (or ever calculated) are the costs of fitting out and donating the *E. A. Stevens* and for any construction and other activities between 1862 and the death of Edwin Stevens.

In June 1885, the *Army and Navy Journal* reported that her engines were sent to the coal mines of Pennsylvania and her bolts went to make shotgun barrels. A bell, dated 1841, was the only intact remnant of the great ship.[6] Forty-four years had come and gone and the Hoboken monster was at last put to rest.

The last half of the 1860s saw little construction of any kind. The last of the *Monadnock* class, *Canonicus* class, and light drafts were completed by late 1866. Work was suspended on the *Kalamazoo* class and *Puritan* late in 1865.

Two other armor-plating projects were in the works. Two of the fast wooden-hulled cruisers begun in 1863, to be named *Hassalo* and *Wautauga*, were to be given light plating "in the space occupied by the guns." This was "to resist shells, but not of sufficient weight to interfere with the nautical qualities of the vessels."[7] Neither of these vessels was actually built.

The steam sloop *Niagara*, the largest vessel of the prewar navy, was to become an ironclad. Her decks were to be raised and twenty 11-inch guns were to be placed on her main deck, protected by an armor belt. It appears that this project got little farther than the drawing of the plans.

The major ironclad projects undertaken in the 1870s involved the *Puritan* and the four *Monadnock*-class wooden monitors. These five vessels were "rebuilt" by the navy over a period of some twenty years, with the *Puritan* the last commissioned, late in 1896.

The resulting vessels, of course, were totally new: little if anything was carried over from the original Civil War ships. As the construction of these ships extended well into the era of the "New Navy" it will suffice here to describe their building up until about 1885—the end of the "Old Navy."

In 1874 Congress, spurred on by the *Virginius* affair, authorized $849,045 for "completing the repairs of such double-turret monitors as the Secretary of the Navy should select."[8] The *Puritan*, still on the stocks, and the *Monadnock* class were selected and contracts were let as follows. *Puritan* and *Miantonomoh:* John Roach, Chester, Pennsylvania; *Amphitrite* (formerly *Tonawanda*): Harlan and Hollingsworth, Wilmington, Delaware; *Monadnock:* Phineas Burgess, Continental Iron Works, Vallejo, California; and *Terror* (formerly *Agamenticus*): William Cramp of Philadelphia.

Painting of the Stevens battery under construction. The ram bow is not shown in the hull plans. (Stevens Institute of Technology)

As of 1876 the general plan for the *Monadnocks* was to replace their wooden hulls with iron, their 5-inch laminated plating with 7 inches of solid, their simple engines with compound to attain 10 knots, and add freeboard and storage. The *Puritan*'s hull form was to be changed to lessen her draft and 12 inches of solid plating was to supplant her laminated side armor. Her freeboard was to be increased to allow the use of her guns in all weathers, and the second turret, removed from the original vessel during the Civil War at Ericsson's insistence, was to be replaced. The battery was to be four "41 ton" rifles.[9]

If there was any doubt that this was indeed new construction the navy received a bill in August 1876 for the cutting up and burning of the "old vessel" *Amphitrite*.[10] More importantly, each firm received three contracts for each monitor. The first was for the erection of the iron hull frames in readiness for plating, the second was for the plating, and the third was for building the machinery.[11]

The method used by the navy to pay for these "repairs" is a complete story in itself, involving the "Roach, Robeson, Robbers" scandal and the general aura of malfeasance that accompanied the second Grant administration. It appears, however, that the wrongdoing in the case of these vessels was exaggerated and was probably generated in part by the rather unusual method used to pay the contractors. Because of the fiscal shortages endemic during these years, the navy paid a portion of the bills for these ships in the form of scrap at a fixed ratio of scrap metal to newly rolled iron. Along with the metal, numerous discarded vessels, such as the old *Roanoke* and seven of the light-draft monitors, became part of the payment structure.[12] These methods raised questions among the public as to the

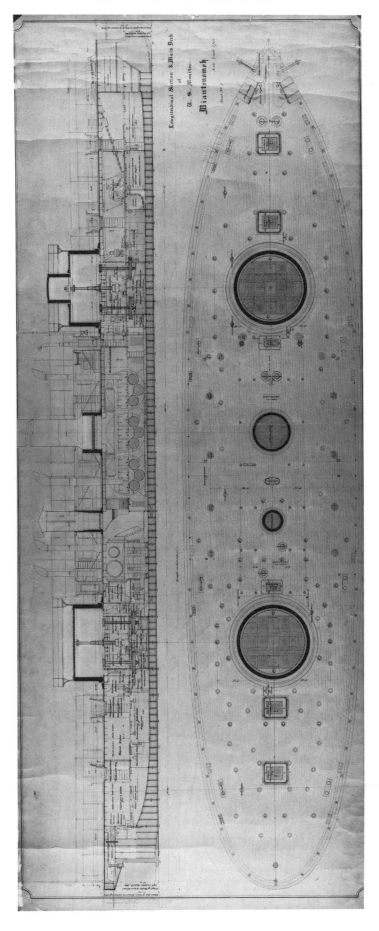

actual value of the materials being turned over to the contractors, along with exaggerated claims as to the true condition, for instance, of the vessels built late in the war and found to be of rotting wood.

In 1880, after the scandals had died away and the money (or barter) available to the contractors had been expended, the five ships were retrieved for completion by the navy. Mare Island received the *Monadnock;* Brooklyn, the *Terror, Puritan,* and *Miantonomoh;* and Norfolk, the *Amphitrite.*

The *Miantonomoh* departed the Roach yard at Chester, in 1880. She was the first launched. Between perpendiculars, she was still 250 feet long, and her breadth was 55 feet 10 inches. The new iron hull no longer had the hips and overhang of the original monitors. Instead, there was a formidable ram at the forefoot, the armor was located in a recess along her sides, and there was a double bottom (the first in the navy).[13]

The armor itself was solid iron: 7 inches thick at the deck line, reduced to 3 inches at the bottom of the belt. Turrets, pilothouse, and armored funnel were not yet built, nor were there guns on board. Two compound engines were built, with 32-inch high-pressure and 48-inch low-pressure pistons, on a stroke of 42 inches. This pair of engines was arranged in a V with the piston rods crossing in an X configuration, resulting in the pistons for one screw above the crankshaft of the other. For the purposes of duplicating her service draft, she was given chain cables and kentledge in square timber cribs at the locations of the turrets. On trials she made 10.5 knots.[14]

At this point a board was appointed to report on the condition of the other four still incomplete vessels and determine if it was in the "interest of the government to complete them." Given the fact that the Congress had allowed the navy a total of eight new vessels since the end of the war, it was not surprising that the board was not in favor of disposing of the vessels.[15]

The board was not in agreement with the bureaus' plans for their completion, however, frowning particularly on the iron plating and recommending compound (steel-faced) armor. They also recommended long-range 10-inch breech-loading rifles in place of the smoothbore battery and improved watertight bulkheads.[16]

Eventually, all five received breech-loading rifles and either compound or steel armor. Compound side armor for the *Monadnock* and *Amphitrite* was 9

The Miantonomoh *in the late 1870s. This "rebuilt" ship was entirely new, with an iron hull, armor belt recessed into the hull sides, and ram bow. Note the compound engines and cylindrical boilers. Despite this plan, the vessel was without turrets, pilothouse, and armored funnel when she left the hands of the contractor, John Roach. (NARS Plan 138-3-1, National Archives)*

inches, and 7 inches for the *Terror* and *Miantonomoh.* The *Puritan* received Harvey and nickel steel side plating 14 inches thick on the belt. The rifles were not mounted until the 1890s and were the first large-caliber modern guns forged entirely in the United States. The *Puritan* mounted 12-inch, 35-caliber weapons: the other four received 10-inch and 30-, 35-, and 40-caliber guns.[17]

The *Monadnock* was given horizontal triple-expansion engines rather than the compound power plants. These were the most advanced engines to be used in any vessel begun during the era of the old steam navy. She and the *Amphitrite* had four boilers, whereas the remaining pair had six each.

Two, *Amphitrite* and *Monadnock,* had their turrets mounted on armored barbettes, making them marginally drier below decks than the others, and three of the four received a superstructure running from turret to turret. This included wardroom, heads, chart room, officers' cabins, and so on. The *Miantonomoh* had only a hurricane deck, albeit a more elaborate one than that of her Civil War namesake.

Steam operated the steering, turrets, and guns on the *Monadnock* and *Miantonomoh.* An unusual pneumatic system performed these functions on the *Terror,* and hydraulics were used on the *Amphitrite.*

The *Miantonomoh* was launched in 1876, and the three remaining vessels in 1883. *Miantonomoh* was commissioned in 1891; *Amphitrite,* 1895; and *Monadnock* and *Terror,* 1896. All were sold out in the 1920s.

The *Puritan* was considerably larger than the others, at 296 feet 3 inches by 60 feet $1\frac{1}{2}$ inches and 6060 tons. She was launched in 1882 and commissioned in 1896, with ten cylindrical boilers and horizontal direct-acting compound engines (cylinder diameters: 50 and 86 inches; stroke: 42 inches).[18] She served in the Caribbean during the Spanish American War and sold in 1922.

These five monitors represent a motley collection of technologies. Iron hulls and compound engines smacked of the 1860s and 1870s, whereas the breech-loading rifles, double bottoms, and the triple-expansion engines of the *Monadnock* brought them nearly to the twentieth century. John Ericsson's concept of the monitor, however, was a far cry from these completed vessels. His single turret had been abandoned, as well as the low profile possible with decks nearly awash. In any case, the development of a blue-water navy in the last decade of the nineteenth century relegated the coastal defense strategy to oblivion, and along with it the monitor. It also seems obvious that the navy's obsession with completing these vessels had less to do with strategic considerations than with a simple reluctance to part with five major warships in an era of meager appropriations.

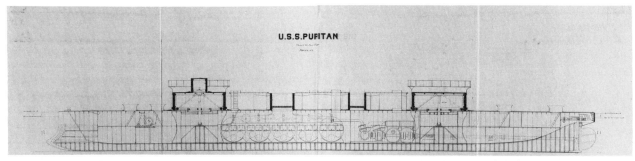

U.S.S. PURITAN

Longitudinal section of the Puritan. *She was launched in 1882 and was 40 feet longer than the* Miantonomoh *and others of her class. Note the breech-loading rifles and cylindrical boilers. This plan, dated 1882, does not reflect the vessel as completed in 1896. (NARS Bureau of Steam Engineering Plan, National Archives)*

The U.S. Navy in the mid-nineteenth century fluctuated between eras of stasis—even reaction—and progressivism. As has been seen both in this and the previous volume, the 1840s were years of experimentation in technology, represented in this volume by the beginnings of the Stevens battery. The 1850s, except for the development of the Dahlgren shell gun, was a decade of complacence—vividly reflected by the lack of reaction to the advent of the European ironclads.

In the war years, the pendulum swung again: the monitors represented a technological breakthrough unmatched in any other navy. Indeed, John Ericsson and Benjamin F. Isherwood, along with others of the era, have been credited with founding the process of technological research and development in the military.[19] No doubt the war itself was the key to the navy's veritable leap of faith in adopting Ericsson's original *Monitor*. There was also a self-made American image being perpetuated and projected to the world in this strange vessel: the myth of "Yankee ingenuity." Ericsson joined a pantheon of men such as Robert Fulton, Samuel Slater, Eli Whitney, Samuel F. B. Morse, and Samuel Colt: practical men of invention who personified the American notion that this brash and, as the British termed it, "go-ahead" nation could teach the old

world the benefits of innovative technological thinking. Indeed, Ericsson described the vessel as this "Yankee notion" intended to awe not only the South but the "Lords of the Admiralty."[20]

The postwar years are generally termed the American naval "Dark Ages." The rebuilding of the large monitors, however, along with the use of up-to-date steam technology in the conventional wooden ships, indicates that the picture was not without redeeming features.

Given these extreme contrasts, it is difficult to give a generalized evaluation of the navy in this era of transition and technological frenzy. Certainly the presence of talented individuals and the willingness of leadership—men such as Gustavus Fox—to allow these men free reign seem to have been the key factors in maintaining a level of technological advancement despite periods of fiscal and bureaucratic inertia. There was, however, a pronounced conservative strain throughout, exemplified by the reluctance to adopt ironclad vessels until the South forced the issue, and earlier, in the dilatory adoption of steam propulsion. On balance, the picture of the navy in the mid-nineteenth century was not as positive as it could have been given the resources and talents available.

Appendix

CONSTRUCTION AND FATE OF VESSELS

NAME	HULL/MACHINERY	LAUNCHED	COMMISSIONED	FATE
CHAPTER 3				
Monitor	Continental/Delamater	30 Jan 1862	25 Feb 1862	Foundered 31 Dec 1862
New Ironsides	Cramp/Merrick & Sons	10 May 1862	21 Aug 1862	Burned 15 Dec 1866
Galena	Maxon & Fish/Delamater	14 Feb 1862	21 Apr 1862	Broken up 1871
CHAPTER 4				
Essex				Sold 29 Nov 1865
Benton		Nov 1861	24 Feb 1862	Sold 29 Nov 1865
CHAPTER 5				
Cairo	Eads	1861	25 Jan 1862	Sunk by mine 12 Dec 1862
Carondelet	Eads	1861	15 Jan 1862	Sold 29 Nov 1865
Cincinnati	Eads	1861	16 Jan 1862	Sold 28 Mar 1866
Louisville	Eads	1861	16 Jan 1862	Sold 29 Nov 1865
Mound City	Eads	1861	16 Jan 1862	Sold 29 Nov 1865
Pittsburgh	Eads	1861	16 Jan 1862	Sold 29 Nov 1865
St. Louis (*Baron de Kalb*)	Eads	12 Oct 1861	31 Jan 1862	Mined 13 Jul 1863
CHAPTER 6				
Roanoke	Brooklyn Navy Yard/Tredegar		29 Jun 1863	Sold 27 Sep 1883
Onondaga	Continental/Morgan Iron Works	29 Jul 1863	24 Mar 1864	Returned to contractor 12 Jul 1867
Miantonomoh	New York Navy Yard/Novelty Iron Works	15 Aug 1863	18 Sep 1865	Broken up 1874
Tonawanda	Philadelphia Navy Yard/Merrick & Sons	6 May 1864	12 Oct 1865	Broken up 1874
Monadnock	Boston Navy Yard/Morris & Towne	23 Mar 1864	4 Oct 1864	Broken up 1874
Agamenticus	Portsmouth Navy Yard/Morris & Towne	19 Mar 1863	5 May 1865	Broken up 1874
Keokuk	J. S. Underhill, NY	6 Dec 1862	24 Feb 1863	Sunk 8 Apr 1863
E. A. Stevens		1844		
CHAPTER 7				
Camanche	Secor/Joseph Colwell	14 Nov 1864	24 May 1865	Sold 22 Mar 1899
Catskill	Continental/Delamater	6 Dec 1862	24 Feb 1863	Sold 8 Jan 1902
Lehigh	Reaney/Morris & Towne	17 Jan 1863	15 Apr 1863	Sold 16 Apr 1904

NAME	HULL/MACHINERY	LAUNCHED	COMMISSIONED	FATE
CHAPTER 7 (continued)				
Montauk	Continental/Delamater	9 Oct 1862	14 Dec 1862	Sold 16 Apr 1904
Nahant	Loring/Loring	7 Oct 1862	29 Dec 1862	Sold 16 Apr 1904
Nantucket	Atlantic/Atlantic	6 Dec 1862	26 Feb 1863	Sold 14 Nov 1900
Passaic	Continental/Delamater	30 Aug 1862	25 Nov 1862	Sold 10 Oct 1899
Patapsco	Harlan & Hollingsworth	27 Sep 1862	2 Jan 1863	Mined 16 Jan 1865
Sangamon	Reaney/Morris & Towne	27 Oct 1862	9 Feb 1863	Sold 16 Apr 1904
Weehawken	Colwell/Fulton Foundry	5 Nov 1862	18 Jan 1863	Foundered 6 Dec 1863
Canonicus	Loring/Loring	1 Aug 1863	16 Apr 1864	Sold 19 Feb 1908
Catawba	Swift, Evans/Niles	13 Apr 1864	10 Jun 1865 (Completed)	Sold 2 Apr 1868, sunk 16 Jan 1880
Mahopac	Colwell/Fulton Foundry	17 May 1864	22 Sep 1864	Sold 24 Mar 1902
Manayunk	Snowden/Snowden	18 Dec 1864	27 Sep 1865 (Completed)	Sold 10 Oct 1899
Manhattan	Colwell/Fulton Foundry	14 Oct 1863	6 Jun 1864	Sold 24 Mar 1902
Oneota	Swift, Evans/Niles	21 May 1864	10 Jun 1865 (Completed)	Sold 2 Apr 1868, blown up 6 Jun 1880
Saugus	Harlan & Hollingsworth	16 Dec 1863	7 Apr 1864	Sold 25 Mar 1891
Tecumseh	Colwell/Fulton Foundry	12 Sep 1863	19 Apr 1864	Mined, Mobile Bay, 5 Aug 1864
Tippecanoe	Litherbury/Greenwood	22 Dec 1864	15 Feb 1866 (Delivered)	Sold 17 Jan 1899
Dictator	Delamater/Delamater	26 Dec 1863	11 Nov 1864	Sold 27 Sep 1883
Puritan	Continental/Allaire	2 Jul 1864		Broken up 1874
CHAPTER 8				
Chillicothe	Brown/McCord & Junger	1862	5 Sep 1862	Sold 29 Nov 1865
Tuscumbia	McCord & Junger	12 Dec 1862	12 Mar 1863	Sold 29 Nov 1865
Indianola	Brown/McCord & Junger	4 Sep 1862	14 Jan 1863	Sold 29 Nov 1865
Lafayette	W. D. Porter/unknown	1848/24 Sep 1862	27 Feb 1863	Sold 28 Mar 1866
Choctaw	W. D. Porter/unknown	1855/27 Sep 1862	23 Mar 1863	Sold 28 Mar 1866
Eastport		1852/17 Jun 1863	9 Jan 1863	Destroyed 26 Apr 1864
Avenger	New Albany, IN U.S. Army		29 Feb 1864	Sold 29 Nov 1865
Vindicator	New Albany, IN U.S. Army		24 May 1864	Sold 29 Nov 1865
CHAPTER 9				
Osage	Eads/Union	13 Jan 1863	10 Jul 1863	Mined 29 Mar 1865
Neosho	Eads/Union	18 Feb 1863	13 May 1863	Sold 17 Apr 1873
Ozark	Hambleton, Collier/McCord	18 Feb 1863	18 Feb 1864	Sold 29 Nov 1865
Marietta	Tomlinson/Hartupee	4 Jan 1865	16 Dec 1865 (Completed)	Sold 17 Apr 1873
Sandusky	Tomlinson/Hartupee	17 Jan 1865	26 Dec 1865 (Completed)	Sold 17 Apr 1873
Chickasaw	Gaylord/Fulton	10 Feb 1864	14 May 1864	Sold 12 Sep 1874
Kickapoo	G. B. Allen/Fulton	12 Mar 1864	8 Jul 1864	Sold 12 Sep 1874
Milwaukee	Eads/Fulton	4 Feb 1864	27 Aug 1864	Mined 28 Mar 1865
Winnebago	Eads/Fulton	4 Jul 1863	27 Apr 1864	Sold 12 Sep 1874
CHAPTER 10				
Casco	Atlantic/Atlantic	7 May 1864	4 Dec 1864	Broken up 1875
Chimo	Adams/Adams	5 May 1864	20 Jan 1865	Broken up 1875
Cohoes	Continental/Hews & Philips	31 May 1865	19 Jan 1866 (Delivered)	Broken up 1874
Etlah	McCord/McCord	3 Jul 1865	12 Mar 1866	Sold 12 Sep 1874
Klamath	Hambleton/Moore & Richardson	20 Apr 1865	6 May 1866 (Delivered)	Sold 12 Sep 1874

NAME	HULL/MACHINERY	LAUNCHED	COMMISSIONED	FATE
CHAPTER 10 (continued)				
Koka	Wilcox & Whiting	18 May 1865	28 Nov 1865 (Delivered)	Broken up 1874
Modoc	Underhill/Underhill	21 Mar 1865	23 Jun 1865 (Completed)	Broken up 1874
Napa	Harlan & Hollingsworth	26 Nov 1864	4 May 1865 (Completed)	Broken up 1874
Naubuc	Perine/Dolan & Farron	19 Oct 1864	27 Mar 1865	Broken up 1874
Nausett	McKay/McKay & Aldus	26 Apr 1865	10 Aug 1865	Broken up 1874
Shawnee	Curtis & Tilden	13 Mar 1865	18 Aug 1865	Broken up 1875
Shiloh	McCord/McCord	14 Jul 1865	12 Mar 1866 (Delivered)	Sold 1874
Squando	McKay/McKay & Aldus	31 Dec 1864	6 Jun 1865	Broken up 1874
Suncook	Globe/Globe	1 Feb 1865	27 Jul 1865	Broken up 1874
Tunxis	Reaney/Reaney	4 Jun 1864	12 Jul 1864	Broken up 1874
Umpqua	Snowden/Snowden	21 Dec 1865	7 May 1866 (Completed)	Sold 12 Sep 1874
Wassuc	Lawrence/Lawrence	25 Jul 1865	28 Oct 1865 (Completed)	Broken up 1875
Waxsaw	Denmead/Denmead	4 May 1865	21 Oct 1865 (Completed)	Broken up 1874
Yazoo	Cramp/Merrick	8 May 1865	15 Dec 1865 (Completed)	Sold 5 Sep 1874
Yuma	Hambleton/Moore, Richardson	30 May 1865	6 May 1866 (Delivered)	Sold 12 Sep 1874
Kalamazoo	New York Navy Yard/ Delamater			Broken up 1874
Shackamaxon	Philadelphia Navy Yard/ Pusey & Jones			Broken up 1875
Passaconaway	Portsmouth Navy Yard/ Delamater			Broken up 1884
Quinsigamond	Boston Navy Yard/ Alantic			Broken up 1884
Dunderberg	Webb/Etna	22 July 1865		Returned to Webb 1867
CHAPTER 11				
Puritan	Roach/Morgan	6 Dec 1882	10 Dec 1896	Sold 26 Jan 1922
Amphitrite	Harlan & Hollingsworth	7 Jun 1883	23 Apr 1895	Sold 3 Jan 1920
Monadnock	Continental/Vallejo	19 Sep 1883	20 Feb 1896	Sold 24 Aug 1923
Terror	Cramp/Cramp	24 Mar 1883	15 Apr 1896	Sold 10 Mar 1921
Miantonomoh	Roach/Morgan	5 Dec 1876	27 Oct 1891	Sold 26 Jan 1922

Notes

Works frequently cited have been abbreviated as follows:

DANFS	*Dictionary of American Naval Fighting Ships*
JFI	*Journal of the Franklin Institute*
NARS	National Archives and Records Service
ORN	*Official Records of the Union and Confederate Navies in the War of the Rebellion*
OSF	Old Subject File
RG	Record Group
SecNav Reports	*Annual Reports of the Secretary of the Navy*

CHAPTER 1. IRONCLAD PRECEDENTS: PRE–CIVIL WAR PROPOSALS AND THE STEVENS BATTERY

1. Lossing, *Pictorial Field Book of the War of 1812*, 974–75.
2. Baxter, *Introduction of the Ironclad Warship*, 8.
3. Hutcheon, *Robert Fulton*, 134.
4. Canney, *The Old Steam Navy*, vol. 1, *Frigates, Sloops, and Gunboats*, 4–5.
5. Hutcheon, *Robert Fulton*, 145–46.
6. "Uriah Brown," 29th Cong., 2d sess., 20 Jan. 1847, H. Rept. 36.
7. *SecNav Reports*, 1847, 362–66.
8. "Uriah Brown," 1847, H. Rept. 36.
9. Baxter, *Introduction of the Ironclad Warship*, 30, 53, 227.
10. NARS Plan 80-7-15 (James Marsh floating battery); Baxter, *Introduction of the Ironclad Warship*, 8–9; Lossing, *Pictorial Field Book of the War of 1812*, 976.
11. Ridgely-Nevitt, *American Steamships on the Atlantic*, 26; Renwick, *Treatise on the Steam Engine*, 283.
12. Orth, "The Stevens Battery," 761; Baxter, *Introduction of the Ironclad Warship*, 9.
13. Canney, *The Old Steam Navy*, vol. 1, *Frigates, Sloops, and Gunboats*, 4–5.
14. Baxter, *Introduction of the Ironclad Warship*, 20–23; Tucker, *Arming the Fleet*, 177–78.
15. Tucker, *Arming the Fleet*, 183–84; B. Crowninshield to John Rodgers, 29 Feb. 1818, RG 45, Entry 8; L. Warrington to A. Upshur, 30 Oct. 1841, RG 45, Entry 28. The latter discusses Lt. William Porter's audacity in opening up one of these projectiles and indicates the "engagement" to secrecy was not per regulations but only in the original agreement between Stevens and the board.
16. Bauer, *New American State Papers: Naval Affairs*, 4:206.
17. Bauer, *New American State Papers: Naval Affairs*, 4:704–7.
18. "Construction of the Steam Frigate Fulton," 25th Cong., 2d sess., 1837–38, H. Exec. Doc. 433, letter no. 99.
19. *SecNav Reports*, Nov. 1843, 562–63.
20. "U.S. Screw Steamship Princeton," *JFI* 25, no. 6 (June 1853): 382.
21. Orth, "The Stevens Battery," 95; Committee on Naval Affairs, 16 Mar. 1852, 32d Cong., 1st sess., S. Rept. 129, 1; *Harbor Defense*, 27th Cong., 2d sess., 15 Mar. 1842, H. Rept. 448, 11–12.
22. L. Warrington to A. Upshur, 13 Jan. 1842, Letters from Board of Naval Commissioners, RG 45, Entry 28; *Harbor Defense*, H. Rept. 448, 11–12; Orth, "The Stevens Battery," 95.
23. *Harbor Defense*, H. Rept. 448, 12–15.
24. Contract between Robert L. Stevens and Abel P. Upshur, Secretary of the Navy, 10 Feb. 1843, RG 217, Entry 232; Canney, *Old Steam Navy*, vol. 1, *Frigates, Sloops, and Gunboats*, Appendix B.
25. Contract, Robert L. Stevens and Abel P. Upshur, Secretary of the Navy, 10 Feb. 1843, RG 217, Treasury Department Records, Entry 232.
26. Ibid.; Bennett, *Steam Navy of the United States*, Appendix B.
27. Contract, Robert L. Stevens and John Y. Mason, Secretary of the Navy, 14 Nov. 1844, RG 217, Entry 232.
28. Ibid.
29. Report on Stevens's Battery, 16 Mar. 1852, Committee on Naval Affairs, in Bauer, *New American State Papers: Naval Affairs*, 10:263; *SecNav Reports*, Dec. 1849, 433–34.
30. Report on Stevens's Battery, 16 Mar. 1852, Committee on Naval Affairs, in Bauer, *New American State*

Papers, 10:263; "Building of a War Steamer by R. L. Stevens," 27th Cong., 3d sess., 27 Jan. 1843, H. Doc. 98.

31. *U.S. Nautical Magazine and Naval Journal* 3 (Oct. 1855–Mar. 1856): 212–13; Orth, "The Stevens Battery," 95.
32. Ibid.; Bennett, *Steam Navy of the United States*, 58, 59, 70.
33. Baxter, *The Introduction of the Ironclad Warship*, 220. The quote was from a Philadelphia newspaper and appeared in the *Gazette* on 23 Mar. 1861.
34. United States Military Commission to Europe, 1855 to 1856, *Report on the Art of War in Europe* (The Delafield Report), 7 May 1858, 172.
35. Among the NARS records scanned for the mid-1850s were letters in Record Group 45, including Captain's Letters (M125), Letters to Chiefs of Bureaus (M480), Letters from Chiefs of Bureaus (M518), Squadron Letters (M89), Area File (M625); and various entries in Record Group 19 (Bureau of Construction and Repair). Periodicals included the *Journal of the Franklin Institute*, *U.S. Nautical Magazine and Naval Journal*, and the *New York Times*. See Sprout and Sprout, *The Rise of American Naval Power*, 150.

CHAPTER 2. IRONCLADS INCHOATE, 1861

1. Still, *Iron Afloat*, 10–11.
2. Baxter, *Introduction of the Ironclad Warship*, 222; Lossing, *Pictorial History of the Civil War*, 1:312.
3. Still, *Iron Afloat*, 10–11.
4. Ibid.
5. Baxter, *Introduction of the Ironclad Warship*, 219.
6. J. Lenthall to I. Toucey, 4 Feb. 1861, RG 19, Entry 49.
7. Baxter, *Introduction of the Ironclad Warship*, 221.
8. R. Bristol to G. Welles, 16 Apr. 1861, Gideon Welles Papers, Library of Congress.
9. T. Rowland to G. Welles, 30 May 1861, Welles Papers; Specification of C. W. Whitney's Iron Mail Clad Floating Battery or Steam Gun Boat, 23 Apr. 1861, NARS 80-11-28.
10. Baxter, *Introduction of the Ironclad Warship*, 239–40.
11. J. Lenthall, 11 May 1861, quoted in Baxter, *Introduction of the Ironclad Warship*, 242.
12. *Report of the Secretary of the Navy in Relation to Armored Vessels*, 1864, 1.
13. J. Laird to G. Welles, 30 May 61, Welles Papers, box 4, New York Public Library.
14. Draft of Gunboat by Mr. Lenthall, *Annual Report of the Secretary of War*, 37th Cong., 3d sess., 1 June 1861, H. Exec. Doc. 1, 87.
15. Weigley, *Quartermaster General of the Union Army*, 241; M. C. Meigs to G. McClellan, 17 June 1861, Montgomery Meigs Papers, Library of Congress; Plan for Gunboat "with iron plates," by S. M. Pook, 2 July 1861, neg. no. 92-x-8, RG 92, Entry 1403.
16. *Report of the Secretary of the Navy in Relation to Armored Vessels*, 1–2.
17. Ibid.
18. Sloan, *Benjamin Franklin Isherwood*, 50.
19. *Report of the Secretary of the Navy in Relation to Armored Vessels*, 2.
20. "Particulars and Performance of the U.S. Steamer *Wyoming*," *JFI* 38 (Oct. 1859): 267–68.

21. NARS Plan 80-1-4.
22. NARS Plan 80-10-17.
23. Plans for "Armored Steam Corvette," by John W. Nystrom, 29 Aug. 1861, RG 71, Entry 76.
24. Ibid.
25. Ibid.
26. NARS Plan 80-8-11.
27. Memorandum, n.d., Welles Papers, box 5, New York Public Library.
28. *Report of the Secretary of the Navy in Relation to Armored Vessels*, 5–7.
29. Ibid., 3.
30. Ibid., 3–4.
31. Ibid.
32. Ibid., 5.
33. G. Welles to C. H. Davis, 11 Feb. 1863, RG 45, M480.
34. "Report of Naval Board on the Stevens Battery," *JFI* 43 (Mar. 1862): 152–53.
35. Ibid.
36. Ibid.
37. *Scientific American* 5, no. 9 (31 Aug. 1861): 129.
38. Ibid.; "The Stevens Battery," n.d., description found at Stevens Institute of Technology (SIT), Hoboken, N.J.
39. Orth, "The Stevens Battery," 8–9.
40. "Report of Naval Board on the Stevens Battery," 150.
41. "The Stevens Battery" (SIT).
42. "Report of Naval Board on the Stevens Battery," 156–62.
43. Still, *Iron Afloat*, 50–51.

CHAPTER 3. FIRST-GENERATION COASTAL IRONCLADS: NEW IRONSIDES, GALENA, AND MONITOR

1. Bennett, *Steam Navy of the United States*, 272–74.
2. Earliest references to the ship delete the word *New* from her name and *Ironsides* was her original official designation. Eventually the popular usage prevailed.
3. William H. Roberts, "The Neglected Ironclad: A Design and Constructional Analysis of the USS *New Ironsides*," *Warship International* 26, no. 2 (1989): 110; "Editorial: The USS Armored Frigate *New Ironsides*," *JFI* 53, no. 2 (Feb. 1867): 79.
4. NARS Plans 107-9-12K and 107-9-12M; "Editorial: *New Ironsides*," 76.
5. "Editorial: *New Ironsides*," 76–77.
6. Lambert, *Warrior: Restoring the World's First Ironclad*, 67–69.
7. "Editorial: *New Ironsides*," 77.
8. Roberts, "The Neglected Ironclad," 111–12; "Editorial: *New Ironsides*," 77; B. H. Bartol to J. Smith, 9 Jan. 1862, RG 71, Entry 5; Plan and Specifications of bulkheads, B. H. Bartol, with letter from Bartol to J. Smith, 9 Jan. 1862, RG 45, OSF, AD box 51.
9. NARS Plan 1206, RG 74.
10. Hill, *Twenty-six Historic Ships*, 330; NARS Plan 1206, RG 74; J. Lenthall to C. Stribling, 23 Apr. 1863, RG 19, Entry 52; J. Lenthall to C. Stribling, 5 Oct. 1863, RG 19, Entry 54.
11. Roberts, "The Neglected Ironclad," 111.
12. "Editorial: *New Ironsides*," 76.
13. J. Smith to G. Welles, 24 Apr. 1862, RG 71, Entry 1.
14. Roberts, "The Neglected Ironclad," 110–11.
15. Gun deck of *New Ironsides*, NARS Plan 1206, RG 74.

16. "Editorial: *New Ironsides*," 77–78; Roberts, "The Neglected Ironclad," 110–11; *Scientific American* 9, no. 15 (10 Oct. 1863): 231.
17. NARS Plan 107-9-12M; T. Turner to S. Dupont, 6 Feb. 1863, *ORN* 13:646–47.
18. Sail Plan, NARS Plan 67-9-12L, RG 19.
19. Roberts, "The Neglected Ironclad," 114, 133.
20. Hill, *Twenty-six Historic Ships*, 330.
21. Roberts, "The Neglected Ironclad," 114, 119, 121; T. Turner to S. Dupont, 19 Jan. 1863, *ORN*, 13:518–19; W. Radford, Sailing Quality Report, RG 45, OSF, AD box 52; Roberts, "The Neglected Ironclad," 130.
22. T. Turner to S. Dupont, 19 Jan. 1863, *ORN*, 13:518–19.
23. S. C. Rowan to Dahlgren, 3 Oct. 1863, *ORN*, 15:25–26.
24. Tucker, *Arming the Fleet*, 221; Naval History Division, *Civil War Naval Ordnance*, 5.
25. S. C. Rowan to Dahlgren, 13 May 1864, *ORN*, 14:605.
26. "Editorial: *New Ironsides*," 80–81; T. Bishop to S. Rowan, 9 Sept. 1863, *ORN*, 14:555–56; S. Rowan to J. Dahlgren, 10 Sept. 1863, *ORN*, 14:553–54.
27. Roberts, "The Neglected Ironclad," 125.
28. *DANFS*, 5:58–59.
29. *DANFS*, 5:59; J. Thomas Scharf, *History of the Confederate States Navy*, 758.
30. Porter, *Naval History of the Civil War*, 716.
31. Bennett, *Steam Navy of the United States*, 272.
32. S. H. Pook to C. Bushnell, Sept. 1861, NARS Plan 28-6-3, RG 19; "Specifications for Bomb Proof Steam Screw Gun Boats as Proposed by Cornelius S. Bushnell & Co.," 28 June 1861, Bushnell Papers, New-York Historical Society; *Scientific American* 6, no. 15 (19 Apr. 1862): 244.
33. "Specifications," Bushnell Papers; "Proposed Plan for Bomb Proof Steam Gunboat," NARS Plan 28-6-2J; "Gunboats, June, 1861," NARS Plan 79-5-21; Isherwood, *Experimental Researches in Steam Engineering*, 2:452.
34. NARS Plans 79-5-21 and 28-6-2J; Baxter, *Introduction of the Ironclad Warship*, 253; Christley, "Mystic River Builds an Ironclad," 130–31.
35. J. Smith, H. Paulding, and C. H. Davis to G. Welles, 6 Sept. 1861, RG 71, Entry 1.
36. "Cross-section at Engines," NARS Plan 28-6-2C.
37. "Specifications," Sept. 1861, NARS Plan 28-6-3; plan by S. H. Pook, Miscellaneous Letters, RG 71, Entry 5.
38. NARS Plans 28-6-2H, 28-6-2C, 28-6-2J.
39. Christley, "Mystic River Builds an Ironclad," 132; Diary of William Ellery Maxson, G. W. Blunt White Library, Mystic Seaport Museum.
40. Maxson diary, G. W. Blunt White Library, Mystic Seaport Museum; T. Rowland to J. Winslow, 4 Dec. 1861, Griswold Papers, Monitor Book, Smithsonian Institution.
41. J. Smith to J. Winslow, 5 Dec. 1861, Griswold Papers, Smithsonian Institution; Contract Addendum, n.d., Griswold Papers, Smithsonian Institution; J. Smith to C. Bushnell, 3 Dec. 1861, RG 45, OSF, AD box 51; S. Pook to J. Smith, 21 Jan. 1862, RG 45, OSF, AD box 51.
42. J. Smith to S. Pook, 8 March 1862, RG 45, OSF, AD box 51; J. Faron to J. Smith, 31 March 1862, RG 45, OSF, AD box 51; Maxson Diary, G. W. Blunt White Library, Mystic Seaport Museum.
43. J. Smith to S. Pook, 21 Oct. 1861, RG 45, OSF, AD box 51.
44. "Deck Log of *Galena*," April 1862, RG 24.
45. L. Goldsborough to G. Fox, 24 and 28 Apr. 1862, in Thompson and Wainwright, *Correspondence of Gustavus V. Fox* 1:263, 265; J. S. Misroon to L. Goldsborough, 22 Apr. 1862, *ORN*, 7:257.
46. *Battles and Leaders of the Civil War*, 2:269.
47. Ibid., 1:711; Faust, *Encyclopedia of the Civil War*, 227.
48. *Battles and Leaders of the Civil War*, 2:269.
49. J. Rodgers to L. Goldsborough, 16 May 1862, *ORN*, 7:357; "Deck Log of *Galena*," 15 May 1862, RG 24.
50. R. E. Gieson [Surgeon] to J. Rodgers, 16 May 1862, *ORN*, 7:358–59.
51. J. Smith, H. Paulding, C. H. Davis, to G. Welles, 6 Sept. 1861, RG 71, Entry 1.
52. J. Lenthall to C. Stribling, 13 May 63, RG 19, Entry 52; J. Lenthall to C. Stribling, 13 and 30 May 1863, RG 19, Entry 54; NARS Plan 78-3-3X.
53. *DANFS*, 3:7.
54. Clark, *My Fifty Years in the Navy*, 166. This statement was made by Rodgers himself to Rear Admiral Clark and quoted in a book published in 1917; no doubt it was not verbatim. Clark's decription of its impact on him, however, is so powerful that one cannot doubt that the gist is accurate.
55. Church, *The Life of John Ericsson*, 249–50; Beale, *Diary of Gideon Welles*, 1:214. Yet another version quoted in the 1885 *Magazine of American History* ("Building of the Monitor" by Francis B. Wheeler), involves the mediation of Messrs. Griswold and Winslow on behalf of Ericsson and Bushnell. This story, incidentally, gives Winslow entire credit for convincing the department of the merits of Ericsson's scheme. See *Project Cheesebox*, 1:70–71.
56. Church, *The Life of John Ericsson*, 1:238–41.
57. J. Ericsson to G. Fox, 5 Oct. 1875, Fox Papers, New-York Historical Society.
58. "Letter from the Secretary of the Navy transmitting . . . information . . . in relation to . . . the *Monitor*," 40th Cong., 2d sess., S. Exec. Doc. 86, 6–8.
59. Baxter, *The Introduction of the Ironclad Warship*, 261–62.
60. Eskew, "Our Navy's Ships and Their Builders, 1775-1883," 426.
61. "The Ericsson Battery," *Scientific American* 5, no. 21 (23 Nov. 1861): 331.
62. Peterkin, *Drawings of the USS Monitor*, 66–78, 186-201.
63. "Specifications of an Impregnable Floating Battery," *Project Cheesebox*, 1:101; Peterkin, *Drawings of the USS Monitor*, 180–89.
64. Peterkin, *Drawings of the USS Monitor*, 178–81; Thompson, "The Design and Construction of USS *Monitor*," 228–34.
65. J. Ericsson to J. Smith, 17 Dec. 1861, *Project Cheesebox*, 1:168; Peterkin, *Drawings of the USS Monitor*, 136–65.
66. Peterkin, *Drawings of the USS Monitor*, 184–85.
67. Ibid., 186–87.
68. J. Ericsson, "Specification of an Impregnable Floating Battery," *Project Cheesebox*, 1:105.
69. NARS Plan 26-8-21; "The Ericsson Battery," *Scientific American* 5, no. 21 (23 Nov. 1861): 331.

70. Peterkin, *Drawings of the USS Monitor*, 214–15; Thanks to Sam Hicks, whose expertise in CAD three-dimensional drawing enabled the visualization and drawings of the *Monitor* used in this chapter.
71. Peterkin, *Drawings of the USS Monitor*, 230–31.
72. "Specifications," *Project Cheesebox*, 1:101.
73. J. Ericsson to J. Smith, n.d., ibid., 1:137.
74. Peterkin, *Drawings of the USS Monitor*, 190–91; *Scientific American* 9, no. 22 (12 Dec. 1863): 372.
75. "I. N.," "The Monitor Ironclads," 1864, *Project Cheesebox*, 2:520. "Isaac Newton" was an Ericsson apologist.
76. Chapelle, *History of the American Sailing Navy*, 200; Baxter, *The Introduction of the Ironclad Warship*, 188–94; Stern, *Confederate Navy*, 158–59.
77. Ericsson to Smith, 25 Oct. 1861, *Project Cheesebox*, 1:106–7, 159; Thompson, "Design and Construction of USS *Monitor*, 225; Isaac Newton, "Shot Proof Vessels: Ericsson's Battery," *JFI* 43, no. 2 (Feb. 1862): 81.
78. *Project Cheesebox*, 1:107–8; Peterkin, *Drawings of the USS Monitor*, 448–49, 467–69.
79. "Specifications," *Project Cheesebox*, 1:106–7; Ericsson to Smith, 27 Sept. 1862, ibid., 127; Ericsson to Smith, 25 Oct. 1862, 159; Peterkin, *Drawings of the USS Monitor*, 435–47.
80. Peterkin, *Drawings of the USS Monitor*, 435–45, 489–91.
81. J. Ericsson to J. Smith, n.d., *Project Cheesebox*, 1:133; Peterkin, *Drawings of the USS Monitor*, 472–73.
82. Peterkin, *Drawings of the USS Monitor*, 293–95; *ORN*, series no. 2, vol. 1, 72.
83. *Project Cheesebox*, 1:109; *Scientific American* (12 Dec. 1863): 373; Isherwood, *Experimental Researches in Steam Engineering*, vol. 1, plate 16; Newton to Jeffers, 2 June 1862, *ORN*, 7:450; Goldsborough to Fox, 6 June 1862, *ORN*, 7:455–56.
84. "Specifications," *Project Cheesebox*, 1:110; NARS Plan 26-8-21.
85. Ericsson to Smith, 18 Oct. 1861, Ericsson Papers, Library of Congress; Plan 19, Oct. 1861, RG 71, Entry 5, box 447, Miscellaneous Letters.
86. Stimers to Smith (telegram), 17 Feb. 1862, RG 45, OSF, AD box 47.
87. NARS Plan 26-8-20, 28 Sept. 1861?; Miller, *USS Monitor: The Ship That Launched a Modern Navy*, 54.
88. Thompson, "Design and Construction of USS *Monitor*," 225; Peterkin, *Drawings of the USS Monitor*, 511–50.
89. Daly, *Aboard the USS Monitor, 1862*, 25–27, 48, 62.
90. Thompson, "Design and Construction of USS *Monitor*," 237.
91. Beach, *The United States Navy*, 297.
92. Jeffers to Goldsborough, 22 May 1862, *ORN*, 7:410–13.
93. Daly, *Aboard the USS Monitor*, 232–33; Peterkin, *Drawings of the USS Monitor*, 66–78.
94. *Project Cheesebox*, 3:435–41.
95. J. P. Bankhead to S. P. Lee, 1 Jan. 1863, *ORN*, 8:349.
96. Church, *The Life of John Ericsson*, 2:115.
97. W. L. Barnes to Griswold, 31 Dec. 62, Griswold Papers, Smithsonian Institution.

CHAPTER 4. RIVERBOATS OF WAR: WOOD- AND IRONCLAD CONVERSIONS, 1861–1862

1. King, *Lessons and Practical Notes on Steam*, 159–70.
2. A. M. Pennock to J. B. Hull, 12 Sept. 1862, *ORN*, 23:353–54.
3. D. Porter to G. Welles, Nov. 1863, *ORN*, 25:595–96.
4. A. M. Pennock to S. L. Phelps, 19 Mar. 1863, S. L. Phelps Papers, Missouri Historical Society.
5. *ORN*, ser. 2, vol. 1, 46, 168.
6. Quoted in Theodore Roscoe and Fred Freeman, *Picture History of the U.S. Navy* (Bonanza Books, 1956), entry no. 903.
7. RG 92, Entry 1403, box 39.
8. Paul H. Silverstone, *Warships of the Civil War Navies*, 158–59.
9. J. Rodgers to G. Welles, 7 Sept. 1861, *ORN*, 22:319.
10. S. L. Phelps to J. Rodgers, 21 July 1861, *ORN*, 22;290; ibid., 25 July 1861, 292; Silverstone, *Warships of the Civil War Navies*, 158–59.
11. *Battles and Leaders of the Civil War*, 1:453–54; E. Stanton to C. Ellet, Jr., 27 Mar. 1862, *ORN*, 22:680.
12. *Battles and Leaders of the Civil War*, 1:453–54.
13. "Naval Vessels," 7 May 1868, 40th Cong., 2d sess., Exec. Doc. 280.
14. C. Ellet, Jr., to Lt. W. McGunnegle, 27 Apr. 1862, *ORN*, 23:79.
15. Lossing, *Pictorial History of the Civil War*, 2:588–89; *ORN*, 23:523–24, 608.
16. *ORN*, ser. 2, vol. 1, 79; Wegner, "S.X.," 49–51.
17. Ibid., 49.
18. Ibid., 50–52; Moore, *Rebellion Record*, 4:76, 78.
19. Moore, *Rebellion Record*, 4:78; *Battles and Leaders of the Civil War*, 1:364.
20. T. Adams to M. C. Meigs, 5 Mar. 1862, RG 92, Entry 1403, box 40; W. D. Porter to A. H. Foote, 20 Apr. 1862, RG 92, Entry 1403, box 39; Wegner, "S.X.," 51–53; G. D. Wise to A. H. Foote, 25 May 1862, *ORN*, 23:106.
21. Way, *Way's Packet Directory, 1848–1983*, 154, 343; *ORN*, ser. 2, vol. 1, 79; Moore, *Rebellion Record*, 4:78; Gosnell, *Guns on the Western Waters*, 52.
22. Wegner, "S.X.," 51.
23. W. D. Porter to G. Welles, 6 May 1862, *ORN*. 23:83: "Only one penetrated the outer hull, or sponson."
24. Wegner, "S.X.," 50–54.
25. C. Caldwell to D. G. Farragut, 20 Sept. 1862, *ORN*, 19:319–20.
26. Ibid.
27. Ibid.
28. *ORN*, ser. 2, vol. 1, 79–80; Wegner, "S.X.," 52.
29. D. G. Farragut to G. Welles, 25 June 1863, *ORN*, 20:314.
30. E. Bates to J. Eads, 17 Apr. 1861, Eads Papers, Missouri Historical Society.
31. J. Eads to G. Welles, 29 Apr. 1861, *ORN*, 22:278.
32. *ORN*, 22: 277–80.
33. J. Eads to G. Welles, 8 May 1861, G. Welles Papers, Library of Congress.
34. J. Fremont to J. B. Eads, n.d., Eads Papers, Missouri Historical Society; Barton Able to J. B. Eads, 3 Sept. 1861, Eads Papers.

35. James B. Eads, "Recollections of Foote and the Gunboats," in *Battles and Leaders of the Civil War*, 1:339–40.
36. J. Eads to E. Bates, 10 Nov. 1861, Eads Papers, Missouri Historical Society; J. Greer to D. D. Porter, 30 Apr. 1863, *ORN*, 24:613.
37. Silverstone, *Warships of the Civil War Navies*, 155; J. Eads to G. Welles, 29 Apr. 1861, *ORN*, 22:278; J. Eads to E. Bates, 10 Nov. 1861, Eads Papers, Missouri Historical Society.
38. J. Eads to E. Bates, 10 Nov. 1861, Eads Papers, Missouri Historical Society; Plan, Deck, and Profile, USS *Benton*, Smithsonian Institution.
39. *ORN*, ser. 2, vol. 1, 44.
40. A. Pennock and R. Stembel to A. Foote, 17 Jan. 1862, and A. Foote to G. Welles, 22 Jan. 1862, RG 45, M89, reel 123; A. Foote to M. Meigs, 15 Jan. 1862, RG 92, Entry 1403, box 39.
41. Telegrams, A. Foote to M. Meigs, 24 Jan. 1862, and H. A. Wise to A. Foote, 28 Jan. 1862, *ORN*, 22:520; C. H. Davis to G. Welles, 16 July 1862, *Report on Armored Vessels, 1864*, 407; D. D. Porter to G. Welles, 31 Dec. 1862, ibid., 420).
42. Tony Gibbons, *Warships and Naval Battles of the Civil War*, 13.

CHAPTER 5. CITY-CLASS IRONCLADS

1. G. Welles to J. Rodgers, 16 May 1861, *ORN*, 22:280; G. Welles to S. M. Pook, 20 May 1861, ibid., 281.
2. J. Lenthall, "Memorandum for Gen'l Totten," 1 June 1861, RG 92, Entry 1403, box 39.
3. Ibid; Totten to Scott, 3 June 1861, RG 92, Entry 1403, box 39.
4. Report of the Secretary of War, 37th Cong., 3d sess., 1861, H. Exec. Doc. 1, 90.
5. T. Cunningham to J. Gregory, 28 Jan. 1864, RG 19, Entry 64, box 5; Boggs and Mitchell to Gregory, 27 Jan. 1864, ibid. These obscure vessels were also referred to as armed transports and one was named *Burnside*. The extent of their service is unknown.
6. M. C. Meigs to G. McClellan, 17 June 1861, M. C. Meigs Papers, Library of Congress.
7. Pook Plan, National Archives neg. no. 92-x-8; "Specifications for building a Gun-boat," RG 92, Entry 1403, box 39.
8. "Abstract of Bids," 6 Aug. 1861, RG 92, E 1403, box 39.
9. McGrath and Ashley, *Historic Structure Report: USS Cairo*, 15.
10. Ibid., 73–74.
11. Ibid., 144–50; "Specifications for Building a Gun-Boat," RG 92, Entry 1403, box 39.
12. NARS Plan 92-x-92; McGrath and Ashley, *Historic Structure Report: USS Cairo*, 147.
13. *Battles and Leaders of the Civil War*, 1:434.
14. Geoghegan, "Study for a Scale Model of the USS *Carondelet*," 234; McGrath and Ashley, *Historic Structure Report: USS Cairo*, 144.
15. *Harper's Weekly*, 20 June 1863 (Naval History Center photograph NH58761).
16. Elizabeth Joyner (National Park Service), conversation with author, 2 Mar. 1991, Vicksburg National Military Park, Vicksburg, Mississippi.
17. "Specifications," RG 92, Entry 1403.
18. McGrath and Ashley, *Historic Structure Report: USS Cairo*, 33; J. Rodgers to J. Eads, 10 Aug. 1861, J. Rodgers Papers, Library of Congress.
19. Ibid.
20. McGrath and Ashley, *Historic Structure Report: USS Cairo*, 33, 39.
21. D. D. Porter to G. Welles, 12 Dec. 1862, *ORN*, 23:543.
22. Ibid., 19 May 1864, 26:156.
23. "Description of Drawings for Engines" and drawings by S. H. Whitmore, written description and drawings by A. Thomas Merritt, 1861, RG 92, Entry 1403, box 40.
24. B. Isherwood to G. Welles, 20 July 1861, RG 92, Entry 1403, box 40.
25. King, *Lessons and Practical Notes on Steam*, 158–60.
26. Ibid; NARS Plans 92-x-9 and 92-x-11; American Society of Mechanical Engineers, *USS Cairo Engine and Boilers*, n.p.
27. King, *Lessons and Practical Notes on Steam*, 158–60; NARS Plans 92-x-9 and 92-x-11; American Society of Mechanical Engineers, *USS Cairo Engine and Boilers*, n.p.; J. B. Eads, article in the *Missouri Democrat*, vol. 11, no date, RG 92, Entry 1403, box 39.
28. Moore, *Rebellion Record*, 4:428 (from the *Saint Louis Democrat*, Mar. 1862).
29. McGrath and Ashley, *Historic Structure Report: USS Cairo*, 34; American Society of Mechanical Engineers, *USS Cairo Engine and Boilers*.
30. See *ORN*, ser. 2, vol. 1, under specific ship names.
31. McGrath and Ashley, *Historic Structure Report: USS Cairo*, 34; Information from Vicksburg National Military Park ("Identification colors for chimney bands," credited to Mrs. Edwin C. Bearss from a list by a Mr. Shepard, engineer on the *Carondelet*); Naval Historical Center photo no. 72806; General Order No. 46, D. D. Porter, 11 Apr. 1863, *ORN*, 24:540.
32. *ORN*, 25:162.
33. J. Winslow to A. Foote, 29 Nov. 1861, RG 92, Entry 1403, box 39.
34. *Battles and Leaders of the Civil War*, 1:438.
35. A. Foote to H. Halleck with enclosure by H. A. Wise, 13 Mar. 1862, *ORN*, 22:688–89.
36. *ORN*, 23:171–81.
37. W. T. Sherman to D. D. Porter, 28 May 1863, *ORN*, 25:38–39.
38. G. M. Bache to D. D. Porter, 29 May 1863, *ORN*, 25:38.
39. Porter, *Naval History of the Civil War*, 323.
40. J. G. Walker to D. D. Porter, 12 Jan. 1863, *Report on Armored Vessels, 1864*, 428.
41. A. H. Foote to G. Welles, 15 Feb. 1862, *ORN*, 22:585.
42. Porter to Welles, 12 Jan. 1863, *ORN*, 8:484; *Report on Armored Vessels, 1864*, 428; Bache to Porter, 29 May 1863, *ORN*, 25:38–39.
43. Silverstone, *Warships of the Civil War Navies*, 152.
44. Ibid., 151.
45. Ibid., 153.

CHAPTER 6. SECOND-GENERATION COASTAL IRONCLADS, 1862

1. Baxter, *Introduction of the Ironclad Warship*, 275.
2. Lenthall to Welles, 13 Mar. 1862, RG 19, Entry 49.

3. "Building Instructions for an Iron-Clad Steam Battery," NARS Plan 142-10-14; Baxter, *Introduction of the Ironclad Warship*, 274.

4. "Building Instructions for an Iron-Clad Steam Battery," NARS Plan 142-10-14; Isherwood, *Experimental Researches in Steam Engineering*, 1:160.

5. Ibid.

6. "Specifications of the Iron Armature and Other Exterior Iron Work of a Steam Battery," 20 Dec. 1861, NARS Plan 142-10-14; Baxter, *Introduction of the Ironclad Warship*, 187, 189.

7. "Specifications of the Iron Armature and Other Exterior Iron Work of a Steam Battery," 20 Dec. 1861, NARS Plan 142-10-14; Baxter, *Introduction of the Ironclad Warship*, 276.

8. J. Griswold to J. Ericsson, 24 Jan. 1862, Griswold Papers, "Monitor Book," Smithsonian Institution; Baxter, *Introduction of the Ironclad Warship*, 279–81.

9. J. Laird to G. Welles, 30 May 1861, Welles Papers, New-York Historical Society.

10. Baxter, *Introduction of the Ironclad Warship*, 270.

11. Ibid., 273–74.

12. D. Martin to Lenthall, 9 Jan., 6 Feb., 7 Feb., 18 Feb., 25 Jan., 21 Feb. 1862, RG 19, Entry 61; Beale, *The Diary of Gideon Welles*, 1:291.

13. T. H. Galliger to A. H. Foote, 29 Mar. 1862, and J. Smith to T. H. Galliger, 16 July 1862, RG 45, OSF, AD.

14. Report from Isherwood, Lenthall, E. Hartt, and D. Martin, 10 May 1862, RG 45, M518, reel 17.

15. Ibid.

16. Ibid.

17. J. Smith to G. Welles, 10 May 1862, RG 71, Entry 1.

18. J. Lenthall and B. Isherwood to G. Welles, 17 Mar. 1862, RG 19, Entry 49.

19. Ibid.; Baxter, *Introduction of the Ironclad Warship*, 303.

20. B. Isherwood to G. Welles, 19 Mar. 1862, RG 45, M518; J. Lenthall and B. Isherwood to G. Welles, 19 Mar. 1862, RG 19, Entry 49.

21. Ibid.

22. Contract and Specifications, Novelty Iron Works, 3 Apr. 1862, RG 217, Entry 232; *Scientific American* 7, no. 4 (26 July 1862): 57.

23. *Scientific American* 7, no. 4 (26 July 1862): 57.

24. B. Isherwood to G. Welles (annotation by J. Lenthall), 19 Mar. 1862, RG 45, M 518; *Scientific American* 8, no. 5 (31 Jan. 1863): 73–76; NARS Plan 1-10-18.

25. *Scientific American* 7, no. 4 (26 July 1862): 57.

26. Ibid., vol. 7, no. 23 (6 Dec. 1862): 362.

27. Ibid., vol. 8, no. 5 (31 Jan. 1863): 74–75.

28. Ibid., vol. 7, no. 4 (26 July 1862): 57.

29. Goldsborough Board Report, *SecNav Reports*, 1869, 158; NARS Plans 1-10-18 and 79-2-31.

30. Reprinted in *Army and Navy Journal*, 3 Oct. 1863, 87.

31. B. Sands to G. Welles, 11 July 1863, *ORN*, 9:119.

32. Deck Logs, USS *Roanoke*, 1863–65, RG 24.

33. Alden, "Born Forty Years Too Soon," 257.

34. Ibid.

35. Annotation by G. Fox on B. Isherwood to G. Welles, 19 Mar. 1862, RG 45, M518.

36. T. Zeller to Gregory, 15 Jan. and 15 Feb. 1863, and T. Zeller to J. Lenthall, 27 Sept. 1862, RG 19, Entry 64.

37. *Scientific American* 9, no. 69 (8 Aug. 1863): 83; T. Zeller to Gregory, 15 Jan. 1863, RG 19, Entry 64.

38. J. Lenthall to Gregory, 25 Apr. 1863, RG 19, Entry 52; A. Henderson, to Gregory, 30 Nov. 1863, RG 19, Entry 64; Henderson to Sewell, 20 Jan. 1864, RG 19, Entry 64.

39. Board Report on Ironclad Proposals, 10 May 1862, RG 45, M518; "L'Onondaga, Garde-Cote Cuirasse a Deux Tourelles," *Revue Maritime et Coloniale*, February 1870, 107.

40. J. Lenthall to Gregory, 28 Apr. 1863, RG 19, Entry 52; *Scientific American* 8, no. 21 (23 May 1863): 330; ibid., vol. 9, no. 6 (8 Aug. 1863): 83.

41. Board Report on Proposals, 10 May 1862, RG 45, M518; NARS Plan 1-9-38.

42. NARS Plan 1-9-38.

43. Sewell to Gregory, 17 July 1863, RG 19, Entry 64; C. Wilkins C—— [illegible] to Gregory, 1 Aug. 1863, RG 19, Entry 64.

44. Ibid.

45. *Certain War Vessels Built in 1862–1865*, 57th Cong., 1st sess., 17 June 1902, S. Rept. 1942, 42–43.

46. NARS Plans 1-9-37 and 1-9-38.

47. "Naval Vessels," 40th Cong., 2d sess., 7 May 1868, H. Exec. Doc. 280, 9.

48. Gregory to Lenthall, 24 Feb. 1864, RG 19, Entry 64; A. Henderson to Sewell, 20 Jan. 1864, RG 19, Entry 64.

49. D. D. Porter to W. A. Parker, 2 Dec. 1864, *ORN*, 11:120.

50. J. K. Mitchell to S. R. Mallory, 3 Feb. 1865, *ORN*, l:11, 670.

51. "L'Onondaga, Garde-Cote Cuirasse a Deux Tourelles," 98–108.

52. J. Lenthall to Philadelphia, Portsmouth, Boston, and New York navy yards, 9 July 1862, Fox Papers, New-York Historical Society.

53. G. Welles to J. Dahlgren, 3 Aug. 1862, RG 45, M480.

54. *Army and Navy Journal*, 31 Oct. 1863, 158.

55. Van Dusen, *Connecticut*, 37.

56. *Army and Navy Journal*, 24 July 1869, 774.

57. J. Lenthall to Portsmouth, Philadelphia, New York, and Boston navy yards, 9 July 1862, Fox Papers, New-York Historical Society.

58. J. Lenthall to Portsmouth, New York, Boston, and Philadelphia navy yards, 2 Sept. 1862, Fox Papers, New-York Historical Society; Lenthall to Pearson, 2 Sept. 1862, RG 181, Entry 16.

59. NARS Plans 101-10-5 and 136-9-49.

60. Ibid.

61. J. Lenthall to yards, 9 July 1862, Fox Papers, New-York Historical Society; NARS Plan 136-9-39; Bureau of Steam Engineering Plans, NARS, *Miantonomoh;* "Le Miantonomoh, Monitor a Tourelles des Etats-Unis," *Revue Maritime et Coloniale* 19 (Mar. 1867): 546.

62. NARS Plans 104-3-32 and 136-9-49.

63. NARS Plan 101-10-5.

64. *Army and Navy Journal*, 26 Mar. 1864, 517.

65. *SecNav Reports*, 1869, 195.

66. J. Berrien to D. Porter (annotation by Porter), 15 Nov. 1864, *ORN*, 11:600–2.

67. Godon to G. Welles, 31 May 1865, *ORN*, 3:535.

68. F. Bunce to J. Rodgers, 11 and 26 Nov. 1865, John Rodgers Papers (Rodgers Family Papers), Library of Congress; Johnson, *Rear Admiral John Rodgers*, 283–84.
69. J. Rodgers to G. Welles, 8 Jan. and 28 June 1866, and F. Bunce to J. Rodgers, 11 Nov. 1865, Rodgers Papers, Library of Congress.
70. NARS Plan 104-3-32.
71. NARS Plans 104-3-32 and 136-9-49.
72. Ibid.
73. Contract, Novelty Works, 1 Mar. 1863, RG 217, Entry 232.
74. NARS Plans 2-11-53 and 77-3-17.
75. Ibid.
76. Ibid.
77. G. Fox to L. Goldsborough, 16 June 1866, Fox Papers, New-York Historical Society; Church, *Life of John Ericsson*, 2:78–79.
78. Ammen, *The Old Navy and the New*, 421.
79. NARS Plan 2-11-52.
80. *Naval Vessels*, 40th Cong., 2d sess., 7 May 1868, H. Doc. 280, 6–10.
81. "Modifications in regard to Specifications of C. W. Whitney's Vessel," NARS Plan 80-11-28.
82. NARS Plan 107-15-23C.
83. "Specifications of C. W. Whitney's Iron Mail Clad Floating Battery or Steam Gun Boat," NARS Plan 80-11-28.
84. *Scientific American* 7, no. 25 (20 Dec. 1862): 386; NARS Plan 80-11-28.
85. NARS Plan 80-11-28.
86. "Specifications," NARS Plans 107-15-23A and 80-11-28; *Scientific American* 7, no. 25 (20 Dec. 1862): 386.
87. NARS Plan 107-15-23C.
88. *Scientific American* 7, no. 25 (20 Dec. 1862): 386; NARS Plan 80-11-28A.
89. C. Whitney to Gregory, 28 Feb. 1863, RG 19, Entry 64; Gregory to J. Lenthall, 24 Nov. 1863, ibid.; A. Rhind to G. Fox, 10 Mar. 1863, Fox Papers, New-York Historical Society; A. Stimers to Gregory, 22 Nov. 1862, RG 19, Entry 65; Plan, "Ironclad Keokuk," engraving by Charles H. Corbett, 1863, New-York Historical Society.
90. A. Rhind to G. Fox, 20 Mar. 1863, Fox Papers, New-York Historical Society; Gregory to Lenthall, 11 Apr. 1863, RG 19, Entry 64; A. C. Rhind to S. F. DuPont, 21 Mar. 1863, *ORN*, 13:787.
91. A. C. Rhind to S. F. DuPont, 8 Apr. 1863, *ORN*, 14:23–24.
92. A. Stimers to Gregory, 15 Sept. 1862, RG 19, Entry 64; A. Rhind to G. Fox, 29 Mar. 1863, Fox Papers, New-York Historical Society.
93. Letter from Whitney to DuPont, *New York Times*, 21 Apr. 1863, RG 45, OSF, box 50; C. Whitney to Gregory, 11 Apr. 1863, RG 19, Entry 64.
94. Coker, *Charleston's Maritime Heritage, 1670–1865*, 244.
95. Redmond, "The Revenue Steamer *E. A. Stevens* in the Civil War," 155–57.
96. Ibid.
97. Ibid.
98. *The Engineer*, 24 Apr. 1863, 230.
99. Redmond, "The Revenue Steamer *E. A. Stevens* in the Civil War," 156.
100. Ibid.; D. Campbell to Stanton, 17 May 1862, and D. Constable to S. C. Chase, 9 May 1862, *ORN*, 7:367, 332–33; *Scientific American* 9, no. 8 (22 Aug. 1863): 118; *Register of the Commissioned Officers of the United States Revenue Marine to April 1, 1875*, 16–17.

CHAPTER 7. ERICSSON MONITORS: PASSAIC *AND* CANONICUS *CLASSES,* DICTATOR *AND* PURITAN

1. J. Smith to J. Ericsson, 17 Mar. 1862, J. Ericsson to J. Smith, 19 Mar. 1862, RG 45, OSF, box 51.
2. "Specification of an Iron-Clad Shot-Proof Steam Floating Battery," with contract dated 20 June 1862, RG 217, Entry 232, box 49.
3. Ibid.
4. Ibid.
5. J. Ericsson to J. Smith, 30 Mar. and [?] Apr. 1862, *Project Cheesebox* 2:366, 369.
6. "Specification of an Iron-Clad Shot-Proof Steam Floating Battery," RG 217, Entry 232, box 49.
7. Ibid.
8. Ibid.
9. NARS Plans, Bureau of Steam Engineering, *Passaic* class.
10. Ibid.; *Scientific American* 9, no. 22 (12 Dec. 1863): 372.
11. "Specification of an Iron-Clad Shot-Proof Steam Floating Battery," with contract dated 20 June 1862, RG 217, Entry 232, box 49.
12. G. Fox to A. Harwood, 15 May 1862, RG 45, M480, roll 2.
13. S. Stringham to G. Welles, 25 June 1861 and 2 July 1861, *ORN*, 5:745, 758; G. Welles to Stringham, 6 July 1861, *ORN*, 5:770; Tucker, *Arming the Fleet*, 220.
14. *ORN*, 14:357; W. Echols to D. Harris, 9 April 1863, *ORN*, 14, 89; *ORN*, 13:730–34.
15. J. Smith to J. Ericsson, 19 June 1862, RG 45, OSF, AD box 51.
16. Faron to Stimers, 15 Apr. 1863, RG 19, Entry 52; Gregory to Lenthall, 6 Apr. 1863, RG 19, Entry 64; "Coastal Monitors," *DANFS*, 3:759.
17. A. Stimers to Gregory, 15 Nov. 1862, RG 19, Entry 65.
18. Ibid.; T. Griffin to A. Stimers, 30 Oct. 1862, RG 19, Entry 65; "Civil War Naval Ordnance," *DANFS*, 3:805–7.
19. S. P. Lee to Welles, 20 Dec. 1862, *ORN*, 8:311.
20. *ORN*, 8:362–65.
21. S. Collins to parents, 25 Jan. 1863, New-York Historical Society.
22. J. Rodgers to G. Welles, 26 Jan. 1863, *Report on Armored Vessels*, 43–45.
23. J. Rodgers to S. Dupont, 7 Feb. 1863, *ORN*, 8:654; G. Fox to J. Ericsson, 27 Jan. 1863, Fox Papers, New-York Historical Society.
24. P. Drayton to S. DuPont, 22 Jan. 1863, and J. Worden to G. Welles, 20 Jan. 1863, *ORN*, 13:529–30.
25. S. DuPont to Welles, 19 Feb. 1863, P. Drayton to S. DuPont, 24 Feb. 1863, P. Drayton to J. Dahlgren, 8 Mar. 1863, *ORN*, 13: 672–73, 687, 727.
26. P. Drayton, J. Rodgers, D. Ammen, D. Fairfax, and J. Downes to Welles, 24 Apr. 1863, *ORN*, 14:45–48.
27. Johnson, *Rear Admiral John Rodgers*, 245.
28. Ammen, *The Atlantic Coast*, 98–99.

29. Rodgers, Ammen, G. Rodgers, D. Fairfax, and Downes to G. Welles, 25 May 1863, and J. Cornwell to J. Dahlgren, 26 Jan. 1864, *ORN*, 14:215, 589.
30. Hunter, *A Year on a Monitor*, 66.
31. M. Mara to A. Stimers, 22 Sept. 1863, RG 19, Entry 64; Proposal by Secor for *Camanche* modifications, 3 Oct. 1863, RG 19, Entry 64.
32. Rodgers to S. DuPont, 17 June 1863, and W. Taylor, C. R. P. Rodgers, R. Danby, and A. Mackenzie to S. DuPont, 22 June 1863, *ORN*, 14:265–66, 273–76.
33. *SecNav Reports*, Nov. 1876, 280.
34. I. Hanscom to T. F. Rowland, 15 Jan. 1874, RG 19, Entry 72A.
35. Ibid.; NARS Plans 1-10-32 (*Montauk*) and 2-5-36 (*Passaic*).
36. *SecNav Reports*, 1895, 349.
37. NARS Plans 1-10-23B and 2-5-36.
38. Report of Board in the Case of the River and Harbor Monitor *Manayunk*, Court of Claims Case No. 16834, 12 Dec. 1892, RG 19, Entry 188, 1–7.
39. A. Stimers to J. Gregory, 13 Sept. 1862, RG 19, Entry 65; *Manayunk* Board Report, 7.
40. A. Stimers to Z. Secor, 22 Dec. 1862, RG 19, Entry 64; A. Stimers to Lenthall, 3 Feb. 1862 [?], RG 19, Entry 64; "Claim of Secor & Co. & Perine, Secor, & Co., for Alteration in Plan and Delay of Vessels Built for Government" (booklet), 1863, in RG 19, Entry 64; Gregory to Lenthall, 31 July 1863, RG 19, Entry 64.
41. W. Wood to Gregory, 19 June 1865, RG 19, Entry 64.
42. NARS Plan 76-12-30 of *Saugus* shows her at 235 feet, with a 50-inch-wide armor belt and 18 inches less depth than plans of later dates. It is dated October 1862—before the first major changes ordered. NARS Plan 77-9-29 (and others) labeled *Tippecanoe* class show the increased depth, narrower armor belt, and 224-foot length.
43. Stimers to Secor, 18 June 1863, RG 19, Entry 64; *Manayunk* Board Case, RG 19, Entry 188.
44. "Claim of Secor & Co.," 1863, RG 19, Entry 64.
45. There is some disagreement concerning the engines of the monitors, with many sources saying that those of the original vessel and the two following classes were identical. Available plans show the *Passaics* and the *Monitor* with 40-inch pistons and 22-inch stroke (NARS Bureau of Steam Engineering Plans, *Passaic* class; contract for *Monitor*), and the *Canonicus* class with 48- by 24-inch engines (NARS Plan 77-6-36).
46. W. H. Cracknell, "United States Navy Monitors of the Civil War," 286; Bennett, *Steam Navy of the United States*, 349; NARS Plans 76-6-36 (engine), 77-9-9 (inboard cross section), and 77-9-39 (propeller and rudder).
47. Cmdr. Livingston to Gregory, 10 June 1865, RG 19, Entry 64.
48. L. Schenk to Gregory, 9 Feb. 1866, RG 19, Entry 64.
49. NARS Plans 130-10-5 (*Canonicus*) and 1-10-46 (*Ajax*).
50. A. Stimers to Gregory, 4 Feb. 1864, RG 19, Entry 64.
51. W. Parker to G. Welles, 6 Oct. 1864, *ORN*, 10:529.
52. J. Nicholson to D. Farragut, 22 Sept. 1864, *ORN*, 21:665.
53. NARS Plans 130-10-5 and 1-10-36.
54. Godon to Welles, 12 June 1865, *ORN*, 3:545.

55. William S. Dudley, "American Naval Archeology: Past and Prologue," *Pull Together* 30, no. 1 (Spring/Summer 1991): 3 (newsletter of the Naval Historical Foundation and the Naval Historical Center); The National Armed Forces Museum Advisory Board, *USS Tecumseh: Capsule of History*, n.d.
56. J. Lenthall and B. Isherwood to G. Welles, 10 June 1862, RG 19, Entry 49.
57. J. Smith to G. Welles, 23 May 1862, RG 71, Entry 1.
58. NARS Plan 1-9-28a; J. Ericsson to G. Fox, 10 Dec. 1863, Fox Papers, New-York Historical Society.
59. J. Ericsson to W. Wood, 7 Dec. 1864, RG 19, Entry 64.
60. NARS Plan 1-9-27.
61. Church, *Life of John Ericsson*, 2:10.
62. "United States Monitor *Dictator*," *The Artizan* 1, no. 10 (1 Oct. 1867): 218.
63. Ibid., 217; NARS Bureau of Steam Engineering plan (*Dictator*).
64. *Scientific American* 9, no. 18 (31 Oct. 1863): 282; ibid., 12 Dec. 1863, 373; J. Smith, C. Davis, and J. Lenthall to Welles, 31 Aug. 1863, RG 45, M518; NARS Bureau of Steam Engineering plan, *Dictator*.
65. *Scientific American* 9, no. 15 (10 Oct. 1863): 234; ibid., vol. 9, no. 24, (2 Dec. 1863): 373; NARS Bureau of Steam Engineering plans, *Dictator*.
66. Bourne, "On the American System of Turret Ships," 137–38.
67. Beale, *Diary of Gideon Welles*, 1:495.
68. J. Smith (with annotation by J. Lenthall) to G. Welles, 28 Jan. 1864, RG 45, M518.
69. Johnson, *Rear Admiral John Rodgers*, 267.
70. Ibid., 268–70; letter (no signature), 23 Nov. 1864, John Rodgers Family Papers, Library of Congress.
71. Johnson, *Rear Admiral John Rodgers*, 268; Church, *Life of John Ericsson*, 2:17.
72. Johnson, *Rear Admiral John Rodgers*, 269.
73. Ibid., 274–79; E. Robie to J. Rodgers, 21 Mar. 1865, Rodgers Family Papers, Library of Congress.
74. B. Isherwood to G. Welles, 22 Oct. 1868, RG 19, Entry 63.
75. Church, *Life of John Ericsson*, 2:13.
76. Ibid., 12.
77. J. Lenthall to J. Gregory, 4 Nov. 1865, RG 19, Entry 56.
78. Porter to G. Welles, 15 Jan. 1865, *ORN*, 11:601–2.
79. Ibid.

CHAPTER 8. CASEMATED RIVER IRONCLADS AND RAMS, 1862–1865

1. J. Smith to G. Welles, 9 Apr. 1862, RG 71, Entry 1.
2. NARS Plan 28-6-4Q.
3. Contract and Specifications, *Chillicothe*, *Osage*, and *Neosho*, RG 217, Entry 232.
4. Specifications, Contract, and plan, *Chillicothe*, RG 217, Entry 232.
5. Ibid.
6. Ibid.
7. Ibid.
8. Ibid.
9. NARS Plans 28-6-1A and 28-6-1B; J. Lenthall to G. Welles, 24 Feb. 1863, RG 19, Entry 49; Deck Log of the USS *Chillicothe*, Oct. 1862, RG 24.

10. NARS Plan 28-6-1B; J. Walker to D. Porter, 25 Oct. 1862, *ORN*, 23:448–49.
11. J. Walker to D. Porter, 25 Oct. 1862, *ORN*, 23:448–49.
12. NARS Plan 28-6-1A.
13. J. Walker to D. Porter, 25 Oct. 1862, *ORN*, 23:448–49.
14. W. Smith to D. Porter, n.d., *ORN*, 24:246; D. Porter to G. Welles, 26 Mar. 1863, *Report on Armored Vessels, 1864*, 467.
15. W. Smith to D. Porter, n.d., *ORN*, 24:246.
16. Way, *Way's Packet Directory, 1848–1983*, 86.
17. Specifications, Contract, and plan, *Chillicothe*, RG 217, Entry 232.
18. Ibid.
19. NARS Plan 28-6-4M; Specifications, Contract, and plan, *Chillicothe*, RG 217, Entry 232.
20. J. Hull to J. Lenthall, 27 Apr. 1863, J. Brown to J. Hull, 27 Apr. 1863, and D. Porter to J. Hull, 9 Nov. 1862, RG 45, M518.
21. J. Brown to J. Hull, 27 Apr. 1863, RG 45, M518; W. Shirk to D. Porter, 2 May 1863, *ORN*, 24:658–59.
22. J. Brown to J. Hull, 27 Apr. 1863, RG 45, M518.
23. D. Porter to G. Welles, 26 May 1863, *Report on Armored Vessels, 1864*, 522.
24. J. Cronan to Shirk, 30 Apr. 1863, *ORN*, 24:622; D. Porter to G. Welles, 6 Apr. 1863, ibid., 520; K. Breese, J. Shirk, J. Fulton, and N. Dean to D. Porter, 4 Apr. 1863, RG 45, OSF, AC box 25.
25. J. Shirk to D. Porter, 30 Apr. 1863, *ORN*, 24:620; D. Porter to G. Welles (with annotation by J. Lenthall), 8 May 1863, ibid., 658–59.
26. J. Shirk to D. Porter, 2 May 1863, *ORN*, 24:658–59.
27. D. Porter to Welles, 8 May 1863, ibid.; J. Shirk to D. Porter, 22 May 1863, ibid., 25:28.
28. "Naval Vessels", 40th Cong., 2d sess., 7 May 1868, H. Exec. Doc. 280, 10.
29. D. Porter to G. Welles, 16 Feb. 1864, *Report on Armored Vessels, 1864*, 591.
30. NARS Bureau of Steam Engineering Plans; Specifications, RG 217, Entry 232.
31. Specifications, RG 217, Entry 232; Silverstone, *Warships of the Civil War Navies*, 155; *ORN*, ser. 2, vol. 1, 107.
32. J. Hull to C. Davis, 19 Sept. 1862, *ORN*, 23:365.
33. W. Hoel to D. Porter, 11 Apr. 1863, *ORN*, 24:543.
34. NARS Plans 80-1-14, 80-1-15, and 80-1-16.
35. W. Porter to A. Foote, 20 Apr. 1862, RG 92, Entry 1403.
36. Way, *Way's Packet Directory, 1848–1983*, 9.
37. NARS Plan 3438 Black Series, RG 74.
38. Ibid.
39. *Scientific American* 7, no. 10 (6 Sept. 1862): 154; Report, D. D. Porter to G. Welles, 16 Feb. 1864, *Report on Armored Vessels, 1864*, 591.
40. D. Porter to S. Phelps, 6 Mar. 1863, Phelps Papers, Missouri Historical Society.
41. S. Phelps to D. Porter, 14 Mar. 1863, Phelps Papers, Missouri Historical Society.
42. D. Porter to J. Sanford, 6 Feb. 1863, *ORN*, 24:304.
43. D. Porter to S. Phelps, 6 Mar. 1863, Phelps Papers, Missouri Historical Society.
44. S. Phelps to D. Porter, 14 Mar. 1863, and D. Porter to S. Phelps, 6 Mar. 1863, ibid.

45. *ORN*, ser. 2, vol. 1, 124.
46. Way, *Way's Packet Directory, 1848–1983*, 9; NARS Plan 3438 Black Series, RG 74.
47. H. Walke to D. Porter, 17 Apr. 1863, *ORN*, 24:557.
48. C. Underwood to H. Walke, 29 Apr. 1863, *ORN*, 24:623–24.
49. NARS Plan 1213 Red Series, RG 74.
50. M. Meigs to E. Stanton, 6 Mar. 1863, RG 92, Entry 1403.
51. D. Porter to S. Phelps, 4 and 6 Mar. 1863, S. Phelps to D. Porter, 14 Mar. 1863, Phelps Papers, Missouri Historical Society.
52. NARS Plan 1213 Red Series, RG 74.
53. Way, *Way's Packet Directory, 1848–1983*, 86; NARS Plan 1213 Red Series, RG 74.
54. *ORN*, ser. 2, vol. 1, 57.
55. *ORN*, 24:584–85.
56. F. Ramsay to K. Breese, 3 May 1863, *Report on Armored Vessels, 1864*, 508.
57. S. Phelps to A. Foote, 18 Feb. 1862, *ORN*, 22:615; with endorsement by Foote, ibid., 616.
58. A. Foote to M. Meigs, 1 Apr. 1862, RG 92, Entry 1403.
59. *ORN*, ser. 2, vol. 2, 77; D. Porter to A. Pennock, 12 Dec. 1862, ibid., 23:625; D. Porter to S. Phelps, 18 Jan. 1863, S. L. Phelps Letterbook, Missouri Historical Society.
60. D. Porter to G. Fox, Oct. 1863, Fox Papers, New-York Historical Society.
61. Ibid.
62. K. Breese to D. Porter, 12 Nov. 1863, *ORN*, 25:559.
63. D. Porter to G. Fox, 25 Mar. 1864, Fox Papers, New-York Historical Society.
64. Deck Log, *Avenger*, 1864, RG 24; *ORN*, ser. 2, vol. 1, 41.
65. *ORN*, ser. 2, vol. 1, 233.
66. Deck Log, *Vindicator*, 1864, RG 24.
67. S. P. Lee to G. Welles, 29 May 1865, *ORN*, 27:252.

CHAPTER 9. TURRET RIVER IRONCLADS

1. Hartupee and Tomlinson to J. Smith, 19 Apr. 1862, RG 19, Entry 236.
2. NARS Plan 28-6-4G.
3. NARS Plan 28-6-4H.
4. W. Flye to D. Porter, 31 May 1864, *ORN*, 26:340.
5. S. Phelps to D. Porter, 26 Apr. 1863, Phelps Papers, Missouri Historical Society.
6. "Specifications for Engines for Two Small Iron-Clad Gunboats," James B. Eads, RG 217, Entry 232.
7. Ibid.
8. E. Hartt to J. Hull, 18 June 1863, RG 19, Entry 236.
9. J. King, E. Hartt to J. Hull, 1 July 1863, RG 45, OSF, AD box 25.
10. Jos. P. Couthouy to D. D. Porter, 25 July 1863, *ORN*, 25:325.
11. S. Phelps to D. Porter, 26 Apr. 1863, Phelps Papers, Missouri Historical Society.
12. J. Foster to D. Porter, 20 Sept. 1863, *ORN*, 25:423.
13. Contract, George Bestor, 14 May 1862, RG 217, Entry 232.
14. Specifications for *Ozark*, RG 217, Entry 232.
15. Ibid.
16. Ibid.

17. Ibid; NARS Plans 1-8-4 and 1-8-7 (*Marietta* and *Sandusky*).
18. J. Rainbow to J. Hull, 23 Sept. 1865, RG 45, OSF, AC; *Scientific American* 7, no. 25 (20 Dec. 1862): 391; J. Whittaker to D. Porter, 2 Jan. and 10 Feb. 1863, *ORN*, 24:151, 336–37.
19. J. King to J. Hull, 22 Sept. 1863, *ORN*, 25:429–30; J. King to J. Hull, 24 Feb. 1864, RG 45, OSF, AC.
20. W. Cruger [?] to G. Bestor, 29 Oct. 1863, RG 45, OSF, AC.
21. D. Porter to J. Lenthall, 18 May 1864, J. King to B. Isherwood, Mar. 1864, and D. Hasseltine to [?], 13 Apr. 1864 (with annotation by J. Lenthall), RG 45, OSF, AC.
22. Contract (*Marietta* and *Sandusky*), RG 217, Entry 232.
23. Tomlinson & Hartupee & Co., 30 Apr. 1862, RG 19 Entry 236.
24. Specifications, RG 217, Entry 232.
25. Ibid.
26. Ibid.
27. Ibid.
28. H. Loring to W. Wood, 15 Feb. 1865, RG 19, Entry 64.
29. Hearing Report, 5 Nov. 1866, RG 19, Entry 64.
30. A. Case to J. Lenthall, 17 Nov. 1866, RG 19, Entry 64; NARS Plan 1-8-4.
31. NARS Plan 1-8-4; H. Loring and Schenck to Gregory, 26 Mar. 1866, RG 19, Entry 64.
32. G. Welles to J. Smith, 16 Apr. 1862, RG 19, Entry 236.
33. F. Blair to G. Fox, n.d., F. Blair to J. Eads, 6 and 10 Jan. 186-[not legible], Eads Papers, Missouri Historical Society.
34. Contract and Specifications, RG 217, Entry 232.
35. Specifications, RG 217, Entry 232.
36. "Certain War Vessels Built in 1862–1865," 57th Cong., 1st sess., 12 June 1902, S. Rept. 1942, 84–85.
37. Specifications, RG 217, Entry 232.
38. Ibid.
39. Wegner, "Mr. Eads's Turret," 28–29; NARS Plans 80-8-22 and 80-8-23.
40. Ibid.
41. Wegner, "Mr. Eads's Turret," 30.
42. A. Stimers to G. Fox, 2 March 1864, Fox Papers, New-York Historical Society; J. Eads to G. Fox, 30 Mar. 1864, Fox Papers, New-York Historical Society.
43. *Army Navy Journal*, 7 Nov. 1863, 173; J. Eads to G. Fox, 19 Apr. 1864, Fox Papers, New-York Historical Society; J. King to J. Hull, 9 May 1864, RG 19, Entry 64.
44. D. Porter to G. Welles, 13 June 1864, *ORN*, 26: 388; G. Perkins to J. Palmer, 29 July 1864, *ORN*, 21:389; D. Farragut to W. Smith, 1 Aug. 1864, *ORN*, 21:395.
45. Acting Volunteer Lieutenant W. Shankland to G. Welles, 7 Oct. 1864, *ORN*, 21:499.
46. H. Thatcher to G. Welles, 6 July 1865, *ORN*, 22:236.
47. T. Stevens to D. Farragut, 6 Aug. 1864, *ORN*, 21:497; W. Shankland to G. Welles, 7 Oct. 1864, *ORN*, 21:499–500. *Note:* T. H. Stevens was given temporary command of the *Winnebago* for the Battle of Mobile Bay; W. F. Shankland commanded her on the passage from the Mississippi to Mobile.
48. G. Perkins to D. Farragut, 7 Aug. 1864, *ORN*, 21:500–501.
49. G. Fox to D. Porter, 3 Nov. 1863, *ORN*, 25:529–30.

CHAPTER 10. THE FINAL CIVIL WAR IRONCLADS, 1864–1867

1. Church, *Life of John Ericsson*, 2:22–23.
2. J. Ericsson to G. Welles, 8 Oct. 1862, Ericsson Papers, Library of Congress.
3. Ibid.
4. U.S. Congress, "Report on the Light-Draught Monitors," 93.
5. Ibid., 115.
6. Ibid., 93.
7. Ibid., 93, 115, 69.
8. NARS Plan RG 77, Construction File, no. 965.
9. U.S. Congress, "Report on the Light-Draught Monitors," 97; NARS Plan RG 77, Const. File, no. 965.
10. U.S. Congress, "Report on the Light-Draught Monitors," 107–8, 120.
11. J. Ericsson to Welles, 24 Feb. 1863, Ericsson Papers, Library of Congress.
12. U.S. Congress, "Report on the Light-Draught Monitors," 69.
13. F. Gregory to J. Lenthall, 12 May 1864, RG 19, Entry 64; U.S. Congress, "Report on the Light-Draught Monitors," 5.
14. U.S. Congress, "Report of the Light-Draught Monitors," 6.
15. J. Ericsson to G. Fox, 23 July 1864, Ericsson Papers, Library of Congress.
16. W. Wood to [?], 25 June 1864, RG 19, Entry 1254.
17. Wegner, "Alban C. Stimers," 47.
18. W. Wood to Alex Swift & Co., n.d., RG 19, Entry 195, case 6326, *Klamath* and *Yuma*.
19. Ibid.
20. J. Schenck to F. Gregory, 12 Mar. 1866, RG 19, Entry 64.
21. F. Gregory to Cramp, 19 Oct. 1864, RG 19, Entry 64.
22. "Light-Draught Monitors," 68, 96.
23. Beale, *Diary of Gideon Welles*, 2:351.
24. Wegner, "Alban C. Stimers," 22–23.
25. "Light-Draught Monitors," 116.
26. Wegner, "Alban C. Stimers," 45.
27. Ibid., 30.
28. Deck Log, *Casco*, Dec. 1864, RG 24.
29. Deck Log, *Chimo*, Jan. 1865, RG 24.
30. J. Lenthall to H. Paulding, 23 Apr. 1863, RG 19, Entry 52.
31. *SecNav Reports*, Dec. 1864, xxix.
32. NARS Plans 2-6-9, 2-2-9, and 2-1-67.
33. NARS Plans 1-9-14 and 2-2-9.
34. Ibid.; NARS Plan 2-1-67.
35. Canney, *Old Steam Navy*, 1:138.
36. B. Isherwood to G. Welles, 12 Oct. 1865, RG 19, Entry 963; Bennett, *Steam Navy of the United States*, 400.
37. Bennett, *Steam Navy of the United States*, 400; NARS Plan 2-2-9.
38. D. Porter to J. Lenthall, 29 Nov. 1869, RG 19, Entry 61.

39. Beale, *Diary of Gideon Welles*, 2:340–41.
40. Specifications, *Dunderberg*, RG 45, OSF, AD.
41. Contract, ibid.; S. Pook to F. Gregory, 1 Nov. 1862, RG 19, Entry 64.
42. W. Webb to G. Fox, 16 Oct. 1863, Fox Papers, New-York Historical Society.
43. W. Webb to Welles, 19 Sept. 1864, RG 19, Entry 64; W. Wood, F. Gregory, and B. Delano to J. Lenthall, 4 May 1865, ibid.
44. J. Kimball to F. Gregory, 3 Dec. 1863, RG 19, Entry 64; W. Webb to G. Fox, 7 July 1863, Fox Papers, New-York Historical Society.
45. Specifications, *Dunderberg*, RG 45, OSF, AD.
46. Ibid.,; Vessel Plans, Smithsonian Institution, Webb Plan Book.
47. Ibid.
48. Ibid.
49. Ibid.
50. "The Dunderberg Engines," Erastus Washington Smith Papers, Library of Congress.
51. *Dunderberg*, RG 45, OSF, AD.
52. C. Ringgold to F. Gregory, 6 Sept. 1866, RG 19, Entry 64.
53. J. Mullany and W. Buckner to H. Wise, 25 Feb. 1867, RG 45, OSF, AD.
54. Beale, *Diary of Gideon Welles*, 2:604.
55. "Rochambeau: Devis D'Armement," 1868, 1870.
56. *SecNav Reports*, 12 Dec. 1863, xvi; advertisement clipping, 30 Oct. 1862, RG 45, OSF, AC.
57. Report on Ironclad Proposals, RG 19, Entry 49.
58. *SecNav Reports*, 1863, xvi.
59. *Army and Navy Journal*, 3 Oct. 1863, 92; ibid., 30 Oct. 1863, 149.
60. Specifications and plans for 3,500-ton ironclad, NARS Plan 80-9-1.
61. *SecNav Reports*, 1864, xxvii.

CHAPTER 11. THE POSTWAR YEARS: IRONCLADS IN ECLIPSE

1. Orth, "The Stevens Battery," 97.
2. *The Stevens Iron Clad Battery*, 1874, 5.
3. Ibid., 8–10.
4. Ibid., 10–18.
5. Ibid., 29, 45, 46.
6. *Army and Navy Journal*, 13 June 1885, 928.
7. Roberts, "Screw Cruising Vessels of the Union Navy, 1861–1865," 8.
8. *SecNav Reports*, 1878, 26.
9. Bureau of Construction and Repair to SecNav, 15 Nov. 1876, RG 19, Entry 50.
10. Bill from Harlan & Hollingsworth, 26 Aug. 1876, RG 19 Entry 72A.
11. Swann, *John Roach, Maritime Entrepreneur*, 142.
12. Ibid., 143.
13. NARS Plan 138-3-1.
14. "Double Turret Monitors," 46th Cong., 2d sess., 14 May 1880, H. Exec. Doc. 82, 6 and plate D; *SecNav Reports*, 1882, 146–47; NARS Bureau of Steam Engineering Plans, *Miantonomoh* and Class Engines.
15. H. Exec. Doc. 82, 1.
16. Ibid., 7.
17. Alden, *American Steel Navy*, 207.
18. NARS Bureau of Steam Engineering Plans, *Puritan*.
19. Morison, "Inventing a Modern Navy," 91.
20. Church, *Life of John Ericsson*, 1:255.

Bibliography

1. ARCHIVAL SOURCES

National Archives and Records Service, Washington, D.C.

Record Group 19, Bureau of Ships

Entry 49, Letters from Bureau of Construction and Repair

Entry 50, Letters Sent to the Secretary of the Navy

Entry 52, Letters Sent to Officers

Entry 54, Letters to Philadelphia Navy Yard

Entry 56, Letters Sent to the General Superintendent of Ironclads

Entry 61, Letters from Bureau of Construction and Repair

Entry 63, Letters from Commandant of Philadelphia Navy Yard

Entry 64, Letters from Superintendents outside of Navy Yards

Entry 65, Reports from Superintendents outside of Navy Yards

Entry 72A, Letters to Naval Constructor R. W. Steele Relating to Ironclad Vessels, 1875–82

Entry 188, Report of Board in the Case of the River and Harbor Monitor *Manayunk*

Entry 195, Published Court of Claims Records Involving Naval Vessels: Case 6236, *Klamath* and *Yuma*

Entry 236, Proposals to Build or Equip Gunboats, 1861–77

Entry 1254, Circular Letters Sent to Local Inspectors

Record Group 24, Deck Logs of U.S. Naval Vessels

Record Group 45

Old Subject File, 1775–1910

Entry 8, Letters to Board of Naval Commissioners

Entry 28, Letters from Board of Naval Commissioners to Secretary of the Navy

M89, Squadron Letters (microfilm)

M125, Captains' Letters

M480, Letters to Chiefs of Bureaus

M518, Letters from Chiefs of Bureaus

M625, Area File

Record Group 71, Bureau of Yards and Docks

Entry 1, Letters Sent

Entry 5, Letters Received

Entry 76, Plans and Specifications for an Armored Corvette, 1861

Record Group 74, U.S. Navy Bureau of Ordnance Plans

Record Group 77, U.S. Army, Records of the Office of Chief of Engineers, Fortification File

Record Group 92, U.S. Army Quartermaster General

Entry 1403, Water Transportation

Record Group 181, Records of Naval Districts and Shore Establishments

Entry 16, Letters from Bureau of Construction and Repair to Commandant, Portsmouth Navy Yard (Federal Records Center, Waltham, Massachusetts)

Record Group 217, Treasury Department

Entry 232, Navy Contracts

Library of Congress

John Ericsson Papers

Montgomery Meigs Papers

John Rodgers Papers (Rodgers Family Collection)

Gideon Welles Papers

Erastus Washington Smith Papers

Smithsonian Institution

John A. Griswold Papers

New York Public Library

Gideon Welles Papers

New-York Historical Society, New York City

Gideon Welles Papers

Gustavus V. Fox Papers

Cornelius Bushnell Papers

Missouri Historical Society, Saint Louis

James B. Eads Papers

S. L. Phelps Papers

Swedish American Historical Society, Philadelphia

John Ericsson Papers

G. W. Blunt White Library, Mystic Seaport Museum, Mystic, Connecticut

Diary of William Ellery Maxson

2. GOVERNMENT PUBLICATIONS

Messages of His Excellency Theodore F. Randolph, Governnor of New Jersey, to the Legislature, Session of 1870, Trenton, N.J., 1870.

Naval History Division. *Civil War Naval Chronology, 1861–65.* 6 vols. Washington, D.C.: Government Printing Office, 1971.

———. *Civil War Naval Ordnance.* Washington, D.C.: Government Printing Office, 1969.

———. *Dictionary of American Naval Fighting Ships.* 8 vols. Washington, D.C.: Government Printing Office, 1959–81.

Official Records of the Union and Confederate Navies in the War of the Rebellion. 30 vols. Washington, D.C.: Government Printing Office, 1894–1922.

Ordnance Instructions for the United States Navy. Washington, D.C.: Government Printing Office, 1866.

Register of the Commissioned Officers of the United States Revenue Marine to April 1, 1875. New York: "The Nautical Gazette" Press, 1875.

Report of the Secretary of the Navy in Relation to Armored Vessels, 1864.

United States Military Commission to Europe, 1855 to 1856. *Report on the Art of War in Europe* (The Delafield Report). Report by Major Richard Delafield. Washington, D.C.: G. W. Bowman, 1860.

U.S. Congress. "Report on the Light-Draught Monitors." *Report of the Joint Committee on the Conduct of the War.* 38th Cong., 2d sess.

U.S. Congress. House. *Annual Report of the Secretary of War.* 37th Cong., 3d sess., 1861. H. Exec. Doc. 1.

———. *Building of the War Steamer by R. L. Stevens.* 27th Cong., 3d sess., 27 June 1843. H. Doc. 98.

———. *Construction of the Steam Frigate Fulton.* 25th Cong., 2d sess., 1837–38. H. Exec. Doc. 433.

———. *Double Turret Monitors.* 46th Cong., 2d sess., 14 May 1880. H. Exec. Doc. 82.

———. *Harbor Defense.* 27th Cong., 2d sess., 15 March 1842. H. Rept. 448.

———. *Naval Vessels.* 40th Cong., 2d sess., 7 May 1868. H. Exec. Doc. 280.

U.S. Congress. Senate. *Certain War Vessels Built in 1862–1865.* 12 June 1902. S. Rept. 1942.

———. *Committee on Naval Affairs.* 32d Cong., 1st sess., 16 March 1852. S. Rept. 129.

———. *Letter . . . in relation to . . . the Monitor.* 40th Cong., 2d sess., 25 July 1868. S. Exec. Doc. 186.

U.S. Navy Department. *Annual Reports of the Secretary of the Navy.* 1842–88.

3. PERIODICALS

Army and Navy Journal (1863–95)
The Artizan
Journal of the Franklin Institute
Scientific American
U.S. Nautical Magazine and Naval Journal (1853–57)
U.S. Naval Institute Proceedings

4. UNPUBLISHED SOURCES

Eskew, Garnett Laidlaw. "Our Navy's Ships and Their Builders, 1775–1961." [With the approval and cooperation of the Bureau of Ships, U.S. Navy]. Typescript draft, 1962. Naval Historical Center Library.

Roberts, Stephen S. "Screw Cruising Vessels of the Union Navy, 1861–1865." Working paper.

Wegner, Dana. "Alban C. Stimers and the Office of the General Inspector of Ironclads." Master's thesis, State University of New York at Oneonta, 1979.

5. FOREIGN PUBLICATIONS

"Le Miantonomoh, Monitor a Tourelles des Etats-Unis." *Revue Maritime et Coloniale* 19 (March 1867).

"L'Onondaga, Garde-Cote Cuirasse a Deux Tourelles." *Revue Maritime et Coloniale* (February 1870): 95–101.

"Rochambeau: Devis D'Armement." Marine et Colonies, 1868, 1870.

6. BOOKS AND ARTICLES

Alden, John D. *American Steel Navy.* Annapolis: Naval Institute Press, 1972.

———. "Born Forty Years Too Soon." *American Neptune* 22, no. 4 (October 1962): 252–63.

American Society of Mechanical Engineers, *USS Cairo: Engine and Boilers,* 1990.

Ammen, Daniel. *The Atlantic Coast.* New York: Charles Scribner's Sons, 1883.

———. *The Old Navy and the New.* Philadelphia: J. B. Lippincott, 1891.

Ballard, Admiral G. A. *The Black Battle Fleet.* Annapolis: Naval Institute Press, 1980.

Battles and Leaders of the Civil War. 4 vols. New York: Century Magazine, 1887.

Bauer, K. Jack. *Ships of the Navy, 1775–1969.* Troy, New York: Rensselaer Polytechnic Institute, 1969. Additional material supplied by Stephen S. Roberts, editor of the revised edition of this work, *Register of Ships of the U.S. Navy, 1775–1990: Major Combatants* (Westport, Conn.: Greenwood Press, 1991).

Bauer, K. Jack, ed. *New American State Papers: Naval Affairs.* Wilmington, Del.: Scholarly Resources, 1981.

Baxter, James Phinney, III. *The Introduction of the Ironclad Warship.* Cambridge: Harvard University Press, 1933.

Beach, Edward L. *The United States Navy: 200 Years.* New York: Henry Holt, 1986.

Beale, Howard K., ed. *The Diary of Gideon Welles.* 2 vols. New York: W. W. Norton, 1960.

Bennett, Frank M. *The Steam Navy of the United States.* Pittsburgh: Warren & Co., 1896.

Bourne, John. "On the American System of Turret Ships." *Transactions of the Institute of Naval Architects* (23 March 1866).

Bushnell, C. S. *The Story of the Monitor, The Original United States Warship "Monitor."* New Haven: 1899.

Canney, Donald L. *The Old Steam Navy.* Vol.1, *Frigates, Sloops, and Gunboats, 1815–1885.* Annapolis: Naval Institute Press, 1990.

Chapelle, Howard I. *The History of the American Sailing Navy.* New York: W. W. Norton, 1949.

Christley, James L. "Mystic River Builds an Ironclad." *The Log of Mystic Seaport* 32, no. 4 (Winter 1981): 129–38.

Church, William Conant. *The Life of John Ericsson.* 2 vols. New York: Charles Scribner's Sons, 1891.

Clark, Charles E. *My Fifty Years in the Navy.* Boston: Little, Brown, 1917.

Coker, P. C., III. *Charleston's Maritime Heritage, 1670–1865*. Charleston: Cokercraft Press, 1987.

Coletta, Paola E., ed. *American Secretaries of the Navy*. 2 vols. Annapolis: Naval Institute Press, 1980.

Conway's All the World's Fighting Ships, 1860–1905. Edited by Robert Gardiner. Greenwich: Conway Maritime Press, 1979.

Cracknell, W. H. "United States Navy Monitors of the Civil War." *Warship Profile* 36 (Sept. 1973).

Daly, Robert W., ed. *Aboard the USS Monitor, 1862: The Letters of Acting Paymaster William Frederick Keeler, U.S. Navy, to His Wife, Anna*. Annapolis: U.S. Naval Institute, 1964.

Davis, William C., ed. *The Image of War*. 6 vols. New York: Doubleday, 1982.

Faust, Patricia, ed. *Historical Times Illustrated Encyclopedia of the Civil War*. New York: Harper & Row, 1986.

Geoghegan, William. "Study for a Scale Model of the U.S.S. *Carondelet*." *Nautical Research Journal* 17, no. 4 (Winter 1970): 233–35.

Gibbons, Tony. *Warships and Naval Battles of the Civil War*. New York: Gallery Books, 1989.

Gosnell, H. Allen. *Guns on the Western Waters: The Story of River Gunboats in the Civil War*. Baton Rouge: Louisiana State University Press, 1949.

Herrick, Walter R., Jr. *The American Naval Revolution*. Baton Rouge: Louisiana State University Press, 1966.

Hill, Frederic Stanhope. *Twenty-six Historic Ships*. New York: Belknap & Sons, 1905.

Hovgaard, William. *Modern History of Warships*. London: E. & F. Spon, 1920.

Hunter, Alvah F. *A Year on a Monitor and the Destruction of Fort Sumter*. Edited by Craig L. Symonds. Columbia, S.C.: University of South Carolina Press, 1987.

Hutcheon, Wallace S., Jr. *Robert Fulton: Pioneer of Undersea Warfare*. Annapolis: Naval Institute Press, 1981.

Isherwood, Benjamin F. *Experimental Researches in Steam Engineering*. 2 vols. Philadelphia: W. Hamilton, 1863–65.

Johnson, Robert Erwin. *Rear Admiral John Rodgers*. Annapolis: U.S. Naval Institute, 1967.

King, William H. *Lessons and Practical Notes on Steam*. Revised by James W. King. New York: D. Van Nostrand, 1864.

Knox, Dudley W. *A History of the United States Navy*. New York: G. P. Putnam's Sons, 1936.

Lambert, Andrew. *Battleships in Transition*. Annapolis: Naval Institute Press, 1984.

————. *Warrior: Restoring the World's First Ironclad*. London: Conway Maritime Press, 1987.

Lossing, Benson J. *Pictorial Field Book of the War of 1812*. New York, 1869. Reprint. Glendale, N.Y.: Benchmark Publishing Co., 1970.

————. *Pictorial History of the Civil War*. 3 vols. Vols. 1–2. Philadelphia: George W. Childs, 1866. Vol. 3. Hartford: T. Belknap, 1868.

McGrath, Tom, and Doug Ashley. *Historic Structure Report: USS Cairo*. Denver: U.S. Department of the Interior, National Park Service, 1981.

Miller, Edward M. *USS Monitor: The Ship That Launched a Modern Navy*. Annapolis: Leeward Publications, 1978.

Miller, Francis Trevelyan, ed. *The Photographic History of the Civil War*. 10 vols. New York: Review of Reviews Co., 1911, 1912.

Moore, Frank, ed. *Rebellion Record*. 11 vols. New York: various publishers, 1862–66.

Morison, Elting E. "Inventing a Modern Navy." *American Heritage*, June–July 1986, 81–96.

Morison, Samuel Eliot. *"Old Bruin" Commodore Matthew Calbraith Perry*. Boston: Little, Brown, 1967.

Morrison, John H. *History of American Steam Navigation*. New York: Stephen Daye Press, 1958.

Neeser, Robert Wilden. *Statistical and Chronological History of the United States Navy, 1775–1907*. New York: Macmillan, 1909.

Orth, Michael. "The Stevens Battery." *U.S. Naval Institute Proceedings* 92 (June 1966): 92–99.

Penn, Geoffrey. *"Up Funnel, Down Screw!"* London: Hollis & Carter, 1955.

Peterkin, Ernest W. *Drawings of the USS Monitor*. USS Monitor Historical Series, vol. 1, no. 1. Raleigh, N.C.: Department of Cultural Resources; Washington, D.C.: U.S. Department of Commerce, National Oceanic and Atmospheric Administration, 1985.

Porter, David D. *Naval History of the Civil War*. 1886. Reprint. Secaucus, N.J.: Castle, 1984.

Project Cheesebox: A Journey into History. "A Research Manuscript." 3 vols. U.S. Naval Academy, Department of History, Annapolis, 1974.

Redmond, R. A.. "The Revenue Steamer *E. A. Stevens* in the Civil War." *American Neptune* 20, no. 3 (July 1960): 155–66.

Renwick, James. *Treatise on the Steam Engine*. New York: G. & C. & H. Carvill, 1830.

Ridgely-Nevitt, Cedric. *American Steamships on the Atlantic*. East Brunswick, N.J.: Associated University Presses, 1981.

Roberts, William H. "The Neglected Ironclad: A Design and Constructional Analysis of the USS *New Ironsides*." *Warship International* 26, no. 2 (1989): 109–34.

Ronnberg, Erik A. R., Jr. "Webb's Plans of Wooden Vessels." *Nautical Research Journal* 34, no. 2 (June 1989): 62–114.

Scharf, J. Thomas. *History of the Confederate States Navy*. New York: Rogers & Sherwood, 1887.

Silverstone, Paul H. *Warships of the Civil War Navies*. Annapolis: Naval Institute Press, 1989.

Sloan, Edward William, III. *Benjamin Franklin Isherwood, Naval Engineer*. Annapolis: U.S. Naval Institute, 1965.

Sprout, Harold, and Margaret. *The Rise of American Naval Power, 1776–1918*. Annapolis: Naval Institute Press, 1980.

Stern, Philip Van Doren. *The Confederate Navy: A Pictorial History*. New York: Doubleday, 1962.

The Stevens Iron Clad Battery. New York: D. Van Nostrand, 1874.

Still, William N., Jr. *Iron Afloat: The Story of the Confederate Armorclads*. Columbia, S.C.: University of South Carolina Press, 1971.

Swann, Leonard Alexander, Jr. *John Roach, Maritime Entrepreneur*. Annapolis: U.S. Naval Institute, 1965.

Thompson, Robert Means, and Richard Wainwright, eds. *Confidential Correspondence of Gustavus Vasa Fox*. 2 vols. New York: Naval Historical Society, 1920.

Thompson, Stephen C. "The Design and Construction of USS *Monitor*." *Warship International* 27, no. 3 (1990): 222–39.

Tucker, Spencer. *Arming the Fleet: U.S. Navy Ordnance in the Muzzle-Loading Era*. Annapolis: Naval Institute Press, 1989.

Van Dusen, Albert E. *Connecticut*. New York: Random House, 1961.

Way, Frederick, comp. *Way's Packet Directory, 1848–1983*. Athens: Ohio University Press, 1983.

Wegner, Dana. "Mr. Eads's Turret." *Civil War Times Illustrated* 12, no. 6 (October 1973): 24–31.

———. "S. X.: The Federal Gunboat *Essex*." *Nautical Research Journal* 19, no. 1 (Spring 1972): 49–51.

Weigley, Russell F. *Quartermaster General of the Union Army: A Biography of M. C. Meigs*. New York: Columbia University Press, 1959.

Index

About the Author

Donald L. Canney received his bachelor's degree from Georgia Southern College in 1969 and did graduate work at Florida State University. He taught history at the high school level before joining the staff of *Blue and Gray Magazine*. He has written articles for such maritime history periodicals as *Naval History*, *Seaways*, and *Sea Classics*. His first book, the first volume of *The Old Steam Navy*, was published in 1990.

Canney, who lives in Bowie, Maryland, is the registrar for the historical collections of the U.S. Coast Guard. He is working on a history of early U.S. Revenue and Coast Guard cutters for the Naval Institute Press.

THE NAVAL INSTITUTE PRESS

**The Old Steam Navy, Volume Two
The Ironclads, 1842-1885**

Designed by CR MacLellan and Associates
Baltimore, Maryland

Set in New Baskerville and Old Style Baskerville
by TCSystems, Inc.
Shippensburg, Pennsylvania

Printed on 60-lb. Glatfelter Antique B-16
by John D. Lucas Printing
Baltimore, Maryland

Bound in Holliston Roxite B
by American Trade Bindery, Inc.
Baltimore, Maryland